Picasso
and the
War Years
1937–1945

PICASSO
AND THE WAR YEARS
1937–1945

Steven A. Nash, Editor

WITH

Robert Rosenblum

AND CONTRIBUTIONS BY

Brigitte Baer

Michèle Cone

Michael FitzGerald

Lydia Csatò Gasman

Gertje Utley

THAMES AND HUDSON
FINE ARTS MUSEUMS OF SAN FRANCISCO

Published on the occasion of the exhibition
Picasso and the War Years: 1937–1945

Fine Arts Museums of San Francisco
California Palace of the Legion of Honor
10 October 1998 – 3 January 1999

Solomon R. Guggenheim Museum
5 February – 26 April 1999

Picasso and the War Years: 1937–1945 has been organized by the Fine
Arts Museums of San Francisco, in collaboration with the Solomon R.
Guggenheim Museum, New York. We are grateful to the National
Endowment for the Arts and the National Endowment for the Humanities,
Federal agencies, whose grants have made this exhibition possible. This
exhibition is supported by an indemnity from the Federal Council on the
Arts and Humanities.

First published in the United States of America in hardcover in 1998 by
Thames and Hudson Inc., 500 Fifth Avenue, New York, New York 10110

First published in Great Britain in 1998 by Thames and Hudson Ltd, London

Library of Congress Catalog Card Number 98-60335

ISBN 0-88401-095-3

British Library Cataloguing-in-Publication data
A catalogue record for this book is available from the British Library

Produced by the Publications Department of the Fine Arts Museums of
San Francisco: Ann Heath Karlstrom, Director of Publications and Graphic
Design; Karen Kevorkian, Editor. Frances Bowles and Sharon Vonasch,
proofreaders. Book and cover design by Michael Sumner. Typeset in
Berthold Baskerville at Burning Books, Santa Fe, New Mexico. Assistance
by Melody Sumner Carnahan and John Inserra.

Printed and bound in Hong Kong

FRONT COVER: Pablo Picasso, *Still Life with Skull, Leeks, and Pitcher*
(detail), 14 March 1945, Fine Arts Museums of San Francisco, cat. no. 80.

BACK COVER: Pablo Picasso, *Study for* Guernica *(Head of a Horse),* 2 May
1937, Museo National Centro de Arte Reina Sofia, Madrid, cat. no. 4.

FRONTISPIECE: Picasso in his studio on the rue des Grands-Augustins, 1938.
Musée Picasso, Paris, Picasso Archives. Photograph by Peter Rose Pulham.

Preface

It is with special pride that we at the Fine Arts Museums of San Francisco present the exhibition *Picasso and the War Years: 1937–1945,* documented by the publication of this book. Both are historical events of the first order. They represent the fulfillment of a longtime dream of Steven Nash's, exhibition organizer and Associate Director and Chief Curator at the Fine Arts Museums, to assemble for the first time in this country an exhibition on this fascinating and under-studied period of Picasso's work when art and history dramatically conjoined.

From our internal perspective, the exhibition advances further our museums' mission to embrace more fully in our collection and programs the most creative and intellectually challenging art of the twentieth century. From the point of view of scholarship and historical information, we expect the exhibition and book to make a significant and lasting contribution.

Although many exhibitions and publications have examined different aspects of Picasso's prodigious career, ours is the first in the United States to focus specifically on the period between the Spanish Civil War and the end of World War II, when Picasso's art intensely reflected the global holocaust and the strain of life under the German Occupation of France. A similar exhibition took place approximately ten years ago at the Ludwig Museum in Cologne, but ours benefits from the extensive new research on this period of Picasso's life and work that is made possible largely by the systematic organization in recent years of the Picasso Archives at the Musée Picasso, Paris, and its vast holdings of correspondence, photographs, press clippings, and other pertinent documents. Our organizational team is greatly indebted to the staff at the Musée Picasso for all the help they provided in making these holdings accessible.

Despite the fact that it contains some of his most personally expressive and, ultimately, characterisitic work, Picasso's war period has not received attention from scholars and collectors commensurate with its importance. Understandably, this owes in part to the art's dark, grim, and challenging qualities that have not been popularly accepted as have other more colorful or pleasurable emotional aspects of his stylistic development. Also important is Picasso's having personally retained a significant proportion of the work from this period, and its passing after his death directly into the private collections of his heirs, keeping sizable portions from general public awareness. *Guernica,* one of the landmark achievements of this period, is, of course, well known to anyone interested in Picasso and modern art, and certain other key works from this era – e.g., *The Charnel House,* variations of the Weeping Woman, *L'Aubade, Night Fishing at Antibes,* and *Man with a Lamb –* have also attained the status of icons. But many other strong and evocative works from the time remain little known and underappreciated. It is often in these less acclaimed paintings, drawings, sculptures, and prints that we find the most telling messages of Picasso's inner reaction to cataclysmic world events and their effects on his personal world. These are messages of timely relevance, given a general renewed interest in the history of World War II and Nazi cultural policies, augmented by the efforts of contemporary artists to address political and social realities.

Through the works in this exhibition and book we see a remarkable record of the interaction of art with historical events. No other artist of the twentieth century left so sustained a visual account of the devastating effect of war on life and the human spirit. For a comparable achievement, one must look back to the work of Picasso's revered countryman Francisco de Goya, whose accounts of atrocities in the Napoleonic wars in Spain almost 150 years earlier have much in common with Picasso's modern updates of the language of loss, struggle, sorrow, and commemoration. We hope through our project to promote greater public understanding and appreciation of what Picasso achieved.

In the accompanying acknowledgments Steven Nash has thanked the many individuals who helped in one way or another with the enormous logistical and research effort that lies behind this project. I add my own voice of thanks to his and also single out for special commendation the outstanding organizational work that Steven Nash himself has done. We are particularly grateful to our colleagues at the Solomon R. Guggenheim Museum, New York, especially Robert Rosenblum, Thomas Krens, and Lisa Dennison, for their help and support, to the many lenders to the exhibition, and to those sponsors who helped make it all possible. Thank you.

HARRY S. PARKER III

Director of Museums
Fine Arts Museums of San Francisco

Acknowledgments

It is axiomatic to note that the organization of a major international exhibition in today's art world requires the assistance of a great many individuals both inside and external to the home institution. For an exhibition on Pablo Picasso, the debts of gratitude for assistance are particularly deep, given the many challenges that any organization is bound to encounter. High insurance values, the frequency of loan requests for well-known works, and the inevitable, central importance of such works in their respective collections help make the securing of necessary loans a particularly daunting task. A great many works by Picasso from the period surveyed in the present exhibition, i.e., 1937–1945, remain sequestered in private collections, their locations unrevealed to recent scholarship and cataloguing efforts. Documentation for this period in general is relatively scarce and often difficult to access, due in part to the disruptions caused by World War II and also to the fact that important materials still reside in private hands or in difficult-to-penetrate government collections.

With these obstacles in mind, it is especially gratifying to be able to acknowledge and thank the many colleagues, collectors, friends, and other individuals connected in one way or another with our enterprise who have all contributed so much to the success of *Picasso and the War Years: 1937–1945.* Chief among these are Dr. Robert Rosenblum, Professor of Fine Arts at New York University and my co-organizer at the Guggenheim Museum,

whose deep knowledge of Picasso, generosity with information, and ready wit made him an ideal partner; and Harry S. Parker III, Director of the Fine Arts Museums of San Francisco, who several years ago recognized immediately the potential importance of the project and lent support throughout its long development. Also crucial to the fruitful realization of the exhibition and its accompanying catalogue are those scholars who shared their knowledge through insightful essays and, in many cases, provided support and information far exceeding that expected of an essayist: Brigitte Baer, Michèle Cone, Michael FitzGerald, Lydia Gasman, and Gertje Utley. A sabbatical leave granted by Harry Parker and the Sabbatical Committee of the Fine Arts Museums of San Francisco allowed me to travel to France for critically important research in the summer and autumn of 1997, a trip made possible by a grant from Robert and Carole McNeil of San Francisco. For all of their help with loans, organizational advice, and access to crucial materials in their museum archives, I am especially indebted to the staff at the Musée Picasso in Paris: Gérard Régnier, Director; Brigitte Léal, former Curator; Hélène Seckel, Curator; Dominique Dupuis-Labbé, Curator; and Anne Baldessari, Curator of Archives and Library, and her extremely helpful staff, especially Sylvie Fresnault. From staff members at the Solomon R. Guggenheim Museum in New York, Robert Rosenblum and I enjoyed invaluable cooperation and help, but I especially want to thank Thomas Krens, Director; Lisa Dennison, Deputy Director and Chief Curator; Fiona Ragheb, Assistant Curator; and Diane Dewey, Administrative Assistant. The long process of archival and bibliographic research for the exhibition was greatly facilitated by the helpful cooperation of staff at the Library and Archives of the Hoover Institution for War, Revolution, and Peace at Stanford University, who also lent materials to a historical gallery to provide an introduction and contextualization for the Picasso exhibition, and the Stanford University Art Library. I am particularly grateful to Elena Danielson, Archivist at the Hoover Institution, and Alexander Ross, Head Librarian at the Stanford University Art Library. Of course, no exhibition is possible without the participation of lenders. To the many individuals and institutions who generously parted with valued treasures long enough for them to appear in the exhibition, we are profoundly grateful. They are all acknowledged elsewhere in this catalogue.

Certain colleagues who played particularly key roles in the conceptualization and development phases deserve special recognition and thanks: to Brigitte Baer (again) for giving me the courage to proceed with what seemed at the outset to be an impossibly difficult project; Maya Widmaier Picasso, for sharing with me her memories of life with her father during the Occupation; Kirk Varnedoe, for assisting with loans in a way that went far and beyond the call of duty; Albert Elsen, in memoriam, for first introducing me to the depths of meaning behind Picasso's *Man with a Lamb*; Ichiro Suyama, for the extraordinarily helpful role he played in facilitating loans from Japan; and Carol Nash, who helped with the project in untold ways.

The following all assisted with research, loan arrangements, photography procurements, or some other aspect of the project: William Acquavella, Doris Ammann, Alexander Apsis, Mami Asano, Abigail Asher, Stephanie Barron, Felix Baumann, Douglas Baxter, Martha Beck, Christoph Becker, Heinz Berggruen, John Berggruen, Ernst Beyeler, Ivor Braka, Gilberte Brassaï, Emily Braun, Elisa Breton, Aldis Browne, Sven Bruntjen, Annette Bühler, Andrew Butterfield, Whitney Chadwick, Michel Cohen, Patrick Cooney, Elizabeth Cowling, Bertrand Davezac, Kurt Delbanco, Emmanuel Delloye, James Demetrion, Douglas Druick, Philippe Durey, Claude Duthuit, Anne d'Harnancourt, Caroline de Lambertye, Guillermo de Osma, Laure de Gramont, Yves de Fontbrun, Gilbert Edelson, Anne Faggionato, Sarah Faunce, Richard Feigen, Michael Findlay, The Honorable Thomas Foley, Kate Ganz, Tony Ganz, Carmen Giménez , Richard Gray, Harriet Griffin, Barbara Guggenheim, José Guirao, John Herring, Paul Herring, Tony Judt, Mary Kadish, Shinji Kohmoto, Edith Kramer, Jan Krugier, Anne Lampe, Quentin Laurens, Duncan MacGuigan, Joshua Mack, Loïc Malle, Robert Mnuchin, Frederick Mulder, Martin Muller, David Nash, Congresswoman Nancy Pelosi, Anthony Penrose, Robert Pincus-Witten, Joachim Pissarro, John Richardson, Rona Roob, Angela Rosengart, Nan Rosenthal, Cora Rosevear, Margit Rowell, Bernard Ruiz-Picasso, Dodie Rosekrans, Marc Selwyn, Remy Squires, Jeremy Strick, Charles Stuckey, Masayuki Tanaka, Gary Tinterow, Phyllis Tuchman, Ludwig Ullmann, Gordon VeneKlasen, Doug Walla, Margit and Rolf Weinberg, Michael Werner, Stephen Wirtz, James Wood, and Mary Zlot. To each and every individual listed, I am most grateful. To anyone I have inadvertently omitted, I offer my apologies for the oversight.

Many staff members at the Fine Arts Museums of San Francisco have worked long and hard on this exhibition and catalogue. I am deeply grateful to them for their professionalism and dedication, and for the team spirit with which they approached the project. In particular, I would like to acknowledge the following: Kathe Hodgson, Director of Exhibitions Planning, supervised many of the logistics of exhibition administration; Karen Kevorkian, Editor of the Museums' Publications Department, copyedited the catalogue and managed the myriad details of its production in collaboration with Ann Karlstrom, Director of Publications and Graphic Design; Exhibition Assistants Danny Hobson and Laurel Fredrickson provided indispensable help with historical research, compilation of loan records and photographs, and manuscript preparation; Bill White, Exhibitions Designer, oversaw the exhibition installation, and Bill Huggins, Lighting Designer, managed the lighting; Therese Chen, Director of Registration, managed the assemblage of loans and tour arrangements, including details of shipping, couriers, insurance, and National Indemnification; Allison Pennell, Librarian, tracked down many bibliographic references; Ron Rick, Chief Designer, provided the exhibition graphics; Vas Prabhu, Director of Education, helped organize the ambitious program of educational activities connected with the exhibition; Carl Grimm, Head Paintings Conservator, and others on the conservation staff, including Tricia O'Regan, Assistant, provided conservation examinations of the paintings and worked skillfully to return certain of the works in the exhibition to more presentable condition; Elisabeth Cornu, Objects Conservator, and Debra Evans, Paper Conservator, helped with conservation and installation matters; Barbara Boucke, Director of Development, and Debbie Small, former Development Associate, both worked on raising funds for the exhibition; Joseph McDonald, Photographer, provided new photography for the catalogue; Suzy Peterson, Secretary to the Chief Curator, in addition to assisting with the preparation of catalogue manuscripts, helped in innumerable tasks connected with research and documentation; Pamela Forbes, Director of Media Relations, and Barbara Traisman, Media Relations Officer, coordinated all public relations and advertising programs; Sherin Kyte, Legion Administrator, oversaw logistics at the California Palace of the Legion of Honor, where the exhibition took place in San Francisco. Michael Sumner contributed his considerable talent to the design of the catalogue, assisted by Melody Sumner Carnahan; meticulous editorial assistance was rendered by Frances Bowles and Sharon Vonasch. The skills and high standards of all of these individuals were clearly manifested in all aspects of the project.

Of course, the exhibition would not have been possible without the generous financial support of several sponsors. For their underwriting and the confidence they showed in our proposals, we are most grateful to the National Endowment for the Arts and the National Endowment for the Humanities, Federal agencies, and for indemnification of the exhibition, to the Federal Council on the Arts and Humanities.

STEVEN A. NASH

Associate Director and Chief Curator
Fine Arts Museums of San Francisco

Introduction:
Picasso, War, and Art

Steven A. Nash

. . . artists who live and work with spiritual
values cannot and should not remain indifferent
to a conflict in which the highest values of
humanity and civilization are at risk.
—Picasso to the American Artists' Congress, 1937

No, painting is not made to decorate apartments.
It is an offensive and defensive instrument
of war against the enemy.
—Picasso to Simone Téry, 1945[1]

War as a subject rarely makes for great art. The horrifying reality of humans slaughtering humans too easily overwhelms artistic efforts to witness or memorialize such events, rendering trivial the results. One thinks of Goya, Delacroix, Callot, and Rubens as artists of earlier epochs who managed to convey the pain, loss, and degradation of war in ways forever compelling. In the twentieth century, this "era of violence," as Churchill put it, where war has reached previously unimaginable dimensions of destruction, the challenge to artists is more important but more daunting than ever. Society relies most commonly on the chilling, on-the-spot immediacy of photography and film to feed its collective understanding and memory of war. We must ask if it is really possible for sculptors or painters to take the measure of horrors such as Dachau or Hiroshima.

Picasso, for the most part, did not try. Aside from his great *Guernica* of 1937 and *Charnel House* of 1945–46, which respond respectively to the savage Nazi bombing of a Basque town and to news of the German concentration camps, his work from the war-torn years of 1937 to 1945 essentially ignores specific world events. Yet no other artist of the twentieth century left so sustained and moving a visual record of the corrosive effect of war on the human spirit and its toll on human life. His achievement was to create a modern alternative to history painting. As he explained to an American war correspondent who sought him out at his studio in Paris just days after its liberation:

I have not painted the war because I am not the kind of painter who goes out like a photographer for something to depict. But I have no doubt that the war is in these paintings I have done. Later on perhaps the historians will find them and show that my style has changed under the war's influence. Myself, I do not know.[2]

His "style," in fact, did not change dramatically to accommodate this new expressive task. The basics of the visual vocabulary he employed throughout the war years – the stylizations, spatial disruptions, deformations of natural form, and coloristic choices – are evidenced in one way or another in earlier work. What changed were the degrees of exaggeration to which Picasso pushed them and the personal messages they served. Through a repertoire of traditional themes – still life, portraiture, landscape, and the nude – Picasso referenced the war in ways often oblique but powerful. A dark mood entered his work, not totally unrelieved by brighter, more hopeful, and even humorous moments, but tending toward a bleak, dimly lit world of contorted forms, claustrophobic spaces, and grayed-down colors, in which recurring iconographies build a picture of life strained to the brink of survival and beyond. As Picasso put it, in a typically trenchant remark about his expressive language during the war years, "you see, a casserole too can scream."[3] Through his treatment of quotidian subjects, refracted through the lens of private trauma, he captured a portrait of an era that rises above the strictly personal to comment memorably on life in the shadow of war and the spiritual negativism that resulted, when traditional religion was futile and the ancient furies, all too alive for Picasso, wreaked havoc on humanity. The more narrowly autobiographical or hermetic focus of much of Picasso's art at this point expands into a give-and-take with history and an interaction with momentous world events.

THE POLITICALIZATION OF PICASSO'S ART

Picasso's productivity during the years 1937–45 remained surprisingly high, despite the social upheavals going on around him. Throughout the Spanish Civil War, which he experienced only from a distance, his routines of work and relaxation followed long-established patterns, with most of the fall, winter, and spring seasons spent in Paris and summers on the Riviera. Early in 1937 he established a new studio in the seventeenth-century mansion at 7, rue des Grands-Augustins (fig. 1), but he also continued to live and work at his apartment at 23, rue La Boétie for several more years and to make occasional visits to his studio in Ambroise Vollard's home at Le Tremblay-sur-Mauldre. Even after the outbreak of World War II, during the twelve months Picasso spent in the coastal town of Royan and the four years in occupied Paris, he continued to turn out work with accustomed profusion.

[page 12]
Pablo Picasso
Still Life with Blood Sausage (detail)
10 May 1941. Cat no. 42.

Although he went through certain periods when he produced little or nothing, the overall record is remarkable. His cataloguer Christian Zervos lists over 2,200 paintings and drawings for the nine years spanning the Spanish Civil War and World War II, and Zervos's compilation is far from exhaustive.

Clearly, the psychological stress of the times actually stimulated Picasso's creative instincts rather than blunting them. He had ample opportunity to leave France before and after its invasion by Germany in June 1940, but chose not to. Although this decision was made more out of passivity than any heroic instinct – "I'm not looking for risks to take," he told Françoise Gilot, "but in a sort of passive way I don't care to yield to either force or terror"[4] – it submitted him to the difficulties of life in France under the Occupation, with the normal hardships of food and fuel shortages, blackouts, and curfews, exacerbated by Picasso's status as a foreigner and a "degenerate" artist who was subject to regular Nazi surveillance. The intriguing but complex and only partially known story of Picasso's position vis-à-vis the Occupation regime will be surveyed later. Of primary importance is the fact that making art constituted for Picasso, in and of itself, a declaration of free will and a sign of human perseverance. His subject matter was not ostensibly antiwar or anti-German. It did not "scream out the truth," as one Resistance writer in Paris exhorted her fellow writers to do.[5] Given the scrutiny under which he worked, expressing too blatantly political a message would have been foolhardy for Picasso even if he were inclined to a more activist role, which he was not, and efforts by some writers to make of him a Resistance worker greatly exaggerate the facts. But in its own way, his work became a private resistance effort, one that carried strong symbolic value for friends and other artists trapped within the same excoriating circumstances. Through its inward journey, it opens a unique window onto the trauma of war and the pressures of life in occupied Paris.

The radicalization of Picasso's art that led to this unique chronicle can be traced to the intensifying political situation in Europe in the mid-1930s. Although much debate has centered on the issue of political and social meanings in Picasso's earlier art, and while it must be recognized that such meanings do exist to varying degrees, it also must be acknowledged that they are distinctly understated and are far from the type of "instrument of war against the enemy"[6] that Picasso eventually prescribed. It is wise to keep in mind Roland Penrose's observation that the "the language of politicians was as foreign to him as the speech of distant tribes."[7] All of that changed in the mid-1930s.

As Hitler solidified his power in Germany, social unrest increased dramatically in France and Spain alike, becoming particularly widespread during the short reign of the Popular Front governments in both countries. From February 1936 to Franco's military mutiny in July that precipitated the Spanish Civil War, Picasso's homeland experienced 113 general strikes, 218 partial strikes, and the burning of over 200 churches and newspapers. Picasso's sensitivity to the deteriorating political situation in Europe was more acute than it had been in similar situations in the past. Undoubtedly this was due in part to Spain's involvement but it was also perhaps attributable to his closer alignment with the Communist Party through respected friends who were members, and his growing conviction that the Communists were an important revolutionary force against some of the social evils he cared most about. This conviction was cemented by the strong antifascist support the Communist Party threw behind the Republican government in the civil war, which eventually, in fact, dominated the Loyalist effort. As is frequently pointed out, Picasso's *Composition with Minotaur,* a gouache from 28 May 1936 that provided a curtain design for Romain Rolland's play *Le 14 juillet* (page 70, fig. 1), translates political sentiment into a mythological scene featuring a dead or dying minotaur held by a fearsome griffin-headed predator (read "fascism"). A slightly later study from 13 June (page 71, fig. 2) brings the focus resoundingly up-to-date with the presence of a throng of protesters who assault a burning building, brandish the hammer and sickle, and exhort one another with raised fists.[8] Numerous other works from 1936

FIG. 1
Eugène Atget, *Hôtel Antoine Duprat, 7 rue des Grands-Augustins* (future apartment and studio of Pablo Picasso) ca. 1900. Albumen-silver print, 8½ × 6¹⁵⁄₁₆ in. (21.6 × 16 cm). The Museum of Modern Art, New York, Abbot-Levy Collection, partial gift of Shirley C. Burden. Copy print © 1998 The Museum of Modern Art, New York.

express a sociopolitical awareness beneath the veil of mythologized subjects and the recurring themes of death, sacrifice, and destruction. Particularly significant is Picasso's killing of the minotaur, his alter ego through whom he had unleashed over the years so much basic instinctual passion, from bestiality and lust to tender love. In April 1936, Picasso had his minotaur pack up and move, pulling a handcart behind him.[9] In several later compositions, he is slain in combat or in sports arenas.[10] Clearly, Picasso's worlds, internal and external, were changing.

One of the earliest works in which this generalized ennui became more specifically focused is the intriguing *Figure* of 28 January 1937 (cat. no. 3). In three drawings from this date, Picasso put on display an amply endowed, fashionably dressed woman with a grotesquely, phallically distorted face.[11] In *Figure,* she is immobilized like a mannequin on an upright, tripod prong aimed menacingly at her sex, while she tongue-kisses a black-masked, putrid sun (the *soleil pourri* of surrealist fame). In her hands she holds a banner on which are drawn the two arms of a drowning victim, while she ignores the plight of the creature actually drowning at her side. Given Picasso's patriotic loyalties, might not this scenario be best interpreted as la France, a vain but impotent and hypocritical consort of evil, who by its non-interventionist policies ignored the plight of the Spanish Republicans?[12]

Such a polemical reading is credible given the seething attack on Franco and his pillaging Fascist troops that Picasso delivered several weeks before in his etchings entitled the *Dream and Lie of Franco* (cat. no. 2). This set of serial images, made to be cut up and sold as postcards or as a folio in support of the Spanish Refugee Relief Campaign, has its iconographical roots in pictorial traditions of religious and military processions, to which Goya among many others importantly contributed.[13] Picasso's title represents another memory of Goya, recalling the *Dream of Lies and Inconstancy* in *Los Caprichos.* While it is often commented that Picasso's prints may take a cue from political cartoons common in the French newspapers of the day or from the traditional Spanish *aleluyas,*[14] his long-standing admiration for Alfred Jarry and the scatological mayhem of the Ubu plays surfaces here as well.[15] The tuberous, polyplike form that Picasso gave Franco bears a striking resemblance to the strange creature in Dora Maar's 1936 photograph of *Père Ubu.*[16] When Alfred Barr wrote to Picasso in 1945 asking him if Franco in these etchings had been inspired by Ubu, his secretary Jaime Sabartés wrote back that "Il affirme s'être inspiré par l'ETRON," meaning roughly that Picasso affirmed the influence of "the old turd."[17]

Similarities have been pointed out between Franco and some of Jarry's own illustrations of his iconoclastic protagonists, and those of other artists seem relevant as well (see fig. 2), although Picasso had prefigured the tuberous form of Franco in

FIG. 2
Pierre Bonnard, drawing of Père Ubu from the *Almanach illustré du Père Ubu (XXe siècle),* (Paris: Ambroise Vollard, 1901).

drawings as early as April and May of 1936.[18]

Picasso worked on the two plates for the etchings in early January and again in June, after the Nazi bombing of Guernica, adding at that time the four final images that relate to his painting on this other subject. The narrative that the images describe is not precisely clear, and the poem that Picasso appended to the set does not shed much light on its meaning. The overall message, however, is unmistakable. In Franco's persona of crowned ugliness, his slaying of horses and confrontation with a bull (Picasso's typical symbols of the Spanish people and tradition), his destruction of beauty both in the forms of a classicized monument and a beautiful young girl, and his hypocritical invocation of religious mission, he emerges as emblematic of the evil of the military, church, and monarchy all in one, a traitor to Spanish tradition and a destroyer of its culture and people.

Given the vehemence of this attack, it is surprising that Picasso, when asked around the middle of January 1936 by the Republican government to prepare a mural for the Spanish Pavilion that was due to open in May at the World's Fair in Paris, chose at first a nonpolitical theme. The earliest sketches he prepared for the project date from 18 and 19 April. They show that he reverted at first to the standard, politically benign theme of an artist and his model in a studio,[19] although in two of these sketches Picasso appended a raised arm holding a hammer and sickle to the body of his earlier sculpture called the *Orator*, indicating that the theme of protest was also on his mind. That so few drawings exist from this stage of work reveals both that Picasso was procrastinating and that he remained indecisive and uninspired over how to fill the dauntingly large canvas (almost 11½ by 26 feet) that was expected of him.

The saturation bombing of the Basque town of Guernica and its civilian population by the Nazis' Condor Legion on 26 April provided Picasso the meaningful theme he previously lacked. It was a subject grounded in the immediacy of horrifying world events but rich in potential for a humanistic protest against the senseless violence of war in general. He set to work with remarkable energy. His first sketches date from 1 May, when the news of what happened in Guernica was still echoing out in sometimes contradictory news accounts, and he turned over his completed canvas to the organizers of the Spanish Pavilion a little more than a month later, well before the delayed opening of the pavilion on 12 July.[20]

The story of Picasso's development of his composition through many drawings and different stages of work on the canvas is well known, and the final painting has been analyzed from many points of view. In the present volume, Gertje Utley examines the complicated political tensions among differing factions and loyalties within the Republican cause at this time, and questions Picasso's precise political motivation. Robert Rosenblum shows how Goya, as an ever-present influence on Picasso during the war years, figured significantly among the many sources he drew upon in constructing his great vision of terror and destruction, and how his imagery ferociously subverts traditional Catholic iconography. For a survey of Picasso's overall wartime production, *Guernica* (pages 40–41, fig. 1) clearly is a landmark achievement that spawned many ideas he further developed and that opened the way for much of the work that followed.

The stark grisaille palette of the painting, for example, that contributes so much to its nocturnal eeriness and helps raise it from the arena of actual, colorful, organic life into a realm of abstract icon, very early set the tone of drab grayness permeating many of Picasso's wartime paintings and drawings. Although foreshadowed in certain earlier works,[21] and undoubtedly influenced by black-and-white photographs and newsreels, this absence of color became a main signifier in Picasso's work during the war years, connoting a long, purgatorial winter of the soul that continued, in fact, although less insistently, into the difficult postwar years of reconstruction. Several emblematic images in the painting – the crying woman, the largely disembodied bull's head, the pointed tongue as a sign of anguish, the torturously distorted hands and feet – have long afterlives in other works. Perhaps most importantly, the imagery has a complex, multilevel quality that avoids direct description and defies easy interpretation, another salient feature of Picasso's wartime production. To a journalist visiting him just after the liberation of Paris he suggested specific symbolic meanings for the horse and bull, while to Alfred Barr Picasso insisted that they were just a horse and just a bull.[22] Such masterworks from the years that follow as *Woman with a Cock, L'Aubade, Charnel House* (cat no. 82), and *Man with a Lamb* (cat. no. 66), have a similar combination of gripping visual imagery and elusive or multivalenced meaning. Although specific connotations such as sacrifice, isolation, fear, or suffering may be communicated, Picasso's approach is always intuitive rather than programmatic, and therefore a single, unequivocal reading of his symbolism is rarely possible. Ambiguity gave Picasso the desired effect of leaving freedom of interpretation to the public. It does not matter that a viewer of *Guernica* may be unfamiliar with the history of Nazi involvement in the Spanish Civil War, or that the bull in *Guernica* can be interpreted alternatively as victim or aggressor. The true meaning of the painting is lifted out of space and time coordinates in the civil war to become a summa on *all* wars and *all* victims.

STEVEN A. NASH   17

Picasso's preoccupation with tragedy in *Guernica* gave way after its completion to themes of a more lighthearted nature – landscapes, still lifes, portraits of friends and family – but he also continued to express his sentiments about the war in Spain, primarily through his long series of paintings and graphics on the theme of the Weeping Woman (see cat. nos. 7–11, 14).[23] A famous group of prints on the subject, featuring images with both autobiographical and political associations, dates from early in July 1937. They are often referred to as portraits of Dora Maar, who had become Picasso's mistress and was regularly present in his studio during work on *Guernica* – she photographed its seven main stages of development – and whose high-strung emotionalism caused Picasso to think of her as "always . . . weeping."[24] They also hark back, however, to events in Spain. Picasso's crying woman is undoubtedly the release of his own lament for all the pain and suffering experienced by the populace of Spain, his own family included. Barcelona, where Picasso's mother and sister lived, was a center of the Republican movement that became one of the main theaters of action. It is possible to tie the image of the weeping woman to the news Picasso received from his mother about street disturbances in the civil outbreaks of May 1937, which described the way that smoke from fires made her eyes tear and nearly asphyxiated the family.[25] That Picasso's father had made one of the sculptural *mater dolorosae* so common in Spain, complete with glass tears,[26] a work the family kept for many years, must have increased for the artist the poignancy of the crying motif and its associations with home. Brigitte Baer has also shown that a work as seemingly apolitical as the large print *Woman with a Tambourine* (cat. nos. 25, 26), with its self-conscious borrowings from Poussin's *Bacchanal before a Herm* and Degas's bathers, also couches veiled references to contemporary events, in particular, the street fighting in Spain.[27]

BETWEEN THE WARS

The war in Spain continued into 1939, but the tide had turned against the Republicans by spring 1938. While Picasso generously supported various relief efforts with cash and the donation of works, feeling on a deeply personal level his country's tragedy,[28] the civil war tended to become a more distant referent in his art from late 1937 onward. In this period, leading up to the outbreak of World War II in September 1939, his work settled into a state of uneasy quietude, during which images of a seemingly pleasurable character – brightly painted seated women, bathing scenes, domestic genres – were balanced by still-life compositions that contemplate such major themes as death, the arts, culture, and civilization. Frequently, however, even his more outwardly hedonistic compositions feature a highly stylized distortion or a dense interweave of pattern and weblike lines that convey confinement, entrapment, or tense emotional states. Together with the still lifes, the gathering malaise in such works corresponds to the deterioration of the political situation in Europe as the continent plunged toward total war. The culminating expression of this distress is the great *Night Fishing at Antibes* (fig. 4 and cat. no. 31). On the one hand, it is an innocent scene of two pretty girls watching men fishing at night by the light of lanterns, and on the other, it is an apocalyptic vision of bursting bombs, death, and erotic fervor.

Three outstanding still-life paintings in this volume display the syncretistic thinking on themes of life and death that characterize this period: *Still Life with Palette, Candlestick, and Head of a Minotaur* from 4 November 1938 (cat. no. 23), *Still Life with Candle, Palette, and Black Bull's Head* from 19 November 1938 (cat. no 24), and *Bull's Skull, Fruit, and Pitcher* from 29 January 1939 (cat. no. 27). Sobering notes of memento mori infuse all three through the decapitated heads of the bull and minotaur (neutralized into sculptures on bases) and the desiccated bull's skull. As iconographical and compositional counterpoints to these emblems of death, Picasso stationed candles in two of the works, the irradiating light offering a vision of illumination and hope. In the third, he provided a juxtaposition of ripe and glowing fruit, a colorful pitcher, and a tree in blossom, all talismans of regenerative life. Open books surmounted by palettes and brushes proclaim the powerful life force of the arts. The colors in all three tend toward a high-keyed, even garish range of blue, green, yellow, and red, another sign of Picasso's basically optimistic expectations of the triumph of good over evil and life over death.

Such works as the *Seated Woman* of 29 August 1938, and the two drawings of *Bathers with Crab* and *Three Figures,* from 10 July and 10 August 1938, respectively (cat. nos. 21, 19, 20), exemplify the linear constriction often seen in Picasso's figure style during these years. The entire pictorial space is enmeshed in a fine web of lines and pattern. In the two drawings, Picasso's compulsive covering of all forms and even open spaces with dark lines from his sharp-tipped pen is particularly suggestive of the webbing of a fishing net. The painting of the *Seated Woman* is a riot of intersecting patterns of line and color tightly confined within the surrounding

FIG. 3
Pablo Picasso, *Woman with a Cock,* 15 February 1938. Oil on canvas, 56⅝ × 46¹¹⁄₁₆ in. (144 × 118.5 cm). Private collection, Switzerland.

architectural frame. From the upwardly spiraling forms of the basket-weave torso, echoed in the basketlike hat, to the harshly outlined facial features and the flattened linearity of hair and dress, every component is jostled into motion, accentuated by the hot, sunstruck, Mediterranean colors. The subjects all relate to relaxed summertime pleasures, and recall earlier times in Picasso's life and work when the political atmosphere was less strained. But the *horror vacui* of their construction hints at psychological rumblings below the hedonistic surface.

This double edge in Picasso's work from 1938–39 is particularly apparent in his two masterpieces of the period, *Woman with a Cock* of 15 February 1938 and *Night Fishing at Antibes,* finished just before Germany invaded Poland (figs. 3–4).[29] In the former, the somewhat moronic appearance of the woman holding the rooster (it is often remarked that her features resemble Picasso's at this time of his life) is at first disarming. Gradually, however, the brutishness of the image makes itself felt through the figure's elephantine head, hands, and legs, the tight grip on the bird, and the proffering of a cup to catch the sacrificial blood, all intensifying the anticipation of a ritualistic killing. The woman takes on more and more the identity of a seated priestess whose plying of death is routine and heartless.

Such imagery provides a clue to the true meaning of the large *Night Fishing at Antibes,* a work that has been analyzed from almost as many different interpretive points of view as *Guernica.*[30] By now, it seems clear that it is far more than the innocent summer idyll or an exposition of heatedly sexual gamesmanship that some authors suggest. Especially when considered in the context of earlier and later war-related works, it looms as a haunting prophecy of impending doom.

The painting was started inauspiciously enough. In strolls around the quays of Antibes with Dora Maar, Picasso had witnessed scenes of fishermen working in their boats in the harbor at night, spearing fish lured to the water's surface by the bright light of their lanterns. This motif became Picasso's point of departure. At the right side of

FIG. 4
Pablo Picasso, *Night Fishing at Antibes,* August 1939. Oil on canvas, 81 × 136 in. (205.7 × 345.4 cm). The Museum of Modern Art, New York, Mrs. Simon Guggenheim Fund. © 1997 The Museum of Modern Art, New York. Cat. no. 31.

FIG. 5
Nicolaes Berchem, *Landscape with Crab Catchers by Moonlight,* 1645. Oil on canvas, 23¾ × 31½ in. (60.3 × 80 cm). Courtesy of Trafalgar Galleries, London.

the composition, he inserted two brightly dressed young women standing along the ramparts of the harbor, identified by Dora Maar as herself and her artist friend Jacqueline Lamba, wife of André Breton.[31] In the background to the left can be seen two towers, one from the château Grimaldi, later to become the Musée Picasso, and the other a nearby bell tower.[32]

It has been suggested that the composition may owe something to a boating scene of *Bathers* in the Louvre attributed to Nicolaes Maes,[33] but a closer parallel is found in a painting by Nicolaes Berchem entitled *Landscape with Crab Catchers by Moonlight* (fig. 5), widely known through engravings by Dancker Danckerts and François Denis Née.[34] The symbolism of fishermen in a boat, of course, has particularly strong Christian connotations. One pictorial example of this tradition that could have attracted Picasso's attention is the fresco of the *Miraculous Draft of Fishes* in San Pedro de Sorpe in Catalonia, published by Picasso's close friend Christian Zervos in 1937 in his book on Catalonian art (fig. 6).[35] Picasso's general interest in early Catalonian art is well documented, and further comparisons can be drawn, for example, between the flattened, simplified rendering of the fish and crab in *Night Fishing* and denizens of the deep in the Apocalypse tapestry in the Cathedral of Girona, also published by Zervos.[36]

The relevance of Christian teachings of the Apocalypse and Christ the fisherman, with its converse reference of Christ as fish and sacrificial victim, takes on greater probability in light of Picasso's distinct interpretive twist on his subject. His nighttime lighting, shot through with blacks, dark blues, and purples, has its own deeply ominous effect. The lights around the boat do not just glow, but, rather, explode with light, much like shells bursting in air. The two fishermen, one leering over the edge of the boat and the other poised, about to drive his four-pronged spear into a fish, have a savage, menacing quality. And the thrusting of the spear, highlighted in the lower center of the composition, provides the central theme visually and figuratively, summoning thoughts of sudden death from above that we cannot help but link to the menace of wartime bombardment. Even the two girls become caught up in the frenzy of explosive emotion. As if the message behind the one on the right obscenely licking the double ice-cream with her pointed tongue were not clear enough, Picasso represented her head as a giant phallus, perhaps, as he had many times in the past, correlating sex and violence, ecstasy and death. Another note on mortality is sounded by the triangular fluttering moths that swarm around the boat, attracted to their deaths by the light of the lamps. These brightly lit creatures and the lamps, too, seem to be

FIG. 6
Miraculous Draft of Fishes (detail), from San Pedro de Sorpe, 12th century. Fresco. Museu Nacional d'Art de Catalunya, Barcelona.

as much celestial bodies as earthly objects, adding to the scene another portentous quality of something "read in the stars."

The largest canvas Picasso painted for many years after *Guernica, Night Fishing at Antibes* is also one of the most telling documents of his own fears of war and the ferocity of aerial bombardment. It is an amazingly prescient anticipation of the blitz-krieg about to be unleashed on Europe.[37]

THE HOLOCAUST BEGINS: PICASSO IN ROYAN

That Picasso was expecting the political situation in Europe to deteriorate further in 1937 is shown by his dispatch of Marie-Thérèse and Maya to summer in the coastal town of Royan, north of Bordeaux. Not only was Royan distant from possible military targets, it also was well situated if a sudden exodus from France by boat were deemed necessary. Just a few days after returning to Paris from Antibes, Picasso himself departed for Royan with his chauffeur Marcel, Sabartés and his wife, Dora Maar, and his dog Kazbek.

Provincial life generally did not agree with Picasso, at least in large doses, but he would remain in Royan for almost a year, with fairly frequent trips back to Paris to keep in touch with developments there. Except for occasional landscapes or works based on personal experience, such as the drawings inspired by Picasso's observations of horses being led along rural roadways for the dismal prospects of military service,[38] his work in Royan is not place-specific. Instead, starting almost immediately after his arrival, it mirrored through familiar subject matter a new depth of despair and anguish that connects directly to the outbreak of World War II. This work set the tone of Picasso's output for the next several years.

In an album of drawings Picasso began on 30 September, the first pages are devoted to grim sketches of a flayed sheep's head, which lead compositionally to the large ink drawing of 1 October (cat. no. 34).[39] Isolated in inky blackness, monumental in presence and unflinching in its portrayal of cold, hard lifelessness, this drawing introduces a series of still-life compositions with skulls that date mostly from early in the Royan period (cat. nos. 34–37). Whereas Picasso had moderated his memento mori subjects from 1938 with the hope-filled symbols of books, palettes, and candles, these still lifes dating after the outbreak of World War II are single-mindedly, unremittingly concerned with one subject – death. Skulls either bleached white, or red with the blood of flesh, are shown singly, or combined with a slab of meat, or piled with an insouciant disregard of balance that mocks even more the dumb victims of recent violence. Devoid of any interrupting details, the surrounding spaces in these works sometimes have a glow of hot red or orange that increases even more their emotional intensity. In their starkness, these works relate back to Goya's still-life paintings of butchered animal parts and Cézanne's compositions of skulls.[40] For Picasso, they mark the first of a lengthy series of varied works on the motif of the skull, both animal and human, that runs throughout the war years and provides a primary vehicle of expression.

Stylistically, these Royan still lifes display a generally harsh or purposefully crude drawing of form and paint handling that reinforces the blunt-ness of message. Another stylistic and iconographic

saw that the head resembled a German helmet."[42]

Such distortions look back to Picasso's work from the late 1920s, when surrealism rose as a powerful influence on his art and he responded with inventive female anatomies meant more to menace than to please. In the wartime period, however, Picasso somehow makes us feel that his figures are actually distorted humans rather than fictive, fully imaginary creations. The powerful disorientations that can result are evident, for example, in the famous *Woman Dressing Her Hair* in the Museum of Modern Art (fig. 8). Picasso here revisited a motif found repeatedly in his work in images of self-absorbed bathers, one that comes

departure of the period is the darkly limned, torturous deformations of female anatomy that set in, embodying the distorting, transformative powers of wartime emotion. In a relaxed mood, when he was drawing his young daughter Maya, for example, Picasso might reprise a delicately classicizing mode from earlier years.[41] Generally, however, the women in his art from this time take on a monstrous quality, with heads reworked into dog faces or skulls and bodies verging more toward skeletons or cadavers than living creatures. In some sketches (e.g., fig. 7), we seem to witness the evolution of a relatively naturalistic head into a ghastly skull-like incubus. In reporting to Daniel-Henry Kahnweiler an anecdote about one such work, Picasso admitted the subconscious proddings behind them: "When the Germans arrived in France, I was in Royan, and one day I did a portrait of a woman . . . and when the Germans arrived a few days later, I

ultimately from a long tradition of depictions of the Birth of Venus (see fig. 9). Nineteenth-century academic artists such as Adolphe-William Bouguereau and Louis Perrault had rendered the image of Venus wringing her hair as a sugary cliché,[43] but Picasso gave it the force of a battering ram.

As we can now trace in Picasso's Royan sketchbooks, this composition began early in 1940 with a series of lithe, Matissian drawings of a nude with her arms raised, but by 14 March it had evolved into a far more contorted form.[44] Further studies for the figure date from 3–8 June 1940,[45] and a final overall sketch, which may actually postdate the painting, is inscribed 19 June (fig. 10).[46] As William

Rubin has pointed out, the purpose of the extreme transfigurations in the imposing bather that Picasso finally committed to canvas was "to suggest psychic conflict through somatic dislocation."[47] Confined within a tight, cell-like space and illuminated against nighttime shadows by an artificial raking light, she looms powerfully, taking on all at once the personae of prisoner, victim, and oppressor. She is a mountain of flesh, but in Picasso's cold light seems to be as much carved stone as organic matter. Her exposed ribs on one side suggest starvation, while the massiveness of her elephantine legs, huge abdomen, and tumescent head and breasts lend her brute force. It has to be remembered that

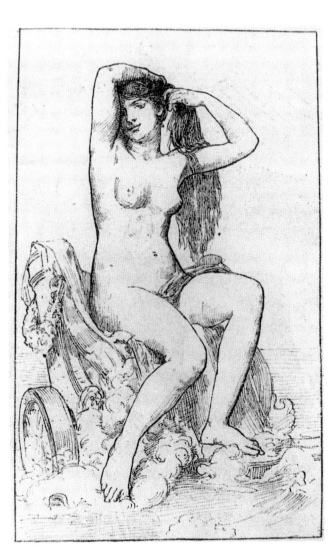

FIG. 9
Louis Perrault, *Venus*, ca. 1890. Reproduction in *Salon de 1890, catalogue illustré.*

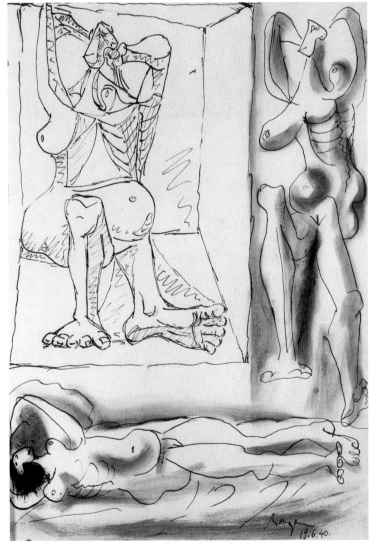

FIG. 10
Pablo Picasso, *Sketches of Nudes,* 19 June 1940. Pen, ink, and ink wash on paper, 16 ¼ × 11 ¹³⁄₁₆ in. (41.3 × 30 cm). Musée Picasso, Paris. M.P. 1880, folio 11R.

Picasso worked on his canvas at the same time that Hitler was overrunning the Low Countries and crossing into France. Nightmares were coming true; to his, Picasso gave flesh and bones.

Another good indication of the despair and shock that for Picasso accompanied the outbreak of war is found in such rapid notebook sketches as those seen in figure 11 and on page 63, figure 9. Both come from a sketchbook dated 30 September to 29 October 1939, now in the Musée Picasso.[48] The latter shows a thick web of lines somewhat similar to those in certain drawings from the late 1920s, when Picasso was beginning to conceive linear sculptures made from armatures of wire or welded rods. Here, the hint of a figure inhabits the web, but it is absorbed into a flurry of disorienting vectors and contradictory perspectives that build to a sense of all-enveloping chaos. In the other sketch, Picasso produced his own variation on a traditional religious theme that can be read as a gruesome Mother and Child or perhaps Mary Magdalen contemplating a skull (see fig. 13). The woman holds on her lap the skull of a sheep wrapped inauspiciously in newspaper. The large lace or ruffled collar suggests seventeenth-century attire, and the stylizations of the figure again express Picasso's interest in Romanesque art (compare fig. 12), although the radio and buffet in the background make it clear that this is really a contemporary drama. To add a darkly bitter and sardonic note, Picasso shows the woman wiggling her fingers through one eye socket and the open jaw of the victimized sheep. If any religious significance resided in the motif for Picasso, it could only have been the mocking of Christ and, with it, Christian promises of salvation.

PICASSO IN OCCUPIED PARIS

Picasso could easily have fled France, had he chosen to do so. Specific offers to help him emigrate came from Mexico and the United States, but perhaps the thought of all the difficulties involved in relocating himself, his art, and all the significant others in his life discouraged him from taking action. At any rate, he had decided by the summer of 1940 to remain in France, and on 23 August he left Royan to return permanently to Paris, Marie-Thérèse and Dora Maar following soon after. For a long while, Picasso split his time between his apartment in the rue La Boétie and studio in the rue des Grands-Augustins. Since travel across Paris had become more difficult with the Occupation, he finally transferred completely to the rue des Grands-Augustins, probably by early 1942. Dora Maar lived around the corner in the rue de Savoie, and he installed Marie-Thérèse and Maya in an apartment a short walk across the river on the boulevard Henri-IV. His son Paulo was living in Switzerland under the watchful eye of Bernhard Geiser, but his wife Olga, from whom he had separated in 1935, remained in Paris, at least at first, despite Picasso's efforts to persuade her also to relocate to Switzerland.

FIG. 11
Pablo Picasso, *Sketch of a Woman Holding a Sheep's Skull,* October 1939. Pencil on paper, 8½ × 6 ¹¹⁄₁₆ in. (21.7 × 17 cm). Musée Picasso, Paris. M.P. 1990–111, folio 51R.

FIG. 12
Mother and Child, altar front, Spanish, Catalan, 12th century. Fresco (detail).

FIG. 13
El Greco, *The Repentant Magdalen,* ca. 1577. Oil on canvas, 42½ × 39⅞ in. (108 × 101.3 cm). Worcester Art Museum, Worcester, Massachusetts, museum purchase.

Picasso's activities in occupied Paris, and his conduct vis-à-vis the Occupation regime, have been the subject of much conjecture, supporters at one end of the spectrum trying to make of him a Resistance hero and critics at the other attempting to tar his reputation with accusations of collaboration.[49] Neither extreme is accurate. Although Picasso's biography during the Occupation still remains an incomplete mosaic, based on scattered documentation and often secondhand reports, an overall picture has begun to emerge. It provides the image of an artist who tried to survive as best he could in order to continue his work. Picasso remained active in certain social and cultural circles, but attempted to keep a low profile to avoid attracting attention from those authorities in whose eyes he was a degenerate, foreign artist linked more than any other figure to subversive, even "Jewish" factions of modern art.[50] Picasso lived under the oppressive weight of German surveillance, manifested most blatantly by occasional searches of his studio by Nazi soldiers. He was even summoned like other citizens to register for the Service de travail obligatoire (STO), which could have resulted in his transfer to Germany for work as a laborer.[51] It is clear that Picasso's financial well being allowed for privileges that eased the discomfort of life made grim by Occupation shortages, and that his status as a famous artist respected around the world brought from certain quarters a favoritism that, although difficult to identify precisely in terms of source, helped on occasion to keep him safe. In general, however, he sought to heed the advice of his friend André-Louis Dubois and try to "remain invisible."[52]

The public life of culture and the arts in occupied Paris was more plentiful than might be assumed. A look at the entertainment pages of a wartime newspaper such as *Comoedia,* for example, reveals just how lively the cultural world remained, with numerous concerts, theatrical presentations, art exhibitions, and films playing at any one time. The artistic content was decidedly conservative, and the criticism that accompanied it markedly right wing, but, on the surface at least, an air of normality prevailed, even if much of the patronage came from Occupation forces.

Picasso's role in this cultural scene obviously diminished from prewar levels, but remained significant. Books about him continued to appear, despite stringent censorship by the Germans, including *Picasso: Seize peintures 1939–1943,* with text by Robert Desnos, which came out late in 1943, and the second volume of Christian Zervos's catalogue raisonné, which appeared in 1942. Picasso provided illustrations to several books of poetry and essays published during the war, such as Georges Hugnet's *La Chèvre-Feuille* (Paris, 1943) and Robert Desnos's *Contrée* (Paris, 1944). To the underground surrealist publication *La Main à plume,* he supplied financial support, illustrations, and a photograph of *Head of a Bull* for the cover of the summer 1942 issue. The dealer Martin Fabiani had taken over plans for the publication of Picasso's illustrations to Buffon's *Histoire naturelle* after Vollard's death in 1939, and managed to bring this famous project to fruition in 1942. Picasso also published the occasional print, as with the Galerie Louise Leiris edition of *Combat in the Arena* in 1943 (cat. no. 12). Works by Picasso came up at public auction, sometimes fetching huge prices, and contrary to what is often reported, paintings by Picasso frequently appeared in exhibitions in wartime Paris.[53] Picasso himself claimed that, owing to a request from the Spanish embassy for an interdiction, the Occupation authorities prohibited him from exhibiting publicly, and an often repeated story tells of the forced removal from public view of a painting by Picasso during an opening at the Galerie Charpentier.[54] But while it is true that no one-man exhibition took place, his works could be seen in many shows around the city, and a fairly extensive behind-the-scenes commerce took place with his art, as Michael FitzGerald discusses in his essay in this book. Moreover, Picasso's name frequently appeared in the art press, most often as a target for reactionary diatribes by collaborationist critics but occasionally in more positive invocations of his work as a standard of achievement.

In his private life, Picasso also was far from reclusive. Sabartés and Brassaï provide vivid accounts of the many visitors to Picasso's studio.[55]

He occasionally went to the cinema and theater and frequented the cafés around his quartier on the Left Bank, usually running into friends such as the Zervoses or Paul Eluard and his wife Nusch. He dined with friends almost every day at his favorite restaurants, Le Catalan in the same street as his studio and the nearby Le Savoyard. He was visited frequently by expatriate Spaniards, and his circle of friends and acquaintances included many of the most prominent writers, poets, and cultural figures of the day, some of them active to varying degrees in the Resistance movement, and some of them, like Jean Cocteau, collaborators. The cast of participants for the reading of Picasso's play *Le Désir attrapé par la queue* in March 1944, and the audience that turned out to listen, is a who's who of the Parisian art and literary worlds.[56] He could afford the luxury of a private secretary (not that he paid Sabartés highly), abundant art supplies, black-market chateaubriands at Le Catalan, and, it seems, adequate supplies of coal. With the help of friends he was able to accomplish some unlikely Occupation-era feats, such as the casting into bronze of several large sculptures at a time when bronze was not only in short supply but also was confiscated by the Germans as metal to support their war industry.[57]

Although Picasso was able to maintain a degree of normality in his life, the war was always present. He felt direct, personal dangers posed by the Occupation. He was summoned, for example, to reveal to German officials the contents of his bank vault.[58] Less well known is the fact that, while Picasso was living in Royan, the Spanish embassy in Paris (where officials considered Picasso an enemy due to his anti-Franco stance) posted notices at both his apartment in the rue La Boétie and studio in the rue des Grands-Augustins, claiming these properties for the protectorship of the embassy.[59] Although Picasso showed both loyalty and resolve by attending the funerals of his Jewish friends Chaim Soutine and Max Jacob,[60] he was not someone with great personal courage when faced with threats from police or government agencies, and the prospect of enlistment by the STO must have been truly terrifying. Certainly, any visit he received at his studio by German troops was alarming. Françoise Gilot and André-Louis Dubois reported that they witnessed some of these visits, when searches were made of the studio and works damaged.[61] Gilot tells of repeated German harassment under the pretext of searches for the sculptor Jacques Lipchitz. And while Picasso himself was not always reliable about such details, he told one interviewer just after the liberation of Paris that the last German visitation had been only weeks before.[62]

Attacks in books and the press by collaborationist, anti-Semitic writers such as John Hemming Fry and Fritz René Vanderpyl would have contributed to this oppressive atmosphere.[63] In his 1942 book *L'Art sans patrie, un mensonge: Le pinceau d'Israël,* a Fascist diatribe against Jewish artists and their purportedly damaging effects on modern art, Vanderpyl made Picasso a special target by deceitfully implying Jewish roots through his use of a Picasso painting as his frontispiece! And Picasso's former friend Maurice de Vlaminck, in his famous article vilifying Picasso in the 6 June 1942 issue of *Comoedia,* voiced the increasingly common insinuation that Picasso and his work were somehow linked to the metaphysics of the Kabala and Talmud.[64] That Picasso had no Jewish blood in his family, and had to attest to this, like everyone else, when renewing his identity papers, did not deter his detractors. Such attacks, however, may have made him uneasy over the safety of his mistress Dora Maar, who is said to have been half Jewish.

In the politically complex position that Picasso occupied in wartime Paris, might such pressures have caused him to exercise what influence he had for self protection? There is little doubt that, on certain occasions, one authority or another stepped forward to assist him. The threatened seizure of his property by the Spanish government passed without any known explanation. In the case of the even more consequential summons by the STO, we again have no record of how Picasso was able to avoid complying, although possibly his age – in 1943 he was over the sixty-year-limit placed on workers – had much to do with it. Picasso's friend Maurice Toesca, who worked in the office of the prefecture, assisted with the renewal of his identity papers when Picasso wanted to avoid alerting the Germans and the Spanish embassy by following normal procedures, but Toesca was powerless at higher bureaucratic levels.[65] One possible source of assistance was the German sculptor Arno Breker, a Nazi favorite whose retrospective in Paris in 1942 became a showcase of National Socialist aesthetics and fawning collaborationist enthusiasm. In his memoirs, slanted by self-serving claims of sympathy for the French, Breker takes credit for protecting Picasso when he was accused of supplying money to the Communists in Spain and to Russia through Denmark.[66] And Picasso also was on speaking terms with the two German officers Ernst Jünger and Gerhard Heller, both cultured men who paid unwelcome but unavoidable visits to Picasso's studio.[67] The old story of a visit from the German ambassador Otto Abetz, to whose question about *Guernica* – "Did you do that?" – Picasso supposedly answered, "No, *you* did," is apocryphal.[68]

Given Picasso's hatred of fascism and fear of entanglement with government officials, it is highly unlikely that he would have sought any assistance directly, but his friends, especially Cocteau, might have appealed to German authorities on his behalf. Picasso always "kept his dignity," as Zervos later put it. The perception of compromise, however, fueled rumors of collaboration, lending a note of credibility to the old notion that Picasso's good friends in the Communist Party such as Aragon and Eluard later recruited him as a member and pushed him into the *épuration* proceedings partly to erase any possible confusion over his wartime contacts.[69] Against those who might tar his reputation come the equally indefensible claims that he played an active role with the Resistance or used his art as an aggressive propaganda agent. Picasso was a survivor. To survive was to work, which to him was all important, and this sheer determination took on for fellow artists and friends in Paris an inspiring heroic value, a symbolism that spread after the Liberation to a much broader realm. Jacques Prévert spoke gratefully of Picasso's decision to stay in Paris as "an act of courage,"[70] and Louis Parrot wrote, "Solely by his presence among us, he gave hope to those who would have ended up doubting our chances of survival," adding that his example warranted the thanks of all the intellectuals and artists of France.[71] The acknowledgment that Christian Zervos wrote of Picasso's inspirational role during the war is even more revealing and moving for its frankness. To correct inflated reports of Picasso's involvement with the Resistance, Zervos wrote to Alfred Barr:

Everything that has been recounted is bad journalism and for the most part false. The anecdotes are false. The participation of Picasso in the Resistance is false. Picasso simply preserved his dignity during the Occupation, as millions of people here did. But he never got involved in the Resistance. Consider that his work in itself is the greatest form of resistance, not only against an enemy but against millions of pretentious imbeciles. . . . Do not let yourself be influenced by nonexistent heroics. There were heroes in France, but they either paid with their lives or ask that there be silence for their actions.[72]

When an opportunity for public exposure of what Picasso had actually produced during the war finally came with the Liberation of Paris in August 1944, critical reception of the work had to contend with unusual forces. Picasso's international renown was suddenly greater than ever, but based on publicity rather than art. His new work, which had not been widely seen, held surprises even for his supporters, and strong political factors also came into play.

Fighting had barely subsided in the streets of Paris when Picasso returned to his studio in the rue des Grands-Augustins from Marie-Thérèse's apartment on the Right Bank, where he had spent the last days of the conflict. While there, he produced his personal celebration of the street fighting and Liberation, an interpretive copy of Poussin's *Triumph of Pan* (figs. 22–23).[73] Almost immediately, Allied soldiers and war correspondents began to stream to Picasso's studio to meet him and pay their respects. Interviews quickly appeared in publications as varied as *Art Digest, Vogue* (with wonderful photographs by Lee Miller, see figure 14), *The New Statesman and Nation,* and the *San Francisco Chronicle.*[74]

Just weeks after the Liberation, the artist André Fougeron, a member of the French Communist Party and a Resistance worker, started developing plans to honor Picasso at the 1944 Salon d'Automne, to become known popularly as the Liberation Salon.[75] Such an exhibition offered the perfect opportunity to celebrate Picasso's work and also the symbolic values of free will and perseverance against oppression for which it had come to stand, and the artist personally selected seventy-four paintings and five sculptures to show, all from recent years. A likely subtext eventually accompanying the plan was a capitalization on Picasso's prestige to further the cause of the Communist Party. Although Picasso had not yet committed himself to membership, at least not publicly, it is more than coincidental that his enlistment and its announcement took place with much fanfare on October 4 and 5, timed to precede the opening of the Salon d'Automne by just one day.[76]

The plans laid by party officials in league with certain of Picasso's friends succeeded probably

FIG. 14
Lee Miller with Pablo Picasso in his studio in the rue des Grands-Augustins, August or September 1944. Photograph by Lee Miller.

more than they dared hope. The story is now well known of the anti-Picasso manifestation staged in the Salon galleries by a gang of mostly student-aged visitors, spurred by a combination of reactionary objections to Picasso's aesthetics and politics, in which numerous paintings were actually taken down from the walls. Political views aside, Picasso's wartime art would have come as a shock to many Parisians who were not overly familiar with his work in general, let alone the tormented vision of recent years, made even more aggressive by comparison with the pallid niceties seen throughout most of the rest of the Salon. In a rapid countermanifestation, other young people agreed to stand guard in the galleries. Letters of praise for Picasso from Le Front national des étudiants and Comité national des écrivains appeared in the media, and various critics chimed in with support for Picasso and his political stance.[77] Simultaneously, Picasso received publicity in the newspapers for his contributions to various benefit events and participation in *épuration* proceedings against collaborationist artists.[78] His celebrity reached new heights, and the "parti aux 75,000 fusillés," as the Communist Party became known in reference to its Resistance losses, had scored a strategic coup.[79]

Not surprisingly, truly objective discussion of the pros and cons of Picasso's wartime production had little chance in this heated atmosphere, and critical debate tended to polarize around two opposite positions: fawning acceptance by political sympathizers and vehement rejection by aesthetic conservatives or, worse, those who saw Picasso and his art as antithetical to the purity of true French traditions, so important, they would say, to uphold and promote at this time of national reinvigoration.[80] Various vehicles arose, however, to spread the news of his new work internationally. Stories about Picasso at the Salon d'Automne, such as that by G. H. Archambault that appeared in the *New York Times Magazine* on 29 October, often carried illustrations of recent production.[81] The courageous and resourceful Christian Zervos was able to publish by the end of 1944 the latest edition of *Cahiers d'Art* (vols. 15–19, 1940–44), celebrating the work artists had done during the war, with special emphasis on Picasso. An exhibition of *Peintures récentes,* accompanied by a major catalogue, took place at the Galerie Louis Carré in June 1945, and an important exhibition pairing recent paintings by Picasso with work by Matisse opened at the Victoria and Albert Museum in London in December 1945.

The storm of controversy that this latter show provoked in London, where protagonists were far removed from the political agendas surrounding Picasso in Paris, illustrates just how troubling the grim, raw nature of Picasso's wartime work could be. In one characteristic attack on the exhibition, the critic Michael Ayrton wrote:

> *His pictures are now uniformly dung-coloured. . . . Picasso has in fact ceased to practice oil painting as a craft, and any other medium would have done as well for these pictures. . . . He is now engaged upon the intellectual activity of flogging his own clichés to death with one dirty brush.*[82]

Other critics rushed to Picasso's defense.[83] In the exhibition catalogue, a thoughtful assessment of the work by Zervos set it clearly into context:

> *It is because he had the power to compel himself to reduce his awareness of the absolute to a temporal plane that Picasso, through the events and struggles of this time, has been conscious of so many of our greatest problems. . . . [H]e represents humanity, glutted with murder, with hatred, chaos and affliction everywhere. All is calamity, beyond control or understanding. . . . His aim above all is to convey the mighty righteous anger of one who . . . refuses to bow to those forces which threaten it.*[84]

Powerful, uncompromising, and unremitting – these are qualities in Picasso's wartime work that stand out, still today, and that finally override any biographical or political considerations to constitute his true legacy.

THEMES OF THE ARTIST: 1940–44

After Picasso returned to Paris from Royan in August 1940, his productivity declined for several months, and he seems to have produced little or

nothing in the way of paintings, drawings, and sculpture until early in 1941. In what may have been his first work after this readjustment to life in Paris, he painted on 25 January 1941 a small gouache on board of a reclining nude (fig. 15).[85] Although Picasso did not develop the composition any further at the time, it is a milestone study, for it anticipates directly his famous *L'Aubade* and *Reclining Nude,* both from 1942, as well as other works in an important, extended series of reclining nudes (see figs. 16–17 and cat. nos. 51, 53 recto, 75).

The theme of the reclining nude weaves through Picasso's wartime art with several permutations and interpretive twists. As in *L'Aubade,* the nude is sometimes accompanied by a musician. At other times, as with the *Reclining Nude* of 1942, she is asleep, and sometimes the sleeper is accompanied by a companion, male or female, who watches and waits. Another variation is the combination of the nude with a figure who is washing, a theme with its own extended life in the wartime oeuvre.

These nudes vary considerably in stylistic handling and formal associations. In *Reclining Nude and Woman Washing Her Feet* (cat. no. 75), the elongated, twisting figure is rendered in a particularly linear, ideographic manner. In both *L'Aubade* and *Reclining Nude,* Picasso must have had in the back of his mind the pose of Goya's *Nude Maja. L'Aubade,* however, also relates to Ingres's *Odalisque with a Slave* from 1839–40 (fig. 18) and carries over

FIG. 15 [above left]
Pablo Picasso, *Reclining Nude,* 25 January 1941. Gouache on wood, 6 11/16 × 10 1/4 in. (17 × 26 cm). Private collection.

FIG. 16 [above right]
Pablo Picasso, *L'Aubade,* 4 May 1942. Oil on canvas, 76 3/4 × 104 3/8 in. (195 × 265.1 cm). Musée National d'Art Moderne, Centre National d'Art et de Culture Georges Pompidou, Paris.

FIG. 17 [above far right]
Pablo Picasso, *Reclining Nude,* 30 September 1942. Oil on canvas, 51 × 76 3/4 in. (129.5 × 195 cm). Berggruen Collection, Staatliche Museen zu Berlin.

from that source a hint of rich color and luxurious fabric that survives despite the harsh emendations to which Picasso subjected his composition. The modeling of the nude in *L'Aubade* is highly planar, resembling the buildup of form in Picasso's later metal cutouts. In the *Reclining Nude,* by contrast, the modeling has a painterly, solidly three-dimensional quality that contributes much to the figure's powerful presence.

These works have in common a somber air of loneliness. The architectural surroundings are always bleak and confining. Picasso's palette is usually stripped down to a sensually deprived range of browns, grays, and ochers, and his dim illumination casts a nighttime, wintry chill over the pictures. Picasso told Heller and others that he preferred to work at night, and that for the paintings to be understood, they should be seen at night.[86]

No work better exemplifies the mood of bleak subsistence that this cold nighttime light can express than the great *Still Life with Blood Sausage* traditionally dated 10 May 1941 (cat. no. 42), the

first of many powerful still lifes that Picasso produced in occupied Paris. [87] In a typically cubist still-life space, with objects and table top tipped steeply up toward the picture surface and the geometry of walls, table, and curtain providing a shifting field of planes, Picasso laid out under a hanging lamp a stark array of provisions. But this is more than just a simple wartime meal. The centralization of the table under an overhead light gives the composition a definite altarlike quality, with a suggestion of traditional formulas for divine light from above, as seen in so many seventeenth-century religious paintings. The dramatic juxtaposition of the truncated, intestinelike sausage with a large knife strongly invokes a sacrificial slaying, perhaps a reference to Christ's death on the cross. The bottle might contain sacramental wine or, alternatively, the vinegar that was fed to Christ in a sponge as he hung dying. Out of the open drawer, which can be read in this context as in the shape of a coffin or tomb, arises a batch of knives and forks, referred to by Picasso at one point as souls in Purgatory and positioned to resemble small figures gesticulating upward in Last Judgment scenes. Brigitte Baer in her essay in this book provides an alternative reading of the picture as self-portrait. In either case, it extends far beyond straightforward reportage into realms of personal revelation involving the artist's psychic life or thoughts of despair and salvation.

Throughout the wartime period the still life remained a key vehicle of expression for Picasso. Sometimes the works are small, not particularly ambitious exercises that might have afforded him a

FIG. 18
Jean-Auguste-Dominique Ingres, *Odalisque with a Slave*, 1839–40. Oil on canvas mounted on panel, 28⅜ × 39½ in. (sight) (72.1 × 100.3 cm). The Harvard University Art Museums, Cambridge, Massachusetts. Bequest of Grenville L. Winthrop.

brief pleasure through the manipulation of a piece of brightly colored fruit or the outlining of a jaunty pitcher. A well-known series of paintings of tomato plants from August 1944 provides an unusually upbeat note through the abundant patterning of green vines dotted with balls of red, and also reveals a domestic side of Picasso's life, in that tomato plants were commonly grown in window boxes in wartime Paris for a supply of food.[88]

Most often, however, Picasso's still-life compositions were essentially meditations on life and death. The magisterial *Still Life with Steer's Skull and Table* from 6 April 1942 (cat. no. 55), for example, painted with a companion still life to commemorate the recent death of his close friend Julio González, continued the development of his Royan-period memento mori pictures by bringing the viewer close to the gruesome skull of an animal whose death spasms are palpable in the agonized set of its jaw and strangely fanned teeth. Numerous works (e.g., cat. nos. 54, 71, 79, 80, 81, 83) use a human skull in the same role. The one from 14 March 1945 (cat. no. 80) sets the cold white surface of the death head against the organic vitality of green leeks, explained by Picasso to be a substitution for crossed bones.[89] The bulbous shape of the skull, with its huge and empty eye socket, reminds us of Picasso's bronze *Death's Head* from 1941, one of his most gripping wartime sculptures (cat. no. 54). The lightened palette of the painting, however, particularly the stripe of yellow sunlight that grazes the skull, contrasts with the morosity of many earlier works and may indicate the distinctly different emotional temperature that early in 1945 anticipated the end of the war.

The one theme from these years

that outweighs in importance and repetition even Picasso's still lifes is that of the Seated Woman. This motif defines more than any other the intensity of work from the war years. Beginning, as we have seen, in the Royan period and continuing throughout his time in occupied Paris, Picasso returned to the compositional idea of the Seated Woman again and again, wringing from it varied expressive effects and psychological nuances. For Picasso the theme developed into a kind of looking glass that reflected his own internal reactions to people and events around him, whether it be

happiness with a lover or anguish and fear about the war. From his "portraits" of others, an extensive self-portrait of the artist emerged.

Attempts are often made to label these works with specific identifications, and Dora Maar is the person generally named (see figs. 19–20). They most often are, in fact, paintings of "woman" in general. Picasso's smaller bustlength representations also fit into this category. The most common motif, however, is a halflength figure seated in a chair, reminiscent in format of so many portraits of seated popes and cardinals from past centuries. Although amply represented in Picasso's earlier work, the motif took on special meaning for the artist during the war, seemingly because it was a reliable template of psychological investigation. That Picasso told André Malraux, "When I paint a woman in an armchair, the armchair implies old age or death, right?"[90] must be seen as another of his purposefully elliptical aphorisms. Indeed, the range of emotion portrayed in these expressive women runs from humor and joy to utter abjection.

In the former category is the sparkling *Woman Seated in an Armchair* of 12 October 1941 (cat. no. 46). Even though painted during the darkest hours of the war, this work, through its brightly colored patterns, seems to ringingly affirm life. The composition dazzles with its juxtapositions of hot tones – from purple/green combinations to flamelike oranges – and a dynamic play of flattened shapes and energetic line. The sparkling stars in the wallpaper strike a note echoed throughout the rest of the densely packed, painterly surface. The only ominous element is the nail-like eyebrows that seem literally to pin one eye and one side of the face to the background.

The *Portrait of Dora Maar* from 9 October 1942, supposedly painted over a drawing by Cocteau and well known for the striped blouse that Picasso "made up,"[91] shows the extreme range of modes that applies in these paintings. Modeled with a degree of naturalism Picasso generally reserved during these years for women particularly dear to him such as his daughter Maya and Nusch Eluard, Dora stares outward with a wide-eyed look of resignation. The simplified,

FIG. 19 [left]
Pablo Picasso, *Woman with a Cigarette Holder (Dora Maar),* 10 August 1942. Oil on panel, 25 ½ × 21 in. (64 × 53.3 cm). Private collection.

FIG. 20 [above]
Portrait of Dora Maar with Cigarette Holder, 1946. Photograph by Louis Izis. Musée Picasso, Paris, Picasso Archives.

clearly defined planes of the figure and her columnar form give her a sculptural quality not far removed from the *Woman in a Long Dress* of 1943 (cat. no. 73), fashioned by Picasso out of a dressmaker's dummy with a head modeled in clay and an arm from a tribal sculpture.

The figure in *Woman in a Hat Seated in an Armchair* of 23 April 1942 (cat. no. 56), with her jaunty hat, dazed expression, and flattened dislocations of head and torso, has a somewhat comical air, while the *Bust of a Woman* of 15 October 1941 and *Woman in Gray (Paris),* of 6 August 1942 (cat. nos. 47, 60), employ similar but more extreme dislocations and simplifications in the creation of images of women unforgivingly monstrous. Proboscis-like noses resemble the long and slender snout of Picasso's Afghan hound Kazbek. Teeth are bared in open mouths, ready to pierce. Heads are tightly gripped by dark, angular hats and rigid blocks of hair. *Bust of a Woman* appeared just three days after the brightly painted *Woman Seated in an Armchair* from Düsseldorf but represents a drastic shift of emotion from the gay and playful to dark terror.

One of the most famous of these seated figures, the *Woman with an Artichoke* from 1942 (see fig. 21, cat. no. 61), echoes similar notes of distress. On the one hand, she has all the regal bearing of Ingres's *Mme Moitessier* or his Napoleon seated on his throne with raised scepter.[92] She could also be taken for Picasso's housekeeper Inés, sitting with a long-stemmed artichoke meant for dinner. The overall, inescapable impression of the image, however, is threatening power. The monumental scale of the figure is daunting. The sharp fingers on one hand are like claws or an armored glove, and the artichoke has more the look of a club or a German hand grenade. Picasso's palette of dark greens, grays, and browns reinforces the lugubrious mood.

The force behind all these works is the twisting, distorting, deconstructing experience of war. Out of the depths of despair, however, Picasso was able to extract reasons for hope. Beginning with the monumental *Man with a Lamb* of spring 1943 (cat. no. 66), we can find clear if not consistent signs of optimism. Two recent developments in the Allied counteroffensive against Germany – the invasion of North Africa in October 1942 and the surrender of the German Sixth Army in Russia after the Battle of Stalingrad – signaled a decisive change in the fortunes of war. Such events were reported to the French population not by Vichy newspapers but by clandestine papers and the BBC, and Picasso would have been aware of them.

Picasso made his first known studies for the *Man with a Lamb* on 15 July 1942, conflating two figures in the classical scene of tribute-bearing in his print *Paris, 14 July 1942* (cat. nos. 57, 58), which in turn seems to be based on a photograph of a gathering of his family in Spain.[93] Over the next year, he developed his ideas for the sculpture through more than fifty drawings examining details of the man, the lamb, or the compositional ensemble. The last drawings are inscribed March 1943, and although Picasso later told Brassaï that

FIG. 21
Pablo Picasso, *Woman with an Artichoke,* 1942. Oil on canvas, 76¾ × 51¼ in. (195 × 130.2 cm). Museum Ludwig, Ludwig Collection, Cologne. Cat. no. 61.

he modeled the sculpture in February, it must date from March or soon thereafter.[94]

Over the course of development, Picasso changed his conception of the image from that of a young man rather protectively holding a playful lamb to an older man who, standing rigidly upright, grasps and holds out before him a trussed animal straining its head upward. Although Picasso cautioned about the final sculpture that "there's nothing religious about it at all. . . . There's no symbolism in it," and that what he was after was "a human feeling, a feeling that exists now as it has always existed,"[95] much discussion has centered on possible ancient and Christian sources for the sculpture and alternative interpretations.[96] In the composition's final form, it is hard to tell if the lamb is being saved (with connotations of Christ and the Good Shepherd) or is about to be sacrificially slaughtered, as the goat in his earlier drawing (cat. no. 17) had been so ferociously put to death. The fixed expression on the man's face and his tight grip, with huge hands, on the braying, straining lamb suggest the latter. Picasso's "human feeling," however, may come not so much from the man's care of the lamb as from the transcending notion of dedication, as in the ancient story of Abraham and Isaac, and the willingness to make a sacrifice for the greater common good. This message in 1943 would have been powerful and hopeful, and it is little wonder that Picasso kept the *Man with a Lamb* in the center of his studio for the rest of the war and often posed with it, as a centerpiece of his wartime art, with postwar visitors (see fig. 14).

Another optimistic signal is found in the large painting entitled *First Steps* from 21 May 1943 (cat. no. 67). A wobbly but determined child is being helped to take its first steps by a protective mother. Easy sentiment was not a common ingredient in Picasso's wartime work, and here, the strongly architectural quality of his composition, with the mother forming a compact arch over the angular structure of the child, overrides the sweetness of theme. In essence, Picasso stresses not only the innocence of youth but also the hopeful future of a younger generation as it thrives and carries forward.

Even the architectural studies Picasso made of familiar sites and monuments in the immediate environs of Paris strike a sanguine note. These date from mid-1943 onward. Although generally dark and claustrophobically patterned, they concentrate on well-known structures – bridges, Notre Dame, the Vert-Galant – and seem to celebrate the beauty and lasting humanistic quality of this built environment.[97]

Mention has already been made of the work Picasso produced during the street fighting prior to the Liberation of Paris, an event that brought much closer the conclusion of the war and signaled the end of the personal hell that Picasso and his fellow Parisians had endured. His variation on Poussin's

Triumph of Pan (figs. 22–23) is perhaps an allusion to the frenzy of street fighting but most basically seems an expression of ecstatic joy, a vicarious release of emotion unhampered by moderating reason. It is a bacchanalia of the spirit. After the painful distortions found in his earlier Seated Women, Picasso's figures are whole again, albeit stretched and twisted in rubbery configurations that now are emblems of glee rather than debilitation. Cognizant of the healing role that art could play after so devastating a societal disaster, and the need for a restoration of order, Picasso spoke of the importance at this time of an art of discipline. "Very likely," Picasso said, "for the poet it is a time to write sonnets."[98] The war, of course, was far from over, and during the months ahead he continued to produce admonitory memento mori and other stark reminders of political reality. Indeed, some of his darkest and most troubling pictures followed VE Day, during the difficult period of European reconstruction.

Nevertheless, hostilities were near an end by the close of 1944. Early in 1945, Picasso began work on a painting that stands as a counterpart to the *Guernica* of 1937, commemorating the conclusion of the war years just as that earlier masterpiece had marked their beginning. His *Charnel House* (cat. no. 82), worked on over the course of many months, together with his *Monument to the Spanish Who Died for France* (Monument aux Espagnols morts pour la France) (cat. no. 83) from 1945–47, both attempted to conclude this painful period by memorializing victims, including the many on the Spanish side who had given their lives with little or no recognition. In one combined, powerful statement, Picasso exhibited both paintings at the Communist-organized exhibition *Art et résistance* in February 1946, where they spoke propagandistically of mourning, retribution, and the harsh treatment Spanish Republicans had received at the hands of the French government.[99]

The Charnel House has more in common with *Guernica* than just iconography, and Picasso may have thought of the two pictures as pendants that together would stand as bracketing statements around the wartime period. It is one of the largest

paintings Picasso undertook for ten years or so after *Guernica.* As with the earlier work, Picasso restricted himself to a highly restrained palette of grays, black, and white, applied within a linear structure of segmented details that adds a staccato rhythm to the light-dark contrasts. This black-and-white construction may express in part Picasso's debt to the graphic art of Goya, where he had found a similar image of mass carnage,[100] or may also reflect the influence of black-and-white films or photography. Dora Maar claimed that the idea for the painting came from a feature film they had seen together.[101] More convincing is the assertion, first made by Picasso himself, although later questioned by various authors, that inspiration for the painting came from revelations of the atrocities of the German concentration camps. Reports of the camps and other *charniers* had begun to spread

even before the end of 1944, sometimes with the inclusion of photographs of victims.[102] Even a population whose sensitivities were numbed by five years of war was deeply upset by such news.

Part of Picasso's success in producing so strong a brooding effect in this picture is owed to a factor that in the past has been considered a fault, the canvas's *non-finito* condition. Picasso worked on the composition intermittently over a long period of time, and Zervos photographed several different states.[103] Whether he reached an impasse he could not or did not wish to resolve, or whether he considered the composition duly complete, we do not know. Obviously Picasso considered it "finished" enough to sign it and release it for exhibition and sale.[104]

In its final state, in which underlayers of drawing and *pentimenti* are clearly visible and major segments

FIG. 22 [left]
Pablo Picasso, *Bacchanal*, 24–28 August 1944. Watercolor and gouache on paper, 12 × 16 in. (30.5 × 40.6 cm). Present whereabouts unknown.

FIG. 23 [above]
Nicolas Poussin, *The Triumph of Pan*, 1635–36. Oil on canvas, 52¾ × 57¹⁄₁₆ in. (134 × 145 cm). National Gallery, London.

are not painted in – such as the tabletop still life that stands over the massacred victims, the background, and the flames to the right – a ghostly, transparent, insubstantial aspect to the picture creates a trancelike level of consciousness part way between reality and dream.[105] Picasso liked to say that a successful work of art is never really finished.[106] *The Charnel House* may be a purposeful embodiment of this dictum. At any rate, it consummates in highly moving form the humanistic message of concern for the human race that animates so much of Picasso's wartime work. William Rubin has called it a requiem.[107] Like the *Guernica*, it is a timeless monument that has lost none of its power over the past fifty years and stands now as it did at the end of World War II, as a moving indictment of man's brutality to man.

Both the *Charnel House* and *Monument to the Spanish Who Died for France* satisfy Picasso's prescription for an art that could serve as a forceful "instrument of war against the enemy." Both, however, are far more rhetorical than most of his work from the war years, speaking in a declamatory

voice through visual codes that are freighted with traditional meanings that would enjoy immediate public legibility. Most of his imagery from the period is at once more personal and visceral, and political only in terms of a general humanitarianism. Picasso spoke frequently of his interest in investing the simplest objects with clear and elevated meanings, just as Christ had done in his sermons.

> *I want to tell something by means of the most common object: for example, a casserole, any old casserole, the one everybody knows. For me it is a vessel in the metaphorical sense, just like Christ's use of parables.*[108]

Herbert Read's insightful remarks about *Guernica* in 1938 are even more presciently applicable to the art of the following seven years:

> *[Picasso's] symbols are banal, like the symbols of Homer, Dante, Cervantes. For it is only when the widest commonplace is infused with the intensest passion that a great work of art, transcending all schools and categories, is born; and being born, lives immortally.*[109]

Like Van Gogh's potatoes and boots, expressive symbols that Picasso openly admired, his quotidian, nondescript subjects speak loudly. His blood sausages, artichokes, and leeks, sheep skulls intended ultimately for the dog's dinner, casseroles and candles, and anonymous lonely women may not actually *scream* the truth of the war, but they hit their marks of meaning with uncorrupted, penetrating force.

Picasso's Disasters of War: The Art of Blasphemy

Robert Rosenblum

Of the masterpieces at the Prado, in whose Spanish ancestral company Picasso hoped *Guernica* (fig. 1) would eventually be displayed for posterity,[1] none was more relevant than Goya's *Third of May, 1808* (fig. 2), which, although painted six years after the event, still gives the illusion of eye-witness immediacy. Its journalistic title might well have been updated by Picasso to the *Twenty-Sixth of April, 1937* in order to pinpoint the historical reality of the Nazi saturation bombing of helpless civilians as they went about their business at the end of a Monday market day in the ancient Basque capital.[2] Apart from its obvious precedence as a pictorial response to a Spanish national tragedy that involved brutal conflicts not only between foreign and native powers, but also between opposing internal factions, Goya's *Third of May, 1808* also launches on the epic scale of history painting a grim and modern vision of contemporary humanity that, as if in response to a pervasive evil, bitterly parodies Catholic traditions of imagery and morality.

Expanding upon many of the gruesome vignettes Goya recorded in a series of etchings, the *Disasters of War,* the *Third of May* shrilly proclaims an era dominated by the anti-Christ. The central, white-shirted martyr, only one among the endless belt-line of victims, is a mock version of the Crucifixion; his extended palms even display ironically the blood stains of the stigmata, just as his posture of Christian martyrdom is shockingly repeated in the totally lifeless, bloody corpse that lies, face down, below him. Among those about to die is another figure who would outrage Catholic pieties, a tonsured monk who, kneeling, clutches his hands in a prayer that will go unheeded. The malevolent night sky offers no source of light and, below it, the unidentified monastery with a church tower (which recalls the sacred buildings that dominated the silhouette of Fuendetodos,[3] Goya's birthplace) looks like an archaeological relic from a civilization forever extinguished by the human slaughter in the foreground. Replacing the natural light of the sky, a lantern used by the Napoleonic troops targets the captured guerrillas and permits a glimpse of the carnage with photoflash clarity. The widening beam of light from the yellow-and-white lantern, whose colors are echoed in the yellow-and-white clothing of the central victim, almost becomes a surrogate agent of death. While discussing *Guernica* with André Malraux, Picasso himself brought up Goya's painting and stated

FIG. 2
Francisco de Goya, *The Third of May, 1808,* 1814. Oil on canvas,
104⅛ × 135¾ in. (266 × 345 cm). Museo Nacional del Prado, Madrid.

quite clearly, "The lantern is Death."[4]

In the *Third of May,* Christian motifs, poignantly warped by these new realities, are constantly recalled; and as in many of the *Disasters of War,* they evoke the traditional depictions of human suffering that finally lead to redemption. Christ on the Mount of Olives, which Goya in fact would paint in a legible Christian guise some five years later in 1819, giving it to the fathers at the Escuelas Pías in Madrid, is one such theme echoed by the *Third of May* as well as by the first plate, *Sad Forebodings of Things to Come,* of the *Disasters of War,* whose most shocking scenes of torture, dismemberment, and corpse-bearing can be viewed as new, godless mutations of standard Christian iconography. As a young artist, Goya, like the young Picasso, depicted a familiar religious repertory, including the Burial and the Lamentation of Christ (fig. 3), not to mention the Crucifixion itself.[5] These motifs are often present in the *Disasters,* as in the case of the mother carried off to her grave while her lone child, weeping, blindly follows the corpse (no. 50,

[page 38]
Pablo Picasso, *Study for* Guernica *(Mother and Dead Child)* (detail)
28 May 1937. Cat no. 6.

FIG. 1 [pages 40–41]
Pablo Picasso, *Guernica,* May–June 1937. Oil on canvas, 137⅜ × 305⅞ in.
(349 × 777 cm). Museo Nacional Centro de Arte Reina Sofía, Madrid.
On permanent loan from the Museo Nacional del Prado, Madrid.

FIG. 3
Francisco de Goya, *Burial of Christ,* ca. 1770–72. Oil on canvas, 51⅛ × 37⅜
in. (30 × 95 cm). Museo Lázaro Galdiano, Madrid.

Unhappy Mother, fig. 4), or when two uniformed brutes lug a male corpse to the cemetery (no. 56, *To the Cemetery*). And the most barbaric mutilations depicted (no. 33, *What More Could One Do?*) can be seen in the venerable context of saints' martyrdoms, so that the X-shaped, upside-down, dragged, or trussed bodies of the anonymous victims become hideous secular variants on the familiar abundance of uncommon suffering endured for their faith by such saints as Andrew, Peter, and Bartholomew, whose agonies were so often emphasized with close-up realism in the traditions of Spanish Catholic art.

Of the countless ways to interpret *Guernica* and its progeny, Goya's bitter inversions of Catholic imagery and morality offer some major points of departure. His relevance to Picasso must have been reaffirmed in 1935, when the Bibliothèque Nationale held a large exhibition from the Prado of Goya's prints (including the complete *Disasters of*

FIG. 4
Francisco de Goya, *Unhappy Mother,* from the *Disasters of War,* ca. 1812–15.
Etching and aquatint, 6 ¹⁄₁₆ × 8 ¹⁄₁₆ in. (15.5 × 20.5 cm). Achenbach
Foundation for Graphic Arts, Fine Arts Museums of San Francisco.

War), drawings, tapestries, and a few paintings.[6]
Like his old-master compatriot, Picasso, too, was
heir to the rituals and iconography of the church
and, even as a teenager in Spain, rendered in an
often sketchy, Goyesque manner a wide repertory
of Christian themes, from the Crucifixion and
the Annunciation to the Holy Family and Saint
Anthony of Padua. But following as well a tradition
of anti-Catholic parody particularly vital in the
most pious Catholic nations, Picasso, from his
childhood on, would often make irreverent jokes
on these conventional pieties. Already in 1895, the
year of his fourteenth birthday, he made a rapid
drawing of Christ blessing, of all unlikely people,
the Devil (and with his left hand, to boot) (fig. 5);[7]
and before the turn of the century he would make
cartoonlike spoofs on the popular imagery of ex-
votos, offering, for example, in a willfully crude,
folkloric style the ludicrous religious reflex of a
desperate prayer to an apparition of the Virgin in
heaven on the occasion of a very modern automobile accident (fig. 6).[8]

Such minor and youthful demonstrations of the
sinful fun of Catholic blasphemy reached almost
transcendental proportions in *Les Demoiselles d'Avignon* (fig. 7), in which the central whore, seemingly
afloat on a crescent of melon that rises from the
tumbling still life below, is virtually an illustration

FIG. 5 [top]
Pablo Picasso, *Christ Blessing the Devil,* 1895. India ink on paper, 8 ¼ × 10 ¼ in.
(21 × 26 cm). Artist's Estate.

FIG. 6 [above]
Pablo Picasso, *Parody of an Ex-Voto,* 1899–1900. Oil on canvas, 22 ¼ × 16 in.
(56.6 × 40.8 cm). Museu Picasso, Barcelona.

of the phrase later used to describe the painting, "The Apocalyptic Whorehouse."[9] For a Spaniard in particular, this airborne image becomes a shocking paraphrase of one of the most familiar themes in Spanish Catholic art, the Virgin borne to heaven on a crescent moon.[10] Of the countless international and Spanish examples of this motif, one must have been of particular relevance to Picasso, El Greco's *Assumption of the Virgin* of 1577 (fig. 8). Before leaving for the Art Institute of Chicago in 1906, it had made its way to Paris in 1904, where, for two years, it resided at the mecca of modern art, the Galerie Durand-Ruel, frequented by Picasso and every other aspiring artist.[11] With one brilliant, heretical twist, Picasso has wedded his national tradition of visionary Catholicism, exemplified by El Greco, the newly resurrected ancestral hero of Spanish modern art, to a brothel scene. Among other things, he thereby fused the fin-de-siècle concept of woman as virgin or femme fatale,[12] and recalled as well the old quip about the male Spaniard's typical Sunday: mass in the morning, bullfight in the afternoon, and brothel in the evening.

Such a double-entendre may still be understood in the context of the popular humor of Catholic countries that turns nuns into whores and priests into money-grabbing drunkards. But thirty years later, in *Guernica,* Picasso's heretical use of Catholic iconography took on a new and tragic pervasiveness whose sense of total malevolence matched not only its prototypes in Goya, but also the historical events on the eve of World War II. Christian faith has become futile, challenged already at the top of the painting in the sinister source of artificial light that offers the work's only reference to a uniquely twentieth-century reality. Recalling the benevolent double image of a sun/eye with raylike eyelashes first seen in the

FIG. 8 [above]
El Greco, *Assumption of the Virgin,* 1577. Oil on canvas, 158 × 90 in. (401.3 × 228.6 cm). The Art Institute of Chicago. Gift of Nancy Atwood Sprague in memory of Albert Arnold Sprague.

FIG. 9 [below]
Pablo Picasso, *Landscape, Juan-les-Pins,* 1920. Oil on canvas, 20 × 26⅜ in. (51 × 68 cm). Musée Picasso, Paris. M.P. 68.

summer of 1920 in a cheerful Mediterranean landscape view of Juan-les-Pins (fig. 9), this new mechanized light source is both an overhead lamp and an eye, with an electric light bulb for its filamented pupil, as well as an exploding bomb, whose eyelash-like rays bring death and chaos to the living creatures below. But this violation of cosmic natural order extends to the supernatural order as well.[13] Nothing is more familiar as a light source in Catholic art than the heavenly radiance that, often emanating from a dove, the symbol of the Holy Spirit, glows from the central heights of altarpieces that depict a wide range of Christian narratives. To choose only three of many old-master Spanish examples from the Prado, an early foundation for Picasso's infinite storehouse of images, El Greco's *Pentecost* (ca. 1600) (fig. 10), Juan Bautista Maino's *Adoration of the Magi* (1611), and Diego Velázquez's *Coronation of the Virgin by the Trinity* (1641–42) all turn our terrestrial eyes upward to a celestial sun and bird. In *Guernica,* that sun and bird have been destroyed. The unnatural light source, which can be read as pilot's eye, bomb, and flashbulb, becomes both the cause of the

of *Guernica*'s fallen warrior. *Guernica*'s bird, too, is marked for sacrifice, its open beak rhyming with the screaming mouth of the mother at the left, just before the moment it lands on a tabletop.[15] Picasso already had explored similar bird-and-table motifs, perhaps even recalling ironically his painter-father José Ruiz Blasco's kitsch specialty, the painting of pigeons in states of almost human happiness and domesticity.[16] As early as 1912, working in a cubist mode, Picasso painted two dead birds – their wings spread, their stiff feet turned up – lying on a tabletop that is given a triptychlike structure (fig. 12). The upstretched claws of one of the birds reach toward the fragmented cubist letters CHR, which inevitably suggest the word CHRIST. There is something strangely sacramental about this feathered offering, as if the birds were placed on an altar.[17] It was a theme, in fact, that would recur with many variations in Picasso's work before *Guernica*,

havoc below as well as the photographic means of recording and disseminating it through the press, much as the light from the groundborne lantern in Goya's *Third of May* seems both the agent of death and the objective way of disclosing these unspeakable facts for posterity.

As for the bird, it falls in the throes of death not only from its natural element, the sky, but also from its supernatural Catholic symbol of a radiant blaze of light. It may also be a bleak inversion of the message of the *colomba,* the dove in the upper left-hand corner of a manuscript page illustrating the *Deluge* in the Spanish Romanesque *Apocalypse of Saint Sever* (fig. 11).[14] This bird, high on the branch of an olive tree against an intensely yellow sky, signifies the coming of peace to the human and animal victims of cosmic disorder below. Picasso knew well these visionary images from medieval Spain and, as often pointed out, used their flat stylizations and colors, as did Miró, for inspiration, not only in his *Crucifixion* of 1930 but in the treatment

FIG. 10 [top left]
El Greco, *Pentecost (Descent from the Holy Cross),* ca. 1600. Oil on canvas, 108⅝ × 50 in. (275.9 × 127 cm). Museo Nacional del Prado, Madrid.

FIG. 11 [above]
The Deluge, from *The Apocalypse of Saint Sever,* 12th century. Illuminated manuscript. Bibliothèque Nationale, Paris.

especially in 1919–21, when a variety of birds – pigeon, dove, rooster – lie dead or about to be slaughtered on a table. But *Guernica*'s bird, falling from the sky or from its Catholic placement as the Holy Spirit within a reigning, golden luminosity, announces new dimensions of cosmic upheaval.

It is telling that, during the years of the Napoleonic invasion of Spain, from 1808 to 1814, Goya himself painted a series of grisly animal still lifes that included paintings of dead birds – chickens, turkeys, ducks, woodcocks (fig. 13) – brutally plucked, strung up, or trussed like barbaric sacrifices on kitchen counters, the feathered surrogates of the human corpses he was recording at the same time.[18] The triumph of human savagery seems, in these still lifes, to extend even to the domain of butchers and cooks, contaminating the sensuous appeal of earlier kitchen still-life traditions with real blood, pain, and indignities. Already in 1921, Picasso painted a ferocious black dog menacing a bound and helpless rooster in an image so close to violent death that it can hardly be called a "still life."[19] And only months after *Guernica,* on 15 February 1938, Picasso pushed this barbarism further in a painting of a demonic woman who, like a priestess of *Santería,* squats on the floor beside a knife, as with one hand she clutches the wings of a trussed, desperate rooster and with the other a cup for the blood (see page 19, fig. 3). It is an animal sacrifice made still more demonic in a drawing of the same year that depicts a frenzied woman plunging a knife into the throat of a trussed goat, as the blood drips into a bowl on the floor (cat. no. 17).

Guernica's evil inversions of both natural and supernatural law and order reach a sacrilegious extreme at the lower left of the painting, where the dead child is held by the screaming mother, whose open mouth, like the bird's, is directed to a now extinct heaven. Here, Picasso creates a heartrending parody of one of the most familiar of all Catholic images of suffering and redemption, the Pietà. Predictably, this, too, has a specifically Spanish inflection, not only in its extremities of physical and psychological pain, but more particularly in its

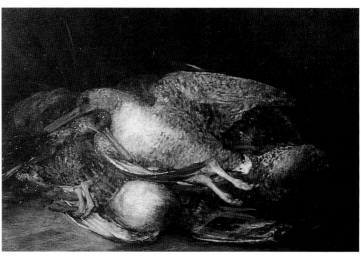

FIG. 12
Pablo Picasso, *Still Life with Dead Birds,* 1912. Oil on canvas, 46 × 65 in. (116.8 × 165.1 cm). Museo Nacional Centro de Arte Reina Sofia, Madrid.

FIG. 13
Francisco de Goya, *Still Life with Woodcocks,* 1808–12. Oil on canvas, 17¾ × 24¾ in. (45.1 × 62.9 cm). The Meadows Museum, Southern Methodist University, Dallas.

allusion to one of the most familiar images in Spanish art, the Virgen de las Dolores or the Virgen de las Angustias (the Virgin of Sorrows or Anguish), as often recreated in Spanish baroque polychrome sculpture and in popular religious art throughout the Hispanic world. The tongue of *Guernica*'s grieving mother is shaped like sharp, pointed metal, a metaphor for a sword (like the one that pierces the flank of the neighboring horse) and an allusion to the piercing metal that intensifies so many Spanish depictions of the Virgin, who, as in Gregorio Fernández's *Virgin of Sorrows,* plunges a sword into her own heart, her radiant halo a painful crown of metallic thorns (fig. 14).

This excruciating image of metal cutting into flesh can be found not only in many of the preliminary studies for *Guernica,* but also in the series of weeping women that followed it.[20] In one preparatory study of 28 May 1937 (cat. no. 6), a mother rushes from a burning building, her sharply pointed tongue directed straight up to the malevolent heavens as she holds a dying child whose chest, along with the mother's protective right hand, seems to have been pierced by a broken sword hurled, like one of Jupiter's thunderbolts, from a stormy sky.[21] Could this be a memory, too, of the centurion's lance that leaves the mark of the fatal wound on Christ's side? And in this drawing, the screaming mother's hair is exactly that, a tumble of real human hair fixed to the paper, a startling new form of collage as well as a survival of the Spanish tradition of including common realities – clothing, blood, hair – in sculptural depictions of Christian themes, whether in the most exalted shrines or in the *pasos,* the popular, lifesize processional figures wheeled through the streets during Holy Week. And in the same spirit of mixing tangible facts and pictorial fictions, Picasso, during the evolution of *Guernica,* added patches of patterned wallpaper as dresses for three of the painting's four women, as well as affixing, according to an unforgettable account by Roland Penrose, a strip of toilet paper to the kneeling woman's exposed buttocks.[22]

As is so often the case with Picasso, such techniques and images often recall the artist's childhood memories. Of surprising relevance here is the

FIG. 14
Gregorio Fernández, *Virgin of Sorrows,* 17th century. Mixed media. La Iglesia de la Vera Cruz, Valladolid, Spain.

fact that Picasso's father had once created his own Virgin of Sorrows from a bust of Venus acquired at a flea market. By covering the pagan head with a plaster-dipped cloth, adorning it with a metal halo and a garland of flowers, as well as adding fake tears and painted eyebrows to the face, he transformed the sculpture into a Spanish religious icon. When, in 1954, Rosamond Bernier went to Barcelona to gather material on early Picasso for the magazine *L'Oeil,* she visited the Picasso family's apartment and photographed many of its contents, including the corner shelf upon which this conversion of an antique deity to Catholicism still resided like a holy image. On seeing the photo, Picasso commented that he had always loved this odd work, that it was a "collage avant la lettre."[23]

The motif of the Virgin of Sorrows is one that casts its painful shadow across many of the drawings, prints, and paintings of convulsively sobbing women that Picasso continued to make during the aftershock of *Guernica.* More specifically, many of them appear to have as the physical source of pain long, pointed darning-needle shapes that, replacing their original function as symbols of female handiwork, actually pierce the tear ducts, releasing at times the kind of comma-shaped tears frequently represented in Spanish polychrome sculpture by bits of shaped glass. And as often happened with Picasso, these implicit allusions to old-master art would become ever more explicit in his later work. In a lithograph dated 2 March 1959, he actually

FIG. 15
Pablo Picasso, *Mater Dolorosa* (Jacqueline Roque), 2 March 1959.
Lithograph, 14½ × 10⅝ in. (37 × 27 cm).

made a portrait of his wife-to-be, Jacqueline Roque, as the Virgin of Sorrows, her eyes streaming tears and her exposed heart pierced by swordlike stems of flowers (fig. 15).

Like Joyce, Picasso had a genius for densely layered punning that can take us back through many genealogical tables to a variety of archetypes; and in the case of *Guernica,* this genius is so abundant that later commentators have been able to find cryptic references to everything from Vishnu and the Rape of Europa to Pinocchio and Hitler.[24] But on a more modest level of the kind of speculation Picasso's art will always invite, the multiple references to archetypal Christian themes, shown as a shocking anthology of sacrilegious inversions, fall into clearer focus. The very structure of the painting evokes one of the most familiar formats of Catholic altarpieces, the triptych. A particularly

relevant example, Matthias Grünewald's *Isenheim Altar,* which was published in 1936 for *Cahiers d'Art* by Picasso's friend and cataloguer, Christian Zervos, had already provided constant inspiration for the artist in the 1930s,[25] as it did for other masters of the decade, especially in Germany Max Beckmann and Otto Dix. Dix's triptych with predella of 1929–32, *War* (fig. 16), a gruesome memory of death in the trenches, offered a particularly blasphemous reincarnation of his sixteenth-century compatriot's anguished view of Christian suffering and ultimate redemption.[26]

But there are, of course, other inescapable memories of Christianity in *Guernica.* The dramatis personae, especially given the actual number of women and children who died during the bombing of the city, evoke the Massacre of the Innocents (indeed, the French press could refer to the event as the "Massacre du Peuple Basque"),[27] a theme whose memory is also grimly alive in one of Goya's *Disasters of War* (no. 11, *Nor Do These*). More specifically, both Poussin's and Reni's interpretations of the biblical massacre are often cited as sources of *Guernica.*[28] In addition, the apocalyptic tenor of the whole (which may also be discerned, via El Greco, in the visionary character of *Les Demoiselles d'Avignon*) finds a corollary in the familiar motif of Death on a Pale Horse. The speared, agonized animal in the center of Guernica, beyond its references to the bullring, also evokes the ghostly steed from Revelation who thunders across the earth leaving a trail of death and destruction. It was a biblical image of the end of the world, now consummated through modern warfare, that Picasso's compatriot, José Gutiérrez-Solana (who often exhibited in Paris and who moved there in 1937), had already painted in 1920,[29] probably in the wake of Vicente Blasco Ibáñez's famous novel of World War I, *The Four Horsemen of the Apocalypse* (1916) (fig. 17). And *Guernica*'s horse, placed in conjunction with the decapitated, hollow warrior on the ground, whose eyes and mouth remain open as if in startled revelation, may allude to another Christian theme, the Conversion of Saint Paul, especially Caravaggio's version,[30] although that miracle of revelation would here become a satanic parody, since the would-be convert now looks up with open, yet sightless eyes to an evil apparition.

Providing yet another allusion to Christian iconography, at the right-hand side of the "triptych," is the split-second image of a woman, her dress on fire, falling like a living torch from a window, at the same moment the bird drops to its death from the sky. With her arms stretched to the heavens in agony, the woman seems, among other things, a chillingly apt quotation from the *Disasters of War,* whether as the pair of hands reaching up from the chaos of a crowd escaping through flames (no. 41, *They Escape through the Flames*)[31] or the startling sight of a corpse just as it is hurled into a ditch that serves as a communal grave (no. 27, *Charity,* and no. 30, *Ravages of War*). It is telling that Goya is reputed to have said that the essential qualities of a draftsman lay in the ability to seize the five cardinal points of a figure as it falls from a roof to the ground,[32] and indeed, he often demonstrated this ability to capture the shock of a body falling mid-air. Could Picasso have had this in mind when, like a journalist at the front with a flash camera, he captured the minisecond of horror endured by the flaming woman before she hits the ground?

In any case, her posture, with its painfully stretched arms and exposed palms, first essayed in the drawing of a falling man (27 May 1937; Museo Nacional Centro de Arte Reina Sofia, Madrid), evokes a Crucifixion, especially in conjunction with the Pietà-like left-hand grouping of this triptych. And here, as well, Picasso has maligned the structure of Christian altarpieces, since either one of these themes, the Crucifixion or the Pietà, would conventionally be relegated to the larger, middle section of a triptych, whereas in *Guernica,* both are peripheral, leaving for the central devotional image nothing but the earthbound debris of a new form of destruction from the air. As a further irony, the woman, who, with bared buttocks and one knee dragging, raises her eyes in bewilderment to the skies, is not only a parody of Ingres's painting of Thetis beseeching Jupiter to help her son Achilles in the Trojan Wars below (fig. 18),[33] but also recalls

FIG. 16
Otto Dix, *War,* 1929–32. Mixed media on panel. 103⅞ × 160⅝ in. (264 × 408 cm) (overall). Staatliche Kunstsammlungen Dresden.

the awestruck, kneeling posture of prayer associated with Catholic traditions of rural feminine piety, an expression of wide-eyed, simpleminded faith often recorded by Goya.[34]

Guernica was hardly the first of Picasso's references to the collision between the realities of the twentieth century and the venerable Catholic traditions that had nurtured him in Spain, but his earlier heresies had been more humorous, sporadic, or single-minded in their allusions to Christian rituals and symbols. In *Guernica,* the artist's awareness of the impossible disparity between a new kind of modern warfare and the ancient faith in heavenly redemption through suffering takes on a numbing, apocalyptic vastness that resurrects for our own century the shock of Goya's *Third of May,* yielding a universal vision of the way these holy images from churches and museums had become pitiful anachronisms, to be remembered only by mockery. To be sure, Picasso was never able to repeat the epic sweep of *Guernica*'s proclamation of a new form of anti-Christian evil, but the aftershocks could be felt again and again throughout the war years, in both oblique and direct ways.

Night Fishing at Antibes (cat. no. 31) was completed at the end of August 1939, on the eve of Germany's invasion of Poland on 1 September and the declaration of war. It has been persuasively interpreted by Timothy Anglin Burgard[35] as a painting that, beginning superficially as a Mediterranean genre scene, reveals a wealth of references to the defeat of Republican Spain, to the women in Picasso's private life, and to traditions of Christian imagery.[36] Absorbed here are such canonic images as Raphael's *Miraculous Draft of Fishes,* such works of Spanish medieval art as a scene from the life of Saint Vincent that was surely known to Picasso,[37] and still more of the apocalyptic imagery of the Beatus manuscripts that had so often nourished his imagination. These visions might include the spiraling yellow-orange light at the top of the painting that can be read not only as the fishermen's acetylene decoy lamp that substitutes for solar light, but also as the apparition of a comet or shooting star signaling imminent, airborne calamity. Moreover, the two female spectators on the jetty may be interpreted as a complementary pair of visionary personae. Dora Maar reincarnates the Whore of Babylon, lewdly licking her double-scoop ice-cream cone with the tongue of her ithyphallic head while clutching with her other hand the bicycle's handlebar at the appropriate place in her skirt; and Jacqueline Lamba, André Breton's wife, reincarnates the Woman of the Apocalypse, clothed in the sun, the crescent moon at her feet. Opposed to the pseudosolar blaze in the heavens above, she seems to offer a lunar counterpart to the whore, with a crescent-moon profile superimposed on a face bathed in milky light. Moreover, the central drama of the painting may allude through traditional Christian iconography to the sacrifice of Christ. The fish (here a sole, whose oddly flattened eyes and "face" once prompted Alfred H. Barr to call it the "most Picassoid of fishes")[38] was often read as a symbol of Christ and, when pierced by a trident, became a symbol of the Crucifixion.[39] In *Night Fishing,* the trident, now provided with an extra tine, like a table fork about to attack a platter of fish, becomes a four-pronged spear that is seen at the instant before it claims its sacrificial victim. Meanwhile, the ordinary fish at the left has just swum past the diagonal line tied to the toe of the other fisherman, who, clumsily poised and stupidly staring at the water, offers a foil

FIG. 17
José Gutiérrez-Solana, *The War,* 1920. Oil on canvas, 42 × 32 ½ in. (106.7 × 82.6 cm). Private collection, Madrid.

to the focused, elegant precision of his companion, whose clutched weapon is as unswervingly vertical as a plumb line. Does this would-be genre scene, of an imposing size that rivals *Guernica,* evoke a distorted, wartorn memory of Christian sacrifice in the way that, later in 1943, the noble solemnity of the bronze *Man with a Lamb* (cat. no. 66) would echo back through the Bible to the Sacrifice of Isaac? And might the white-and-yellow lamp that, from the prow of the boat, casts its beams upon the sole echo the lethal lantern in Goya's *Third of May?*

Animal sacrifice, the soul of bullfighting and, for Picasso, a recurrent memory of both pagan and Christian motifs, left its terror, blood, and bones on many works from the war years. Already in April 1939, another bird becomes the victim of a new kind of savagery in the two versions of a ferocious cat (22 [cat. no. 30] and 24 [?] April [Zervos IX, 297]) torturing a fluttering bird whose screaming, open beak and helpless legs echo the desperation of its falling prototype in *Guernica.* On 13 November 1941, Picasso returned to the more familiar prewar theme of a bird – in this case, a white pigeon – lying on what resembles an aerial view of a tabletop whose brilliant reds and yellows assert the Spanish national colors (cat. no. 48).[40] With its outstretched red legs and claws that seem to penetrate the bird's own body like a sword, this ironic dove of peace also evokes an airplane through the unexpectedly smooth, metallic configuration of the taut upper wing, which contrasts to the feathered contour of the lower wing falling toward the earth.

Of the wartime animal victims, few, if any, are more brutalized than the sheep whose heads and skulls make up a grisly sequence that, moving from sketchbook to paintings, Picasso started in Royan on 30 September 1939, at the end of the bleak month that began with an official declaration of war. Ranging from the shadowy, bone-dry skull of a black-and-white india ink drawing (1 October 1939) (cat. no. 34) to the painting of a flayed head whose blood-red tissues seem caught between life and death (4 October 1939) (cat. no. 35), these butcher's trophies add a new dimension to the Spanish tradition of memento mori, painfully appropriate to the outbreak of an ever-expanding war. In her eloquent and detailed account of this series, Jean Sutherland Boggs raised exactly those questions pertinent to *Guernica*'s heretical fusion of Catholic symbolism and Goya's black vision of modern history.[41] Are these slaughtered – in fact, decapitated – sheep or lambs to be read as nightmare mutations of the Agnus Dei, the lamb of God, who might also be resurrected in more hopeful terms in the bronze *Man with a Lamb*?[42] Indeed, Christian iconography offers as many different readings of the lamb as does the most multilayered of Picasso's own images. It may symbolize not only the Crucifixion and the Eucharist, as in Zurbarán's starkly shadowed image of a haloed, woolly lamb with its four legs bound together for slaughter,[43] but also the Resurrection, a redeemed sinner, a faithful member of the flock, or, in still more general terms, a harmless innocence matching that of the dove of peace (or Holy Spirit) that so often is killed

and mysteriously reborn in Picasso's art and life, even in the name of his second daughter, Paloma.[44]

As with *Guernica,* Goya's dark shadow also hovers over these remnants from a butcher's counter. Just as he had depicted the humanoid corpses of birds during the years of the Napoleonic invasion, so, too, did Goya paint an even more gruesome still life of a sheep hacked into a dismembered head, two rib cages, and the end of a joint, a canvas that, with grimly perfect timing for Picasso, was acquired by the Musée du Louvre in 1937.[45] One of Picasso's variations on this morbid theme, 6 October 1939 (cat. no. 36), is particularly close to Goya in its inclusion of a rib-cage fragment, but the head's almost audible scream defies the inertia of Goya's sheep's head and resonates back to the hysterical noise of *Guernica.*

After the screams of war, however, the eerie, eternal silence of death must preside, as it finally does in human terms in Picasso's graveyard climax to these apocalyptic years, the *Charnel House* (cat. no. 82), begun in February 1945, when the end of the war was in sight.[46] The satanic sky, source of the explosive, deathly energy in *Guernica,* has vanished. The upper zone of the canvas is left incomplete, a linear skeleton of a still life – pitcher and casserole on a tabletop – that, by contrast, intensifies the earthbound density of the human dump heap abandoned in the constricted space of a kitchen floor. From these corpses, a suggestion of ghostly fire rises toward the upper right, a memory perhaps of the ovens in the concentration camps, also evoked, in a startlingly direct way, in Picasso's ready-made sculpture of 1945, the *Venus of Gas,* a gas stove he found that recalls both a prehistoric fertility goddess and one of the Nazis' infamous new methods of genocide.[47] For such a scene of the human garbage of warfare, Picasso, of course, could turn to many plates from the *Disasters of War* (especially nos. 18–27)[48] and he may even have had in mind, given the domestic setting with its murdered nuclear family scattered among the now equally inanimate furniture, Daumier's famous lithograph of the slaughter in a bedroom of four members of a Parisian family (mother, father, infant, and grandparent) on the rue Transnonain during the workers' uprisings of 14–15 April 1834. But these memories of art were also reincarnated for Picasso in the present tense of contemporary history through the medium of journalistic photography, just as in 1937 he had turned to news accounts of the bombing of Guernica provided by the French press. Presumably Picasso saw for the first time, in 1945, the realities of the concentration camps as revealed through black-and-white photographs, although it has recently been suggested that it was more likely an earlier photograph of the corpses of Soviet victims, reproduced in the 13 December 1944 issue of *L'Humanité,* that initially triggered his imagination when working on the *Charnel House.*[49] But whatever the case, the *Charnel House,* like *Guernica,* far transcends the particulars of modern historical fact. As a tombstonelike epilogue to the 1937 mural that appeared to launch this universal evil, the *Charnel House* also turns Christianity upside down. The male victim, a father, still bears the marks of his torture, his wrists bound like the legs of the sacrificial lamb in the bronze of 1943. But this binding brutally forces his arms to rise high over his floor-bound head, in a gross distortion of the Crucifixion, a hideous variation on Saint Peter's own inversion of Christ's martyrdom. A stream of blood flows from the dead mother's breast, as if from Christ's lanced side, pointlessly falling onto first one, and then the other, of the dead infant's outstretched hands in another mockery of the Eucharistic blood of Christ received in Holy Communion.

Perhaps the ultimate blasphemy is the way in which Picasso has extracted a skeletal, bone-white cruciform pattern from the painful intersection of the father's bound forearms. This ghost of a cross, rising above the camouflaged chaos of a family of corpses, is a shocking reminder in this makeshift cemetery of a long-lost world. William Rubin once aptly referred to the *Charnel House* as a requiem.[50] But Picasso also tells us that by 1945 there is no longer any church where a mass for these victims can be performed.

FIG. 18
Jean-Auguste-Dominique Ingres, *Jupiter and Thetis,* 1811. Oil on canvas, 131 × 102 ⅜ in. (327 × 260 cm). Musée Granet, Aix-en-Provence.

Death Falling from the Sky: Picasso's Wartime Texts

Lydia Csatò Gasman

That death could fall from heaven on so many, right in the middle of rushed life, has always had great meaning for me. – Picasso, 1967 [1]

The "bombings everyone expected" in Paris at the outset of World War II prompted Picasso's flight to Royan on the coast of the Atlantic. – Brassaï, 1966 [2]

Picasso was not the only one who feared bombings from the air. By the mid-1930s, many observant Europeans had succumbed to the inordinate fear of an apocalyptic air power.[3] During the Spanish Civil War and World War II, Nazi flying machines whose destructiveness far surpassed that of the German Zeppelins and "Gotha" bombers in World War I seemed to enforce the end of Western civilization. Air power was anything but abstract. The flying Death in the famous *Triumph of Death* at the Camposanto in Pisa[4] and the dropping demons in the naïve *Temptation of Saint Anthony,* reproduced in the winter 1937 issue of *Minotaure* (fig. 1),[5] now became real. Death descending from the air was there for all to see, so tangible and tragic that it appeared farcical, a standard subject for cartoons such as the winged skeleton dispatching bombs in the Republican *El Angel de la Paz . . . de los Fascistas!* (fig. 2) and the winged messengers of the gestapo in David Low's *Angels of Peace Descend on Belgium* (fig. 3). Picasso wrote that his "eyes [were] caught by the sky"of war.[6] In his poetic thinking, the sinister planes of the enemy – swooping repeatedly, together with the "sky that lets itself down" (222)* – brushed against him, affecting his psychological makeup, physiological

functions, and power to create. Diving vertically, the "sky [let] its fist fall" (178) on Picasso. His skin, he sensed, was badgered by the buzzing bombers[7]/ "bees . . . of the sky" (210). The "wings of the sky . . . shook off their fleas" (215) onto his being.

Fear of bombs hammering from the sky is altogether different from trepidations that daze the psyche fallen prey to war pressures. While the fear of air raids is rational,[8] in 1940 Marc Bloch witnessed and recorded the "*cold* fear" inspired by air bombing that provokes a far-reaching disorder in the nervous system.[9] Its roots, he concluded, are "very deep in human nature" and manifest a "peculiarly illogical" dimension of the "instinct for self-preservation." Though an attack from the sky is, "probably, in itself, no more *actually* dangerous than many other kinds of peril to which the soldier" or the civilian is exposed, no one is "ever likely to forget the experience" of "dive-bombers," their dreadful "acoustic qualities," in themselves capable of "so work[ing] upon the nerves that they become wrought to a pitch of intolerable tension whence it is a very short step to panic."[10] The point

---

*Numbers in parentheses that follow quotations refer to pages in *Picasso: Collected Writings,* ed. Marie-Laure Bernadac and Christine Piot (New York: Abbeville Press, 1989). Also see note 6.

FIG. 1
José Guadalupe Posada, *Temptation of Saint Anthony.* Relief etching in zinc,
3⅞ × 5¾ in. (9.8 × 14.6 cm). *Minotaure* (winter 1937).

is, Bloch suggests, that the natural assumption of
heaven as the place of God blends into dread of
the sky as the space of bombers. Impacted by
"bombs dropped from a great height," the subliminal wager on heavenly goodness breaks down:[11]
"The combination of weight and altitude gives
them an appearance of almost visible violence
which no shelter, however thick, seems capable of
resisting. There is something inhuman about the
nature of the trajectory and the sense of power."[12]

Picasso himself was not hit by bombs, but they
did strike those with whom he identified. It was
their martyrdom that deep down martyred him,
regardless of his pragmatic selfishness and healthy
appetite for living. The fear of air raids he confessed
to only in his writings was evidently a fear for the
plight of other human beings. They were the "inter-
subject, [or] co-subject"[13] of Picasso's *Guernica* (see
pages 40–41, fig. 1), of shattering passages in his
wartime texts, and of their guarded transpositions
in concurrent art works. As he himself granted
some twenty years after the end of World War II,
"that death could fall from heaven on so many,
right in the middle of rushed life, has always
had a great meaning for me."[14] Science attests that
air-raid terror arises not only from a personal

[page 54]
Pablo Picasso
Cat Seizing a Bird (detail)
22 April 1939. Cat. no. 30.

predicament, but also from the knowledge that
bombs may hit those who are close to you.
Distance from actual bombing can worsen rather
than quell anguish; evil imagined can be more
intolerable than evil endured. Starkly present, it
flees retaliation. Post-traumatic stress disorder is
not uncommonly caused by "accounts of death or
injury (in contrast to direct encounters)." Being
"'confronted' with traumatic events would include
'learning about unexpected or violent death, serious harm, or threat of death or injury'"[15] occurring
in faraway communities to which the (confronted)
individual is loyal.

AIR POWER AND THE RELIGION OF FEAR

Shortly before the Spanish Civil War, Picasso's
friend André Malraux became convinced that "the
next war would primarily be won by air power."[16]
He was acquainted with the Realpolitik behind
"strategic terror bombing,"[17] the military theory
first formulated by General Giulio Douhet in the
1920s,[18] which advocated assaults on civilians and
nonmilitary targets in order to undermine the
enemy's will and capacity to resist. In *Man's Hope*
(published in 1938), confirming Douhet's principle
that merciless pounding from the air inflicts dis-
abling panic, Malraux proclaimed that something
like a new religion of fear was born in Spain under
the "menace of the sky." When he is on the street
and "under fire" from Fascist warplanes, Moreno
says in *Man's Hope,* "I don't believe in 'thinking
things out' or the 'eternal verities,' or anything at
all. I believe only in fear. Real fear, not the sort that
makes one talk, but the fear that sets one running."[19]
In *Man's Hope,* fear of the sky is a quasi-religious fear
of the sublime. During an air raid, people hustling
on the ground are not simply afraid of the actual
German, Italian, or Spanish warplanes, but are
overwhelmed as if by a natural disaster, not bombing but an "earthquake." Air raids cause the "sort
of terror a cataclysm inspires."[20]

Picasso's fear of air raids, though traceable to his
brush with the "Zeppelin alarm" in World War I,
stems directly from his identification with the victims of diving and machine-gunning airplanes serving Franco in the Spanish Civil War. His fright and

FIG. 2
El Angel de la Paz . . . de los Fascistas! ca. 1937–38. Color poster.

FIG. 3
David Low, *The Angels of Peace Descend on Belgium,* 1940. Lithograph.

fury exploded in his dense, edifying texts written during that 1936–39 fratricidal conflagration.[21] Though polysemic and difficult – fragmented/ cubist and "automatic"/surrealist – they refer unmistakably to his dread of the air-and-heavenly power:

[1936]
"sky . . . fear and anguish . . . a child cries" (86); "light black juice chest cabin . . . hiding the fear and the rancor in the smoke of the cigarette" (89); "good and evil . . . the fear the difficulties the fleas" (98); "wing . . . desperate cry" (113); "girl dead of fear" (128); "black liquid [rains] . . . the dead fall drop by drop" (135)

[1937]
"wings spread out [in] the blue [sky] . . . hid[ing] under the bed trembling" (140); "clouds shit . . . horror and despair" (155); "spitting fear and stinking mucous" (156); "the head . . . falls from the [world] ceiling . . . frightened trembling and smelling the warm excrements" (159); "wing[ed] tank stuck in the blue [sky] . . . the rose on her knees dies of fear" (172); "the nest of vipers . . . the desperate cries of birds . . . what horror what distress and what cold in the bones and what unpleasant odor . . . trembling from fear" (173); "dead of fear in their courtly dress stained by tar" (174); "the hairs covering the clouds . . . the cabins offered sacrificed at the redoubled blows dealt by the bulbs bursting between the frozen fingers of the black pole" (175)

[1938]
"already cold and trembling from fear in front of the firing squad" (178); "the void . . . trembling and frozen covered by snow hidden under the armoire" (184); "black ray of the sun knocking at the door" (186); "sun . . . military music . . . frozen of fear" (195)

[1939]
"the blows of scythes dealt by the sun this moment to the table and the floor" (204); "the azure so pure of the pâté of excrements placed on the sky of the night" (208); "sky empty of caresses and laughter" (210); "the infinite center of the void on the skin torn off the house" (211); "the house empties its tripes on the sky" (212).

LYDIA CSATÒ GASMAN   57

It was, of course, the bombing of Guernica that shook Picasso first and marked him forever. After all, *Guernica* remains the paradigmatic outcry against destruction from the air, and it was while completing it in 1937 that Picasso first explained his hypothesis that dark hostile forces control events in the here and now and through them awaken atavistic terrors.[22] In a performance-collage done ad hoc for Roland Penrose and Henry Moore, Picasso dramatized the visceral fear of dive-bombers tumbling from the "blue [sky, which] sets on fire the black of the space" (122); he pinned a "long piece of toilet paper" to the hand of the running woman on the right of *Guernica* to bare what he called the "commonest and most primitive effect of fear."[23] If scatological, this concept was truthful.

PICASSO'S PRAYER TO THE SKY, 1938

In 1938, after mangling Guernica, Franco gained control of the air and was therefore poised for final victory. When Picasso read that "all neighborhoods [of Barcelona] had been hit" in March, he is said to have fearfully reported to Spanish friends in Paris: "My mother is perhaps dead. My loved ones are perhaps dead."[24] The wickedness of the sky reached such a peak for Picasso in 1938 that for the first and only time in his writings he ended the texts he completed that year by imploring and casting a spell on the sky. The "sky bursts and spreads

FIG. 4
Pablo Picasso, *Women at Their Toilette,* 1938. Collage with paint on paper, 117⅞ × 168⅞ in. (299 × 448 cm). Musée Picasso, Paris. M.P. 176.

on the walls and the ceiling its juice of military marches" (193); "vipers," not angels, fly in the "mathematical square of the air" (196); the "sun hidden in a block of ice" is "crushed on the sky by the cries of pain" (196); the "gangrene of the shadow . . . dives" (178), "hiding the aroma of the rays of the rainbow" (180); and a flying Apocalyptic "boat [is] detach[ing] [itself] from the ceiling of the [world]" (195). Nauseated, Picasso cursed the abrasive "light of the ceiling," swearing to extinguish its malice: "throw the ashes of the light of the ceiling into the jaws of the drawing that would like to tear to pieces the illusion of the hoof of shadow" (183).

About a month prior to the steady bombing of Barcelona between 16 and 18 March 1938, when "panic and fear"[25] gripped the civilian population, 1,300 dying and 2,000 being injured,[26] Picasso engaged in a surrealist game of questions and answers. Underlying this written dialogue with himself is the cause-and-effect relation between the Republican "pigeons"/planes of peace and the "dead citizens" of the Spanish nation. Asking what the volitating "veils of pigeons" mean, in a tour de force of eliding and coding Picasso answered that they stand for the Republic's futile efforts to make peace by making war and for the death of the Spanish people. "The veils of pigeons" correspond to the "weapons of the citizens dead in vain buried in the earth and eating the worms of corpses" (180).[27]

Like the running woman in *Guernica* and like Guernico in *Man's Hope,* who "tried to run, but stumbled at every step over heaped up paving stones,"[28] Picasso knew fear and the shame of being afraid. During World War II he hid under a table when he heard what he thought was a bomb blast (in fact an exploding kitchen pot). Marie-Thérèse Walter, remembering this humiliating outburst of panic, remarked that Picasso behaved egotistically and that instead of "protecting our child" thought only of his own safety.[29] Yet his hiding (which was also a leitmotif of his wartime writings), was not an expression of vulgar selfishness. Rather, it manifested Picasso's vivid participation in the psychophysiological reactions of those directly targeted by terrorism from the air.[30] In February 1938, for example, when the Nazi Condor Legion "began to

[11] ciel ciel ciel ciel ciel ciel ciel ciel ciel violet violet ciel ciel ciel violet violet violet ciel ciel ciel violet violet violet ciel ciel ciel ciel violet violet violet violet ciel ciel ciel ciel violet violet violet violet ciel ciel ciel ciel violet violet violet ciel ciel ciel ciel violet vert ciel ciel ciel ciel vert vert ciel ciel ciel ciel noir vert vert ciel marron ciel ciel ciel noir noir noir noir noir blanc blanc noir vert marron ciel ciel

cache dans ses poches ses mains la nuit ciel aloès fleur ciel cobalt de corde livre de chevet ciel cœur éventail violet ciel robe de soir bouquet de violettes violet violet ciel pierre de lune ciel noir vert ciel marron roue de feu d'artifice perle ciel noir jaune vert citronnier noir ciseaux ombre jaune neige vert marron crème remplie d'eau-de-vie un vol de canaris bleu vert noir loup ciel ciel ciel jaune linge brodé vert nuit ciel soufre blanc plat d'argent terre labourée ciel ciel blanc ciel ciel ciel blanc ciel ciel ciel ciel blanc blanc ciel bleu bleu bleu bleu

FIG. 5
Pablo Picasso, printed excerpt from writings from 9 December 1938. Original manuscript is lost. *Picasso: Collected Writings,* ed. Marie-Laure Bernadac and Christine Piot (New York: Abbeville Press, 1989).

dominate the skies"[31] of Spain, Picasso, empathizing body and soul with the casualties of Nazi air raids became (so to speak) the horse as the exemplary victim eviscerated by the bull in his *corridas.* Taking his work as his alter-ego, he wrote: "the bowels [are] pulled out of the painting" (174).

Fear made Picasso hate flying machines. He decided that the balloon hovering in his 26 March 1938 text above an impaled horse had to be downed, filling it not with hot air or lighter-than-air gas, but with the heavy sand of seashores, decomposed corpses, and hourglasses. "Having a beautiful view of the entrails of the disemboweled horse rotting on the lawn for centuries," Picasso writes, further blurting out his urge to fill "with sand the montgolfier" and then "piss upon it" (190–92). He composed this furious text about a week after Barcelona was bombed on 17–18 March by "rebel planes," suffering those two days alone as the headlines announced: "EIGHT HUNDRED KILLED AND A THOUSAND WOUNDED."[32] In the same torturing early spring, Picasso pasted more than twenty maps of the continents on the dress of one of the three figures in his huge synthetic cubist cartoon for a tapestry, *Women at Their Toilette* (fig. 4). This costumed figure is an allegory of the planet Earth, threatened, threatening, and therefore euphemized, a parody of all nations, turning her face away while combing the hair of a dejected feminine icon of Spain – in the spirit of Picasso's "Samson complex"[33] (or, according to his magico-superstitious code, robbing the vital energy). Its mirror image is a Picassoesque woman

holding a desultory "comb for [the] lice"[34] who plot international confrontations.

Beseeching the nations of the world, Picasso cries out: "Listen in the distance in the country the cries of three little girls attacked by vipers" (180) slinging venom from the space of planes. His last 1938 text, written on 9 December, is a prayer and an order to the enemy heaven that it efface its "violent violets" (199) and take on the whiteness of a compassionate blue sky. In that poignant, mystical litany, he writes the word "sky" sixty-six times (199) (fig. 5).

THE PRESS AND THE INTELLECTUALS

Little wonder, then, that at the dawn of World War II Picasso's horror of air power escalated. The illustrated popular daily *L'Excelsior,* which Jaime Sabartés tells us Picasso read every day,[35] may have delivered to him some of the most alarming reports on current events before and during the blitzkrieg against Poland (fig. 6).[36] Even the more respected *Le Figaro*[37] in July–August 1939 would have fomented the anxieties of cerebral and sensitive readers such as Picasso. On 3 August, *Le Figaro* published Hermann Göring's message that, while the "diktat of Versaille" had destroyed the German

DANS VARSOVIE BOMBARDEE

TANDIS QUE LES AVIONS ALLEMANDS S'ACHARNENT CONTRE LA CAPITALE DE LA POLOGNE, DES ENFANTS, QUI N'ONT PU ÊTRE ÉVACUÉS A TEMPS, REGARDENT, LES YEUX AGRANDIS PAR L'EFFROI, CETTE HORRIBLE VISION DE GUERRE. UN GARÇONNET, BLESSÉ AU COURS D'UN PRÉCÉDENT BOMBARDEMENT, SERRE DANS SES BRAS SON PETIT CHIEN.

FIG. 6
Dans Varsovie Bombardée, front page photograph. *L'Excelsoir,* 20 September 1939.

air force, the führer "offered the German people a new" and intrepid Luftwaffe that dwarfed all other air forces.[38] But what must have gripped Picasso even more were *Le Figaro*'s brutal references to the Luftwaffe's raw brawn: its "most modern and powerful," even "unassailable," sway; its unbearably close "maneuvers in the north-west of Germany"; its foreboding, brazen violations of Poland's air space; and the German "bombers and pursuit planes" ready to appropriate for their own use the airfields of neighboring Austria. Picasso's daily reading of *Le Figaro* would have included its accounts of the large-scale defenses against air strikes – 80,000 bomb shelters were being prepared in Amsterdam alone[39] – and their corollary, the awareness of the sky as alien and menacing. In Picasso's imagination, the thousands of bomb shelters must have anticipated thousands of deaths. Shelters against air raids would have been for him like graves prepared in advance.

In August 1939, *Le Figaro* reported ad nauseam on the meticulous preparations in Paris and the rest of France of professional, military, and civilian measures "CONTRE LES ATTAQUES AERIENNES."[40] The imminence of air raids implied by the blackout of Paris that month seemed even more sinister in *Le Figaro*'s discussion and photographic illustration of a grieving "Paris nocturne," where "only the metro, at twenty feet beneath the earth, retained its scintillating brightness."[41]

After the end of August 1939 and particularly after Hitler launched his terror bombing of Poland on 1 September, the French masses, figures in prominent political positions (such as the prime minister, Edouard Daladier), and especially French intellectuals, were profoundly affected by the fear that great cities such as Paris would be demolished by aerial bombardments. The prospect of "strategic terror bombing" stirred the emotions and changed the *Weltanschauung* of Picasso's close friends – Sabartés, Brassaï, and Penrose – as well as of his literary circle and those on its fringes – Georges Bataille,[42] Simone de Beauvoir,[43] André Breton,[44] Blaise Cendrars (see below), Max Jacob,[45] Eugene Jolas,[46] Thomas Mann,[47] Lee Miller,[48] Jean-Paul Sartre (see below), Denis De Rougemont,[49]

André Suarès,[50] and Simone Weil[51] – to name just a few. Suddenly, the commonplace problem of evil was urgent.

In the 5 December 1939 entry of his *War Diaries,* Sartre adopted the theory that Hitler's threat of "total war"[52] was designed to avoid it, by producing and "exploiting the fear" of an "ever-present specter of total war." Sartre suggested the Germans would try to win the ongoing "phony war" by bombarding France with "fear," not with actual bombs: "When Hitler threatens us with a landing in England, an air-raid on London, etc., what is he doing but summoning up the phantom of total war?"[53] Fear, Sartre wrote in his *War Diaries,* is the "most intense emotion – more intense than love. It would be more accurate to say: the most authentic."[54] Authentic and potentially annihilating, "fear" was above all fear of the "skies *with* raiding German planes."[55] In Picasso's emotionally and indecently spontaneous terms it was "the sky of the night empty of caresses and laughter" (210), or the "filthy ass of the sky" (246).

In his sweeping account of air war during the first half of this century, *Sky Memoirs,* Picasso's old friend Cendrars agreed that on 10 May 1940 nothing "but shit" could come out of the "sky above," with its "gleaming buttocks" and "inflamed anus." It was not a Christian dome but an Incan "abyss," an "absolute and deglutitious black," a "black beast, blood, throat, lung, gland," a "living sponge": "I have seen this sponge, seen it with my own eyes."[56]

To disregard the harshness of history as a condition sine qua non of what was written and painted at that time is to betray the solemn truth of events, to mistake literary and artistic difference with indifference to the "boundary situations"[57] of World War II, and to opt for an amoral hermeneutics of creativity. Picasso was hyperconscious of the separate, intrinsic reality of art, its stylistic requirements, its dependence on the history of art, and even on technical accident and chance occurrence, yet he saw no polar opposition between art and life; existence and history were inevitably expressed by the forms and the subject matter of his work. "History . . . holds us by the throat no more and no less" (154), Picasso declared on 10 February 1937, two days after the defeat of the Republicans in the campaign of Málaga, the city where he was born.[58] Later, in 1939, shortly after Franco's final victory, when Hitler's ruthless demand that Danzig be returned to Germany pre-ambled World War II, Picasso saw himself dying:[59] "Between the two windows of the sky this after-noon on the twenty-ninth of the month of April in the year nine hundred thirty-nine . . . dies the pale blue" (201) – the "pale blue" standing for Picasso's past. In this almost wholly concrete vision of his death on the sky of war, Picasso brings back to life the Blue Period of his youth, colored in the "blue of [his] cry for pity";[60] the artist named "Blue," his alias, who found success but lost his decency in Louis Aragon's roman à clef, *Anicet ou le panorama*;[61] and, finally, the glorified Picasso of recent years, still remembered as the painter of the "blue period" in André Breton's *L'Amour fou*.[62]

ROYAN AND PICASSO'S "FEAR OF THE FLIGHT OF PARTRIDGES"

"Don't you know that there is danger that German planes will fly over Paris tonight?" Picasso anxiously prodded Sabartés. It was probably 3 September 1939 in the French capital, about four o'clock in the afternoon, an hour before France's ultimatum to Germany would expire.[63] Picasso's charged question

FIG. 7
Detail of solar eye pectoral, tomb of Tutankhamun, Thebes, eighteenth dynasty. Egyptian Museum, Cairo. Richard H. Wilkinson, *Reading Egyptian Art: A Hieroglyphic Guide to Ancient Egyptian Painting and Sculpture* (London: Thames and Hudson, 1992).

contained his only recorded oral admission that his apprehension, rather than residing in an unfocused fear of war as a whole, was specifically an acute dread of Nazi air raids. His adrenalin up, Picasso warned Sabartés: "I'm going right home to pack my baggage. . . . Pack yours and stop fooling. I'll come for you tonight."[64] Picasso packed hurriedly and "towards midnight" he left in his car, a Hispano Suiza driven by Marcel, in the company of Sabartés and his wife, and Dora Maar. They "sped on at more than one hundred kilometers per hour," and arrived the next morning in Royan on the Atlantic coast near Bordeaux.[65]

Picasso had already chosen Royan, a resort town, as an asylum for Marie-Thérèse and their daughter Maya because it was beyond either the predicted advance of the enemy on land or the significant civilian targets that Göring's Luftwaffe was expected to hit. From Paris, Royan must have seemed to Picasso an almost perfect, Watteauesque island of forgetfulness. In Royan itself *Le Clairon de Saintonge,* a local paper, boasted that on 20 August, a hundred thousand celebrities from France and abroad converged in the city hoping to find there the lost "PAYS DU SOURIRE."[66]

The Royan Picasso found at the beginning of September was, however, a reminder of what he was trying to escape. When his eyes were opened to what was actually happening, he saw a town holding its breath, waiting for the war. "During the first days of September" in the Charentes region (which included Royan), "everything became dra-matic." Instead of tourists, troops arrived with "req-uisitioned vehicles" and horses, while trainloads of "distraught" refugees spilled in from localities close to the German frontier. Paradise was swept by "LA PEUR DES BOMBARDEMENTS."[67]

Bluntly if metaphorically, Picasso's 1939–40 writings convey his mounting phobia of aerial terror. Clouds, for example, morph into bombers and seem to obsess him. The "clouds"/"gods" in Apollinaire's "Couleur du Temps"[68] become "clouds [diving from the] oily slippery sky deprived of all security" (235), the "cloud stopped at the [world's] middle" (254), and "clouds . . . of the sky of the great latrine" (220). The "sky . . .

scratches its thorn [horn] against the iron of the clouds" (217). "Clouds emanate from the filth of . . . the dead sun" (218); "clouds . . . bleed their vomit of stars" (222); "clouds [are] sticky with cries" (221); the "iron of the clouds carts [airplanes][69] . . . wings . . . cold . . . fires" (234–35); the "petrified blazes of the clouds" (239); "burned bones of the clouds" (252) and [crashing] "clouds . . . drag[ging] belly to earth" (253). We begin to understand why "nails [are] tearing the skin of the clouds" (214) and why the "rotten clouds" (220) are decomposed by Picasso's "magic brush" (44).

Even low-flying partridges sow fear on 4 July 1940 in the second chapter of Picasso's "corrida in mourning" (3 July–19 August 1940), a narrative collage of texts informed by the worst early phases of the Battle of Britain. On the face of it, fearing puny, awkward partridges – the "fear of the flight of partridges" (216) – seems absurd. Yet Picasso knew from Ovid the association of the partridge-Perdrix with flying and falling, from Guillaume Apollinaire the partridge as French military jargon for shells fired by cannons in World War I, and from Christian lore its promiscuity and alliance with Satan.[70] Picasso's wretched partridges may have also been a euphemism[71] that diminished for him the supreme Nazi eagles: the Stukas dive-bombing British convoys in the Channel that fourth day of July. Incongruously, they also point to the eventual victors over the German Stukas, the British bombers that attacked the French battleships stationed at Mers El-Kébir near Oran, Algeria, one day before Picasso expressed his fear of the flight of partridges. The British had bombed their former allies in an attempt to prevent the defeated French from delivering the ships to the Germans. The French reading of the incident at Mers El-Kébir as a "stab in the back," "treachery," and "perfidiousness"[72] corresponded to the traditional symbolism of the partridge in Picasso's text of 4 July, which reverberates with the turbulence of Mers El-Kébir, as well as the related storm unleashed by the dive-bombing Stukas in the Channel.

Three days later, in Picasso's text of 7 July 1940, the winged "eyes of the partridge" watch the baleful events on earth from the empyreal "firmament of gazes" (217). The disorienting moment when, at Mers El-Kébir, friend became foe and the Battle of Britain was breaking out would have sanctioned Picasso's speculations on a universal "enemy!":[73] "*that one* far away" (255) who commands all bombings in the "year . . . 1940" (254).[74] That Picasso began his collage-epic, the "corrida in mourning" one day after the Mers El-Kébir affair does not appear to be a mere coincidence. The work's completion on 19 August 1940 may somehow relate to Winston Churchill's famous words, one day later: "Never in the field of human conflict was so much owed by so many to so few."[75] On 30 July as the "First Phase" in the Battle of Britain continued,[76] the "flight of the partridge" leads an aerial dance of death performed by the "black veils of . . . the black ceremonies of the agitated air fanned by the wings of bats" (227).

FIG. 8
Pablo Picasso, page from a sketchbook, 24 July 1940. Pen and blue ink on paper, 16¼ × 11¹³⁄₁₆ in. (41.3 × 30 cm). Musée Picasso, Paris. M.P. 1880, folio 18V

FIG. 9
Pablo Picasso, page from a sketchbook, dated 30 September–29 October 1939. Pen, ink, and ink wash on paper, 8½ × 6¹¹⁄₁₆ in. (21.7 × 17 cm). Musée Picasso, Paris. M.P. 1990-111, folio 17R.

FIG. 10
Pablo Picasso, page from a sketchbook, dated 30 September–29 October 1939. Pen, ink, and ink wash on paper, 8½ × 6¹¹⁄₁₆ in. (21.7 × 17 cm). Musée Picasso, Paris. M.P. 1990-111, folio 11R.

In the same way that angels were divided into nine orders according to their closeness to God in *The Celestial Hierarchy* of Pseudo-Dionysius,[77] the clouds and the eyes of the partridge, along with a host of other flying objects, were implicitly classified in Picasso's texts. They belonged to a hierarchical system dominated by the "winged eye flying like a ball without stopping from the sky to the earth and the earth to the sky" (235). Picasso's winged eye is both an archetypal symbol and a simile of the winged bomber. It descends from the Egyptian (fig. 7) and Renaissance emblems of divine omnipresence, omnivision, omniscience, and omnipotence. Since it flies at the hour of "last judgments" (235), it must also refer to the "many eyes" that "destroy those who are destroying the earth" in the Book of Revelation (4:7; 11:18). The winged eye was not only a traditional emblem. Picasso consecrated it on 13 August 1940, on the

same day Göring launched the main air assault against Britain. On that day, remembered as the Nazi "Day of the Eagle," "wave after wave of German aircraft, 1,485 in all, flew in search of the air stations and aircraft factories which had to be destroyed, and to be destroyed quickly, if invasion was to follow."[78]

Picasso's untitled drawing of gyrocompass-eyes (fig. 8) is perhaps his most ingenious visual adaptation of the ancient winged eye as an emblem of the winged Stukas in the Battle of Britain. Cautious, finding a way through the forest of symbols in his mind, Picasso places on and around skulls rotating gyroscopes inspired by aircraft gyrocompasses, the three-frame directional gyroscopes used to locate with precision targets on the land. Picasso renders more or less accurately these navigational aids as three intersecting circles seen in perspective. But he adds eyes with winglike eyelashes, repatenting

FIG. 11
Pablo Picasso, studies from the verso of *L'Homme au tricot*, 12 September 1939. Pen and ink on paper, 16¾ × 13 in. (42.7 × 33 cm). Private collection.

signal the London Blitz – and the bombing of Berlin by the Royal Air Force. Picasso blinds the gyrocompass-eyes: the "compass with blindfolded eyes" (231).

Picasso's sketchbooks and paintings completed during the Royan period are punctuated by enigmatic transformations of his literary imagery that revolve around the "menace of the wing" (65) and the "infinite void" (210). Thus Picasso's late 1939 "drawings in the air" (figs. 9–10), which bring back his models for the *Monument to Apollinaire*,[80] depict ironically the elusive "architectures of the air built . . . under the order and commandment of perspective authorities" (218). In his texts the "absolute rigorism of the architectural styles of the air [destroys Picasso] . . . rub[bing] the skin and the sweat of the box of cooked earth [that is, Picasso] which hangs up its bowels in the shadow" (231).

In the breezy studies (fig. 11),[81] drawn in Royan on 12 September 1939, volumetric space encloses transparent cones, conic sections, stacks of circles, polyhedrons, hourglasses, running lines, disoriented planes, hatchings, hooks, a sun, and a star. The large balloonlike cone rising above what seems to be a rippling body of water on the right may well picture one of the huge captive balloons on the Atlantic near the coast of the Royan region that detected mines planted by German submarines.[82] Crude and furious, the spatial

them as the gyrocompasses/winged eyes of bombers and death in the air: two spin upon and stare from the large skull at the center and four more float as attributes of the four auxiliary skulls. In the lower right corner, Dora's distorted nude body reclines indolently on a chaise longue. Picasso's gyrocompass-eyes drawing was made on 24 July when, from eight in the morning until the evening, German bombers attacked convoys in the Channel and airfields on the English coast. On 7 November 1940, Picasso reinvoked the winged eye as the "vipers raining the scarabs of their syphilitic rockets on the empty ground" (253).[79] This scene – impossible to forget – is a baroque cipher for the enemy above, syncretizing popular, ancient Egyptian, military, and medical myths and memories to

FIG. 12
Postcard of Royan, late 1920s or early 1930s, showing the harbor (*La Rade*) and the statue of Eugène Pelletan.

architectures in the Royan album Picasso completed between 30 September and 29 October[83] are humorous concepts that give a nod to his thoroughly serious military and cosmological meditations.[84]

PICASSO'S LIFE IN ROYAN, OR
THE PAST IN THE PRESENT

But there was no *guerre,* none of its horrors, in Picasso's everyday life in Royan. The specter of air raids seems to have evaporated in his daily explorations of the city, which were almost literal explorations of the dust that spread over Royan, preserving its past. Clashing with Picasso's flamboyant texts from Royan, where the darkness of the present prevails and is magically blasted by Picasso, Sabartés's recollections of Picasso's repetitive behavior in the city describe a journey into times past, typical of World War II, when anything that had happened before the war could look unbelievably innocent and serene.

Those sections of the city where Picasso lived between 4 September 1939 and 24 August 1940,[85] though altered, still exist. (Royan was severely bombed by England's "Oiseaux de Mort" in 1945.)[86] Today one sees the same long, broad curved beach (the Grande Conche), the same small port with a ferry, the bubbling marketplace (and the "Gare Routière which from the very first day, reminded [Picasso] of the bull rings of Málaga,

FIG. 13
Postcard of Royan, late 1920s or early 1930s, showing the *casetas* on the beach.

Barcelona, or La Coruña"),[87] the same centers that attracted the artist. Two or three times during one day – at about ten o'clock in the morning, at noon, and at sunset – he walked with Sabartés.[88]

Picasso usually ended his walk through Royan with Sabartés on the boulevard Botton,[89] going by the monument of Eugène Pelletan (fig. 12), and then stopping in "the little square in front of the port where the beach promenade meets the rue de l'Hôtel de Ville and the boulevard Thiers."[90] A sense of déjà vu would have been inevitable. For there on the beach of the Grande Conche were the same nineteenth-century-style *casetas* that, transfigured by his childhood projections of fear and desire, had faced him hypnotically as his own secret doubles between 1891 and 1895 on the Riazor Beach in La Coruña.[91] Royan's boxlike *casetas* (fig. 13),[92] fixed on stilts and withdrawn behind stylish, nimble canvas tents whose primadonna striped regalia trailed across the front stage of the Grande Conche, waited for Picasso, soliciting quietly his return to the land of his childhood and early youth. In a split second, Picasso, awe-stricken, suspected that the small houses on the Grande Conche were setting forth a sober epiphany of his past. The little "house bursting with memories" (216–17) that drifted ashore on the Grande Conche was for Picasso an *invitation au voyage,* an entreaty to ride on the "gallop of remembrances" (213) from Royan and the present to far-off places and days long gone. Did he not instantly recognize these rigid small houses as coded emblems of his hypersensitive body?[93] This much is certain: on Christmas Eve 1939, more clearly than ever before – in either his other writings or in the 1927–38 Cabana series – Picasso, like the pilgrims he had painted at La Coruña,[94] said: This little house on the beach is my mortal body harboring my immortal soul; it is the *caseta* made of my flesh that partakes in all human "houses of the flesh" (227). In its innermost recesses, death, the "horns of the sun" fallen from the "sky" and from the "clouds," mingled with and dominated the undying "flow of life" (222).

On that first Christmas Eve of World War II, a wary French nation (and probably the artist himself) listened to the radio broadcast of Prime Minister Daladier's austere evening address censuring Hitler's appetite for universal domination. Picasso's response, however, contrasted with the political perspective Daladier adopted in his outcry against the Nazis' "martyrdom of innocents."[95] Instead, Picasso evaluated the war as aerial blitzkrieg and the aerial blitzkrieg as the war of heaven against the earth, as "death falling from heaven." He did not lay blame on Hitler's Luftwaffe alone. For him, the adversary manipulating the Hitlerian lackeys was the "infinite void" (210), a plenum of sovereign death. It was this void that was in the last instance accountable for the cruel flaying of the vulnerable house substituting for Picasso's body and for "destroy[ing]," he would explain, all human "houses of the flesh."[96]

The nostalgic *casetas* on La Grande Conche, the eerie statue of Pelletan (who, traversing the romantic revolution, became Léon-Michel Gambetta's counselor after the Paris Commune), the "trinkets" at the marketplace in Royan, the dusty antiques at the popular "Hôtel des Ventes," the rubbish exhibited at the "wretched little store" (the spooky "rabbit skin," the magical "nails," the Hermetic "toothless keys," the Darwinian "monkey"), and the wrinkled Lady of the Past wearing dust as

FIG. 14
Pablo Picasso, *Café at Royan*, 15 August 1940. Oil on canvas, 38⅛ × 51⅛ in. (97 × 130 cm). Musée Picasso, Paris. M.P. 187.

makeup[97] – all that solicited Picasso in Royan made concrete for him traces of a warless time in the warring present. Charged with the diffuse meanings he bestowed upon them but stark in their own solidity, all those "found objects" were "*lost object[s]*,"[98] aiding him to see more clearly within himself and materializing the immaterial past he so urgently needed to recapture – a stay against the constraints imposed by the war. The shrines to bygone primitive eras represented for Picasso the temporal framework in which his infantile, irrational, and magical creative selves existed. To reconcile objective time, September 1939 to August 1940, when he lived in Royan, with the subjective time when the child and the magician in the mature and rational Picasso were engaged in creative activities, he had to establish the following equation: the time in Royan equaled the time of his inner creative self, which equaled his wonder-filled past. Finding the "lost" object was, then, to find himself; discovering it was self-discovery. Driven by fear and aiming to alleviate it, Picasso's return to times past in his daily routine and to an unconscious, childish, and magical self in his work coalesced into an appropriate conjunction of existential and creative complementaries.[99]

On 15 August 1940, the day after what the local press described as the assassination of a sentinel guarding the German Kommandatur,[100] a stray bullet penetrated the dining room on the main floor below Picasso's studio at Les Voiliers. The situation was tense. Unknown people, perhaps engaged in pre-Resistance activities, had already several times cut one of the Germans' electric cables near Royan.[101] The Germans threatened "capital punishment" and warned that they would take "hostages" to "guarantee" the "cessation of sabotage."[102] Picasso challenged them in return. The errant bullet of 15 August could only have been fired by the swastika-emblazoned German plane performing acrobatic stunts above the port: "This bullet was shot down from above and at very close range."[103]

Picasso painted the uncanny *Café at Royan* on the day of the stray bullet (fig. 14). This painting is a chilling portrait of the city's Café des Bains, as a midday ghost seen from Les Voiliers. It represents

FIG. 15
Pablo Picasso, page from a sketchbook,
31 December 1939. Pen and blue ink on paper,
6 ⅜ × 8 ¾ in. (16.3 × 22.3 cm). Musée Picasso,
Paris. M.P. 1877, folio 19V.

a paradoxical, luminous but irritated, angular architecture[104] standing empty and as if preserved by the immobilizing torpor of late summer and the stagnation of Royan after the invasion. A translucent icon of the Occupation, the uninhabited Café des Bains, soaked through by the mother-of-pearl light of the town, arises from the substanceless, empty Botton Square that Picasso could see from his studio. Its windows and doors are blank, the colorful striped awnings are lifted but show nothing, the pointed tents on the Grande Conche zigzag in the far background, a forlorn lighthouse dissolves on a jetty in the middle ground, and a flag opens like a crying beak over a schematic boat. Nobody is in or around the café. It evokes the deserted Botton Square where the Germans had played their first concert one day earlier.[105] The vacant *Café at Royan* tells the story of a city whose population is in

hiding after the invader has left. The Sartrean "'Nobody'" inscribed on the blinding "golden ball" (277) gazes at the viewer, wearing the mask of joy magically contrived by the artist from the Café des Bains in *Café at Royan.*

There were moments when Picasso distinctly conceived writing as a substitute for painting and painting as a form of writing. Picasso's Royan texts are written paintings, as meaningful if not as expert as his painted paintings (fig. 15). "Write, man, write. Write no matter what," Picasso urged Sabartés. "Write, and you will see that all your blues will disappear, and that you will feel better."[106]

From *Guernica* to *The Charnel House:*
The Political Radicalization
of the Artist

Gertje R. Utley

In October 1944, shortly after the liberation of Paris, Picasso claimed that he had always stood against tyranny and dictatorship and fought with the weapons of his art, like a true revolutionary.[1] Yet very little evidence of political engagement in his art exists prior to the late 1930s. Even then, Picasso's political radicalization was gradual, progressing from his embrace – yet arguably moderate support – of the anti-Fascist policies of the Popular Front in France and of the Loyalist cause in the Spanish Civil War, to his open commitment to the French Communist Party.

Picasso's contacts with anarchist circles during his formative years in turn-of-the-century Barcelona are certainly at the root of his political inclinations.[2] The paintings of his Blue Period, in their focus on the poor and downtrodden, reflect many of the qualities of contemporary anarchist literature. In their depictions of misery, however, they also engage in the typically symbolist tendency to aestheticize it. Picasso's lifelong opposition to all armed conflict may stem from these early influences as well. Clues to his pacifist stance have been discovered in several of the newspaper clippings in his synthetic cubist *papiers collés*.[3] Though the dogmatic intent of those works is questionable, the reception of cubism by contemporary critics was at times couched in political argument. Some saw anarchist destructiveness in these works; others thought they recognized their reactionary basis.[4]

Following World War I, a momentous event largely ignored in Picasso's oeuvre, his marriage to Olga Khokhlova, the Russian ballerina of Diaghilev's Ballets Russes, introduced him to a life of bourgeois placidity. Only his contact with the radicalized milieu of the surrealists, with figures such as Louis Aragon, André Breton, Georges Bataille, Michel Leiris, Christian Zervos, Tristan Tzara, and in particular Paul Eluard, led him back into the sphere of left-wing political thinking.[5] Eluard, in particular, the first among the surrealists to join the Communists in September 1926, transmitted to Picasso his conception of the responsibility and the militant role of the artist in society.[6] It was Eluard who introduced Picasso to the surrealist photographer and, later, painter, Dora Maar, whose sharp intelligence and strong connections to left-wing radical groups certainly influenced Picasso's political thought.[7]

When ideological differences, and the first round of what would be called *la bataille du réalisme,* divided the surrealists, Picasso remained closer to the Stalinist faction around Aragon. In his first public political stance, taken in 1932, Picasso became co-signatory of a petition in defense of Aragon, convicted for incitement to violence in his poem "Front rouge."[8] This, however, did not impress the Soviet embassy in Paris, which discouraged its government's interest in Picasso in 1933 with the argument that he was little more than a leftist bourgeois.[9]

Still, shortly after the victory of the Popular Front in France, and before the outbreak of the Spanish Civil War, one of Picasso's watercolors, *Composition with Minotaur* (28 May 1936), reveals beneath a wealth of private symbolism his sympathy for the Popular Front, or, at the very least, for its anti-Fascist stance (fig. 1).[10] The watercolor was reproduced and used as the stage curtain for Romain Rolland's play *Le 14 juillet.* In fact, it was specifically created for that purpose, and much of its imagery is derived from the Rolland text.[11]

Romain Rolland's play was selected as the central cultural event of the first 14th of July celebrations by the new Popular Front government, which sought to reemphasize the symbolic force of the storming of the Bastille. Louis Aragon and Jean Cassou, the principal figures behind the Communist-inspired Maison de la Culture, were charged with the organization of the event as early as May 1936.[12] As both were close to Picasso, they probably approached him with the project.

In Picasso's watercolor, a monstrous bird-man carries the seemingly lifeless body of the minotaur, costumed as a harlequin, in a poetic blend of several of Picasso's alter egos. Their macabre progress is restrained by a bearded man, who carries on his shoulders a youth with outstretched arms. Cloaked in the hide of a horse, like Hercules in his lion skin, the man raises his right fist in defiance. At the time, there was no mistaking the symbol of the raised fist as the Communist salute. It also had become the greeting of the Spanish Republicans, a gestural polemic in response to the raised open palm of

FIG. 1

Pablo Picasso, *Composition with Minotaur* (maquette for the stage curtain of *Le 14 juillet* by Romain Rolland), 28 May 1936. Gouache and India ink, 17½ × 21⅜ in. (44.5 × 54.5 cm). Musée Picasso, Paris. M.P. 1166.

the *Hitler-Gruss,* used by Franco's supporters. Moreover, the image of the youth on the shoulders of the older man is taken directly from the ending of Rolland's play, where the child Julie, "our little Liberty," is carried in triumph on the shoulders of the character Hoche, her arms stretched out to the people of Paris. The vulturelike monster, on the other hand, although physically derived from Goya, relates directly to the final words of Rolland's companion play *Danton,* in which the character Saint-Just proclaims, "The Republic will never be pure until the vultures are no more."[13]

Picasso's conscious use of Communist symbols is even more intelligible in a large pencil drawing of a fortnight later, which depicts a youthful crowd storming the Bastille (fig. 2).[14] The mood is part celebratory and part combative: people dance, fists are raised, and banners carry the hammer-and-sickle motifs.

The militant symbolism of Picasso's curtain was carried out in the performance, with the masses played by workers' theater groups. It ended with both actors and audience, fists raised, singing "La Marseillaise" and the "Internationale."[15] In a further gesture of allegiance, Picasso watched the

[page 68]
Pablo Picasso, *The Cock* (detail)
29 March 1938. Cat. no. 15.

march of the *rassemblement populaire* from the balcony of the theater.[16]

Four days later, on 18 July, the Spanish Civil War erupted. There was no doubt which side Picasso would support,[17] yet he hesitated to become personally involved. Even after the Republican government named him director of the Museo Nacional del Prado in September 1936, Picasso did not follow their repeated invitations to come to Spain.[18] Yet he clearly appreciated the honor and, on several occasions, defended the efforts of the Republic to protect Spain's artistic treasures. Years later he would jest that he probably still was the director of the Prado, as nobody had bothered to fire him.[19] Roland Penrose recalls that Picasso's anxiety about the events in Spain was intense; indeed, much of Picasso's work from that period, especially from early 1937, is suffused with anguish.[20] However, like Eluard, who talked about action but restricted his fight to the weapons of his poetry, Picasso largely confined his demonstrations of sympathy to his art.[21] The attitudes of the two

FIG. 2
Pablo Picasso, *Le 14 juillet,* 13 June 1936. Pencil on six assembled sheets of paper, 26 ¾ × 26 ⅜ in. (68 × 67 cm). Musée Picasso, Paris. M.P. 1167.

friends reflected the postulates of the international writers' conference held in Valencia in July 1937, which declared literary activism to be as valuable an engagement in the cause as any action in the field.[22]

Picasso's most obvious political work, and his clearest condemnation of Franco and the church that supported him, are his etchings in comic-strip form, *Dream and Lie of Franco,* of early January 1937 (cat. no. 2).[23] Picasso's caricature of Franco as an absurd and vainglorious bigot and of his calamitous effect on civilization and the civilian population was the expression of his outrage about the victimization of the Spanish people.[24] Picasso's sudden artistic reaction to the war in Spain possibly was aroused by the distressing accounts he received, in early January 1937, from the Spanish poet and essayist José Bergamín, who was the Republic's cultural attaché in Paris.[25]

Why did it take the attack on Guernica to rally Picasso's full commitment to the program of the Spanish Pavilion at the Paris World's Fair of May 1937? By their presence the Republicans envisaged achieving a specific political goal: the reaffirmation of their legitimacy as the elected government of Spain, and the enlistment of the free world in their support. When first approached by a delegation from the Republican government, headed by his friend Josep Lluis Sert, the architect of the Spanish Pavilion, Picasso was less than enthusiastic.

Was Picasso's reluctance prompted by his earlier claim that he would never put his art at the service of an ideology?[26] Or was it caused by his disenchantment with the schism in the Republican camp in Spain, which was plagued by disagreements over its revolutionary mission?[27] According to his nephew Javier Vilato, Picasso knew about and could not ignore the strife between the factions within the Popular Front in Spain, nor the Communists' violent suppression and eradication of the revolutionary elements in the anti-Fascist militias.[28] This would explain his initial reticence to publicly back the Republican government, which by that time was firmly under pro-Soviet Communist control.[29]

It took three months for Picasso to relent and begin work on some preparatory drawings for the

Spanish Pavilion. Even then, his subject, the artist in his studio – although a frequent theme in his oeuvre – appears to reflect Picasso's desire to remain in his ivory tower.[30] Given Picasso's restrained political stance at the time, it is reasonable to assume that in painting *Guernica* (see pages 40–41, fig. 1) he was motivated less by the politics of the Spanish Civil War than by the human drama of the destruction of the Basque town.[31] The senseless brutality of the bombing must have convinced Picasso of the Republicans' argument that the fight against Franco and his allies had to take precedence over internal conflict. Indeed, on 1 May, four days after the bombing of Guernica, Picasso began sketches related to its devastation. In study after study Picasso filtered the destruction of Guernica through the prism of the iconography of the bullfight, the Crucifixion, and the life, love, and death of the Minotaur, all of which had occupied much of his recent work, as well as through images derived from private experience.

Dora Maar's photographs of the different states of the painting in progress reveal that Picasso's concept evolved from a frankly militant vocabulary (fig. 3), to the universal image of suffering of the final version. Here, as in most of Picasso's later so-called history paintings, we are made to empathize with the victims, while the perpetrator is present only in the destruction he left behind. The Spanish government, disappointed with Picasso's insufficiently partisan approach, even considered removing the

canvas from the pavilion, a step prevented only by their fear of adverse publicity.[32] Still, *Guernica* did not totally fail as an instrument of propaganda. The Germans, while dismissing it alternately as the work of either a lunatic or of a four-year-old, were sensitive to its damning message and regarded it as a provocation in form and content.[33]

Picasso donated *Guernica* to the Spanish Republic, and contributed the sum of 150,000 francs he received for expenses to the fund for Republican exiles.[34] The fund also benefited from the proceeds of the many charitable exhibitions of *Guernica* and its related works and from the sale of the limited folio edition of *Dream and Lie of Franco.*[35] Picasso participated in fund-raising efforts such as exhibitions and auctions to benefit Spanish refugees, signed numerous declarations in support of the Republic, and became involved with several refugee relief organizations.[36] He donated milk for the children in Barcelona, helped finance a hospital for Republican refugees in Toulouse, and was particularly active in securing the liberation of Spanish intellectuals from French internment camps.[37] In his postwar painting *Monument to the Spanish Who Died for France* (Monument aux Espagnols morts pour la France) (cat no. 83), Picasso would commemorate the plight of the Republican refugees who, caught between Franco's Spain and Vichy France, had joined the French Resistance.[38] On a personal level, he assisted many friends or even strangers who appealed to his generosity.[39] Most of his donations remain unnamed, in part because of the necessarily clandestine nature of such operations.[40] It seems that even during the Occupation he tried various ways to smuggle money into Spain, an effort that nearly cost him his freedom, if not his life.[41]

When *Guernica* was on view in New York, the Museum of Modern Art emphasized that Picasso himself had denied the painting any political significance, stating simply that "the mural expresses his abhorrence of war and brutality." However, in a letter to the *New York Times,* Picasso was more explicit in his denunciation of General Franco's military insurrection: "In all my recent works of art, I clearly express my abhorrence

FIG. 3
Pablo Picasso, *Guernica,* state II, 1937. Photograph by Dora Maar. Musée Picasso, Paris. Picasso Archives.

of the military caste, which has sunk Spain in an ocean of pain and death."[42] Years later Picasso told his old friend, the poet Rafael Alberti: "The truth of the matter is that by means of *Guernica* I have the pleasure of making a political statement every day in the middle of New York City."[43]

Increasingly, the success of the widely traveled painting conferred upon *Guernica* the status of a public statement against Fascist aggression, and its political potential came to be valued. Whether Picasso was motivated by political or by humanitarian incentives in painting his mural, it was as the painter of *Guernica* that he came to be seen as a politically valuable asset, or conversely, as a liability and even a threat.[44] The process of Picasso's own further radicalization was largely a response to the legacy of responsibility that *Guernica* imposed upon him.

Picasso himself claimed that it took the experience of World War II to make him understand that it was not enough to manifest political sympathies under the discreet veil of mythologized artistic expression.[45] Except for less than a year in Royan, Picasso spent the period of the Nazi Occupation in Paris. Most contemporary witnesses agreed with Eluard that, during the Occupation, Picasso was "one of the rare painters to have behaved properly."[46] Recent rumors accuse Picasso of a privileged position and self-serving contacts with the Germans.[47] But a closer look at these accusations, as well as a more probing inquiry into the political and social realities of life in occupied Paris, show that Picasso indeed preserved the dignity that his friends so admired.[48]

Although Picasso did at times receive members of the Occupation forces at his studio,[49] his reception of them seems to have conformed to Jean Texcier's *Conseils à l'occupé*. In this short manual on proper behavior under the Occupation, Texcier, a militant Socialist, recommended a civilized comportment toward the occupier without, however, initiating any contact.[50] The documented visits by Gerhard Heller, Hans Kuhn, and Ernst Jünger illustrate, in fact, the paradoxical twists and complexities of relationships under the Occupation, for they were accompanied by Jean Paulhan, a

member of the intellectual Resistance and one of the founders of the clandestine Editions de Minuit.[51] The two Germans also visited Braque and Fautrier, whom Heller later watched as he painted one of the Hostage series (e.g., page 105, fig. 8).[52]

It would have been extremely difficult for Picasso to conceal any questionable dealings with the Germans or to receive secret and unrecorded visitors. Picasso was almost constantly surrounded by friends, many of whom lived within the radius of a five-minute walk. Georges Hugnet speaks of shared lunches on a nearly daily basis. Moreover, Picasso's studio provided a meeting place where even members of the underground felt safe. Many of Picasso's friends were anti-Fascists and, with the noted exception of Jean Cocteau, personally involved in, or at least close to the Resistance.[53] André Fougeron, the militant Communist painter, told me that Picasso, who was aware of his Resistance activities, was always accessible when he came to visit.[54] Had there been any question about Picasso's loyalties, André Malraux would scarcely have come to see him while on a clandestine mission for the *maquis*.[55] Nor would his friends Michel and Louise Leiris have introduced him to Laurent Casanova, a four-time escapee from the Nazis, who was in hiding in their apartment. Casanova was a Resistance fighter, a high-ranking member of the politburo of the French Communist Party and rumored to have been Stalin's man in France. A lawyer by training and a man of erudition and considerable charm, he made a great impression on Picasso and may have been influential in Picasso's decision to join the party after the Liberation.[56]

Picasso did not personally participate in the Resistance; however, his close association with the underground through his friends demanded more courage than is generally granted him.[57] We must not forget that Picasso's active and vocal opposition to Franco and his German supporters during the civil war already brought him the notoriety of being "red as the reddest of the Spanish revolutionaries."[58] It is, furthermore, likely that his denunciation as a "degenerate" artist had as much to do with Picasso's political stance as with his artistic

FIG. 4
Scene from the auction of "degenerate art" at the Gallery Fischer in Lucerne, Switzerland. Photograph from a Swiss newspaper. The works by Picasso are *Head of a Woman* (lot 117) and *Two Harlequins* (lot 115).

style. Indeed, many of his paintings that had been sold at the auction of "degenerate" art from German museums in Lucerne, in June 1939, as well as those that were stored in the infamous Salle des Martyrs at the Musée du Jeu de Paume, lack the characteristics that were denounced by the Nazis as "entartete kunst" (degenerate art), and belong to the least distorted among Picasso's oeuvre (fig. 4).[59]

Picasso's well-known political stance excluded him from several exhibitions of Spanish art during the Occupation.[60] At other times, the presence of his paintings in an exhibition could be seen as provocation. For example, in March 1943 he participated in an exhibition on the influence of African art on modern painters, a theme sure to be criticized as "degenerate."[61] Equally provocative

was Picasso's contribution, in May 1944, to an exhibition of artists' palettes in the Galerie René Breteau. Picasso's exhibit consisted of a double page of a newspaper, which was indeed what he used to mix his colors.[62] Picasso must have recalled that, in 1939, a photo of his work table with just such a newspaper palette had been barred by French censors because of the possible political content of the newsprint.[63] Moreover, Picasso could have anticipated that the publication of two of his poems in *Confluences* (Lyon) in November 1942 would be perceived as "striking evidence of literary, spiritual, and moral decadence."[64] This was a dangerous comment in view of the fact that the fight against moral decadence was the banner under which Vichy led its racist and xenophobic politics.[65]

It also required some degree of courage to cooperate with the underground surrealist publication *La Main à plume,* created at the end of August 1941, with the express intent to resist with the weapon of literature. The publication is said to have survived in part because of Picasso's generosity; he gave financial help, provided illustrations, and, for the cover of the summer 1942 issue, "La Conquête du monde par l'image," he contributed a signed and dated photo of his bull's head assembled from the seat and handlebars of a bicycle.[66] It is surely no coincidence that Picasso contributed his talent to illustrate the works of the poets of the Resistance – Paul Eluard, Georges Hugnet, Robert Desnos, and Maurice Toesca – while he apparently refused to work for writers accused of collaborating.

Picasso had told Françoise Gilot that he was not looking for risks to take, but, he added "in a sort of passive way I don't care to yield to either force or terror."[67] His attitude was facilitated by the network of protectors, which he most probably owed to his friendship with Jean Cocteau.[68] Numerous accounts of intellectual life during the Occupation reveal that differences between resisters and collaborators could be shelved when it came to saving the life of a friend, though the tragic case of Max Jacob showed that even the help of the most powerful friends would not always come in time.[69]

Although Picasso's style during the war years was more than ever antithetical to Nazi artistic doctrines, it seems highly overstated to interpret his work as "a barely concealed action against fascism."[70] Picasso later claimed that the war was reflected in his paintings, but he consistently omitted, and in one case even obliterated, clear references to it. In painting out the prison bars, bread, and water jug in the background of *Portrait of Dora Maar* (9 October 1942), Picasso effaced what would have been his most direct allusion to life under the Occupation during those years.[71] But this was true in general. While French artists had freely depicted their militant opposition to the civil war in Spain, there was practically no reflection of the Occupation in their work during those years.[72] André Fougeron's *Rue de Paris 43,* which he exhibited in the Salon des Tuileries in 1943, was among the rare exceptions (fig. 5).[73] Fougeron, who was charged by the Communist underground to create the Front national des arts, found it extremely "difficult to enlist artists to manifest resistance through their painting."[74] Picasso himself wondered why so few artists, as compared to writers and poets, were insurrectionaries: "Is it due to their trade?" he asked. "Were van Gogh and Cézanne really less audacious in mind than Victor Hugo?"[75]

The only truly militant expression to emerge from the artistic resistance was the album *Vaincre.* Assembled by Fougeron, in April 1944, with the collaboration of eight artists (including Boris Taslitzky, who was still in Buchenwald), it formed a collection of aggressive satirical attacks more caricature than painting on Vichy and the Nazis.[76]

After the war, several critics and artists – Picasso's friend the Communist painter Edouard Pignon among them – claimed that any manifestation of avant-garde art during the Occupation should be seen as a veiled resistance to fascism. This is, for example, how the vibrant colors and surrealist abstractions of the "Jeunes Peintres de Tradition Française" came to be viewed.[77] However, the surprisingly liberal attitude of the Germans with regard to the cultural life of Paris deprives this contention of credibility.[78]

In 1944, for post-Liberation Paris, Picasso became the "symbol of regained freedom," *"le porte-drapeau de la France résistante"* (the standard

FIG. 5
André Fougeron, *Rue de Paris 43,* 1943. Oil on canvas, 53⅞ × 37⅜ in. (137 × 95 cm). Private collection. Courtesy Galerie Jean-Jacques Dutko, Paris.

bearer of resisting France).[79] In his highly visible role in all events related to the celebrations of liberation, Picasso headed several delegations honoring the victims of fascism who had died in the Resistance.[80] He was also commissioned to draw the frontispiece for the special volume *Florilège des poètes et peintres de la Résistance,* presented as a token of gratitude by the poets and painters of the Resistance to General Charles de Gaulle.

Most significantly, Picasso was honored with a retrospective of his work at the Salon d'Automne of 1944, a recognition rarely bestowed on a foreign artist. On 5 October 1944, one day before the opening of the Salon, the Communist daily *L'Humanité* announced that Picasso had joined the French Communist Party.[81] The timing of the two events proved to be a most incendiary mix of art and politics in a time of understandably heightened sensibilities. The Salon that year was called the

Salon de la Libération and was clearly supposed to symbolize restored French culture.[82] It could be expected that to offer a foreigner center stage on such a patriotic occasion would generate opposition. Yet the extent of the ensuing uproar, the so-called *scandale du Salon d'Automne*, was unforeseen.[83] Rallying around Picasso, the Communists blamed the demonstration on reactionary initiatives, and compared it to the "intimidation tactics experienced under Nazi occupation."[84] Before the war Picasso had never exhibited in the official salons. His participation in the Salon de la Libération was his first gesture as an artist to manifest his allegiance to the party: it was intended to demonstrate his desire to be in closer touch with the public.

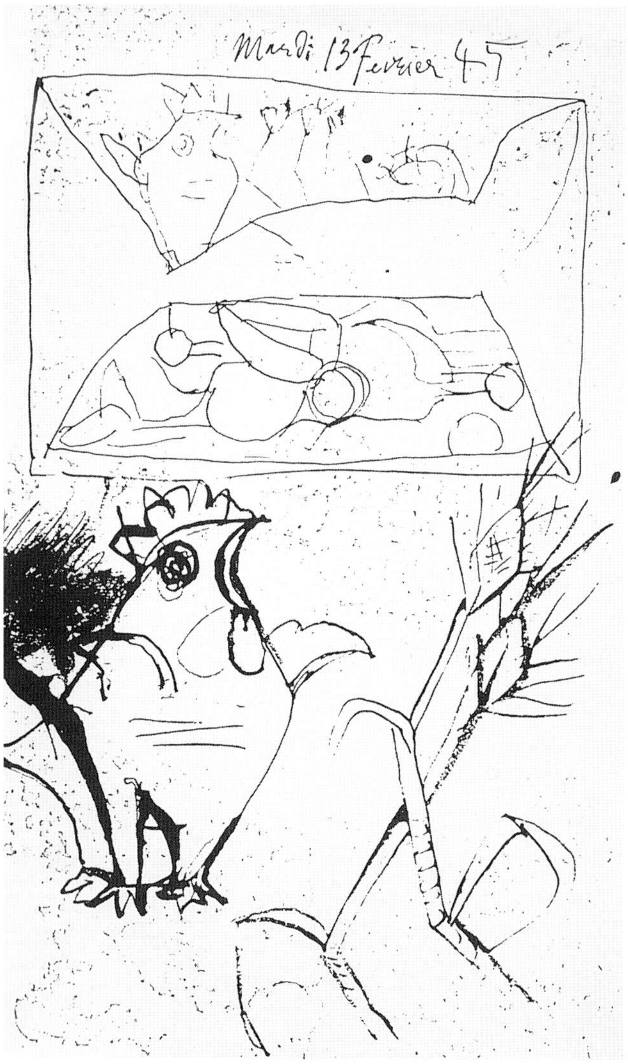

FIG. 6
Pablo Picasso, composition drawing for *The Charnel House,* 13 February 1945. India ink on paper, 12 9/16 × 17 1/8 in. (32 × 43.5 cm). Private collection.

When asked to explain his new affiliation, Picasso's statements echo the unfocused, romantic ideals that led so many intellectuals to join the Communist ranks:

> *I have become a Communist because our party strives more than any other to know and to build the world, to make men clearer thinkers, more free and more happy. I have become a Communist because the Communists are the bravest in France, in the Soviet Union, as they are in my own country, Spain. I have never felt more free, more complete than since I joined. . . . I am again among brothers.*[85]

Undeniably, the experience of the Occupation and the courage of his friends in the Resistance played an important part in Picasso's commitment to communism. Mercedes Guillén recalls how distressed Picasso was about the execution of the Communist journalist Gabriel Péri in December 1941, and how deeply moved he was by Péri's famous last letter. Written moments before Péri's execution, it contained the now legendary phrase that communism prepared "les lendemains qui chantent" (the tomorrows that sing).[86]

Like many others who had joined the party during the war or in the early days of the Liberation, Picasso was no Marxist in the ideological sense of the word; in all likelihood had never even read Marx.[87] As Malraux observed, it was less through the study of ideas than through general osmosis that Marx's ideas spread in France, where communism grew largely out of the revolutionary legacy of 1789.[88] Moreover, the rise of fascism in the 1920s and 1930s, the Communists' opposition to Hitler, and Soviet military support for the Spanish Republican struggle against Franco's insurgency boosted the party's credibility.[89]

In the aftermath of the Liberation, while de Gaulle was seen as the savior of France, the Communists were, for a while, the true beneficiaries of postwar political currents. Never before or after did the Communist Party have such universal appeal in France, and in particular among the French intelligentsia.[90] The Communists' claim to a courageous, if belated, role in the French Resistance

LE DON A LA PATRIE JUIN 1940

FIG. 7
Gérard Ambroselli, *Le don à la patrie juin 1940 (Le Maréshal Pétain)*.
Woodblock on paper. Fonds Pétain. Musée d'Histoire
Contemporaine – BDIC, Paris.

provided moral authority.[91] Moreover, the Soviet Union, as the country that had suffered the heaviest losses, was considered by many French to be the true vanquisher of Nazi Germany.[92] In becoming a Communist, a Frenchman could identify with the victor over fascism and play a role in averting future aggressions against humanity.[93] Recent experience effaced the memory of Stalin's show trials of the 1930s, and for Picasso, too, it seems to have obliterated his awareness of the Communists' brutal suppression of anarchist movements in Spain. From now on he was to subscribe to the Communists' claim that they offered the only viable alternative to Fascism.[94]

Although Picasso was not – and was not expected to be – a major player in the mechanics of party life, he was precious to the party for the prestige his membership conveyed, and useful to the party's image as the champion of a national cultural renaissance.[95] He was valued as an effective magnet in the party's drive to capture the imagination of great numbers of potential supporters and members. Later, in a world divided by the Cold War, his presence was seen as lending legitimacy to the Communists' claim that theirs was indeed the side of culture and peace.[96]

Picasso's formal alliance with the party that proclaimed itself to be the champion of the masses, which clearly expected him to create an art of social and political relevance, had kindled his desire to address his new audience more effectively. He gave fresh thought to the signifying potential of his art, once even comparing it to Christ's use of parables, "so that it would be accessible to the widest possible audience."[97]

In February 1945, Picasso started the first sketchy drawings in preparation for his grim, monochromatic canvas, the *Charnel House,* which was his first attempt to assimilate the political tenor of Communist Party rhetoric into his art (cat. no. 82). In the earliest compositional study (13 February), the group of victims from the *Charnel House* can be recognized in the upper register of the drawing (fig. 6). Above them, cursory lines suggest a hilly landscape where a new crop of wheat and a crowing rooster bespeak renewal sprung from the sacrifice of the victims. In its posterlike use of traditional images of rebirth and resurrection, the sketch conveys the party's militant optimism in a renaissance for which it became the self-declared champion. Although the image curiously echoes similar claims under Pétain (fig.7), its apparent rhetorical intent has a precedent in the second state of *Guernica* – in the declamatory image of the dead warrior holding a sheaf of wheat high before the rising sun (fig. 3).

FIG. 8
Pablo Picasso, *Pitcher, Candle, and Casserole,* 16 February 1945. Oil on canvas, 32 ¼ × 41 ¾ in. (82 × 106 cm). Musée National d'Art Moderne, Centre National d'Art et de Culture Georges Pompidou, Paris, gift from the artist.

GERTJE R. UTLEY 77

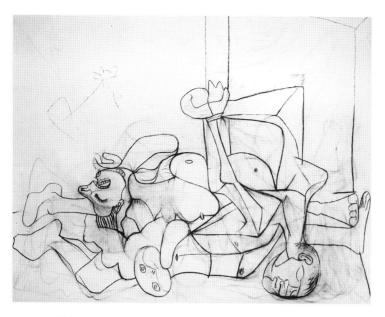

FIG. 9
Pablo Picasso. *The Charnel House,* state I, February 1945.
Photograph by Christian Zervos.

FIG. 10
Pablo Picasso. *The Charnel House,* state II, April 1945.
Photograph by Christian Zervos.

In the finished painting, the scene of death – a pyramid of the massacred bodies of a family – has taken over the major part of the canvas. Open fields have given way to claustrophobic enclosure, and the symbols of renewal have been replaced by a still life, a close citation of Picasso's canvas *Pitcher, Candle, and Casserole* of 16 February 1945, about which Picasso said to Pierre Daix: "You see even casseroles can scream" (fig. 8). Only the candle has been omitted here, in a further and surely conscious obliteration of any token of hope. In studying the proliferation of still lifes with skulls in Picasso's work during the months of February and March 1945, while he was working on the *Charnel House,* it is clear that for Picasso the association between *nature morte* and the meditation on death goes beyond the simple play on words.

The atypically slow progress of the painting, the hesitations, and the presence of so many *pentimenti* seem to exceed the artistic search for formal solutions and enter the delicate sphere of defining a moral and political position. The four photos that Christian Zervos took in February, April, May, and after mid-July of Picasso's work on the painting allow us to follow his progress, and to infer meaning from transformation (figs. 9–12).

The focus of the painting and the object of Picasso's major hesitations is the representation of the male victim. Bound like the lamb in the sculpture of the *Man with a Lamb* (ca. March 1943; cat. no. 66) his neck twisted and elongated in expressive dislocation like that of the horse in *Guernica,* he brings to mind all the personifications of sacrificed innocence in Picasso's artistic vocabulary. The crosslike configuration between his arm and the post to which he is bound and the leanness of his torso call forth images of the sacrifice on Golgotha as much as they do contemporary concentration camp photos. One of his palms is opened in acceptance, like that of the crucified Christ in Matthias Grünewald's *Isenheim Altar* (see page 82, fig. 1); the other is clenched in a fist and provocatively raised in the Communist salute, identifying him with the militancy of the dead warrior in the earliest states of *Guernica.* The consecutive states of the painting reveal Picasso's vacillation between representing the man with open palms or with clenched fists, between the Christian icon of redemption and the Communist symbol for militant strife. This hesitation illustrates Picasso's difficulty in deciding between belief in resurrection based on forgiveness or on the militant call for retribution. The compromise that Picasso chose in the final version (cat. no. 82), one hand

FIG. 11
Pablo Picasso, *The Charnel House*, state III, May 1945.
Photograph by Christian Zervos.

FIG. 12
Pablo Picasso, *The Charnel House*, state IV, after mid-July 1945.
Photograph by Christian Zervos.

clenched, one open, echoes the Communist credo that the belief in the rebirth of France had to coexist with the partisan call for revenge; or in the words of *L'Humanité,* "For the salvation of humanity, hatred – today – is still essential."[98]

In spring 1945, the euphoria over the Liberation was tragically challenged by the full disclosure of Nazi brutalities (Auschwitz was liberated on 19 January 1945), by fear for the lives of hundreds of thousands of French political prisoners still in German captivity, and by the continuation of the war. In France a new war had started: *l'épuration,* the purge of Nazi collaborators as a precondition for the *renaissance française,* was an important item on the agenda of the French Communists. Picasso, whose ties to the party were at their closest during those months, and who had donated the *Charnel House* to benefit one of its charities, shared these sentiments. He was full of scorn toward the artists who, like Derain, Vlaminck, and Othon Friesz, had helped the Germans in their propaganda efforts. On 3 October 1944, the eve of his official enrollment in the French Communist Party, Picasso presided at a meeting of the Comité directeur du Front national des arts, which was held at his studio and at which the punishment of artists and critics suspected of collaboration was demanded.[99]

Picasso's signature under the introductory statement to the catalogue for the Communist-sponsored exhibition *Art et résistance* in early 1946, where the *Charnel House* was first shown, confirms that the painting was meant as a militant call for "justice toward those whose sacrifice secured the survival of France."

The *Charnel House*, unprecedented in Picasso's oeuvre for its brutal imagery, unmitigated by the mythologizing symbolism that pervades *Guernica,* illustrates Picasso's claim that "painting is not made to decorate apartments. It's an offensive and defensive weapon against the enemy,"[100] a weapon Picasso would continue to use on behalf of the Communist Party well into the first decade of the Cold War.

Where Do They Come From – Those Superb Paintings and Horrid Women of "Picasso's War"?

Brigitte Baer

War is generalized catastrophe, and no doubt it was Matthias Grünewald who first and best portrayed the great catastrophe in his *Crucifixion* for the *Isenheim Altar* (fig. 1). Here, probably for the first time, it is not the Man-God who is dying in order to return to his Father, but rather a man, already putrescent, who is dying, abandoned by everyone – by his friends the apostles, his omnipotent Father, and even his mother, who dances the dance of death with her substitute son, the young Saint John.

To be sure, Mary Magdalen, who loves him, weeps at his feet, and Saint John the Baptist, the last prophet, the Precursor (who died because of a woman), points his finger for us all to see the Fate of Man: Ecce Homo. In this painting there is no hope, no possible Resurrection, but only solitude, the hopeless horror of death, and perhaps even the Crucified's scorn and hatred. It is therefore not surprising that the veil of the temple was torn and the sky darkened in broad daylight. Nor is it surprising that this altarpiece was rediscovered in our pessimistic century, which is full of catastrophes. The great catastrophe, for a painter, has always been the Crucifixion (most men, and in any case painters who are or feel themselves to be marginal

and to have a kind of mission, like Jesus, identify with Christ at some time in their lives); when Goya painted his wonderful *Third of May, 1808* (see page 42, fig. 2), he gave the man about to be shot, who is kneeling, Christ's outstretched arms.[1] Faith having been lost, approximately after Rogier van der Weyden, there remains only a more or less complacent identification of the painter with Christ, or, perhaps, of his ego ideal with Christ, or even of the object of his mirror-love, as in W. H. Hunt's obscene *Shadow of Death,* which might be excused because of its time (1873–74).[2]

Picasso also for a time was obsessed with the Isenheim *Crucifixion.* Although he successfully brought chaos and cataclysm into his 1930 panel on this same subject,[3] he did so with irony and even sarcasm. More interesting for our present concerns are the 1932 drawings (e.g., fig. 2), and the last one done on 21 August 1938[4] that led Jean Clair to connect Picasso's *Crucifixion* with a bacchanal, thus establishing the first link in the sequence leading from bacchanal to street fighting (violence, catastrophe, *and* acute pleasure).[5] But the 1932 drawings go further. The 1938 drawing, probably done in a fit of rage against the women who were then pestering him,[6] shows Mary Magdalen cling-

FIG. 1
Matthias Grünewald, *The Crucifixion, Isenheim Altar,* 1512–16. Oil on panel,
105⅞ × 120⅞ in. (269 × 307 cm). Musée d'Unterlinden, Colmar.

ing to the crucified Christ's genitalia while the Virgin drinks the blood spurting from the lance wound in his side. The 1932 drawings show a ripped-apart body, as it is experienced in a severe psychotic episode, which Picasso links with early childhood through his drawing of *L'Epingle de nourice* [*sic*] (the wet-nurse's pin, that is, a safety pin) on which he writes the words to make the reference clear.[7] Some catastrophe, experience of violence, or traumatism from so long ago remains vivid, attached by a safety pin that can never be opened by the little child or later by the adult he is supposed to be.

But this catastrophe has been provoked by curiosity, in particular by sexual curiosity, if we somewhat broaden the scope of "sexual." Who was dismembered and eaten during a bacchanal he was not supposed to see, if not the Pentheus of Euripides' tragedy, *The Bacchantes*? Pentheus did

[page 80]
Pablo Picasso
Woman Seated in an Armchair (detail)
4 October 1941. Cat. no. 45.

not have the right to see those women *and his mother* giving themselves up to the instincts unleashed by the festival. He watched, was imagined to be a wild animal by his own mother (the Earth-Mother who gives life and takes it back), was torn to shreds, and partially eaten.

This is a sort of return to the maternal belly. The mother, as she is seen in the living room or in the children's room, becomes the beast who is hiding with someone behind the second curtain in *Les Demoiselles d'Avignon* (see page 44, fig. 7). After having stimulated such an excitement, which is impossible for a small child to integrate without experiencing a devastating shock, she emerges mad with anger from that lair, her staring, Medusa-like gaze turning the child to stone, for a long time and sometimes for ever.

For one reason or another this catastrophe had been diluted by the young Pablo Ruiz until finally it encompassed all physical violence and thus also war. He shows this clearly in sketchbook 46:[8] two wash drawings representing sex, but what sex! The man really looks as though he were not only raping the woman but also strangling and killing her. At that time the Germans were in Royan, sunbathing in their boxer shorts on the beaches; fat and pink, they pillow fought with the dead, green, putrescent jellyfish (*méduses*) that covered these beaches. The beaches then also were littered with planks from sunken ships, tobacco leaves ruined by salt water, and barrels of port that the local people were tapping, drinking right from the barrels or carrying the precious liquid home in pails and basins; in short, they were wreckers' beaches.[9] All this mess – all this war, violence, all this fear, and shame – all this chaos and the panic it engendered was, for the artist, "caused" by a childish curiosity so deeply buried in the unconscious that it could be expressed only in images.[10]

It is fairly clear that for Picasso war was a matter of "private mythology," as Carl Einstein put it, even if his work especially between 1939 and 1943 "stinks of war."[11] For his work of this period stinks of war, or rather of the German Occupation, more than that of any other artist during the period of crisis that began, in Germany at least, as early as 1930 and did not end, unfortunately, in 1945.

In 1997 Paris saw two enlightening exhibitions about crisis, war, and atrocity (1930–96).[12] They obviously (for me) pointed out that painting is incapable of showing the horror of war in the twentieth century. It is completely impossible. Why? I do not know. Perhaps a painting requires a construction, an "art" (a word Picasso hated) that destroys emotion, at least emotion confronted with such cataclysms.

It may be difficult for Americans even to imagine what it is like to live in one's own country when it is occupied by an enemy like the Germans in World War II. To be sure, some profited from the situation. There were parties, full restaurants, a whole *gai Paris* that swam like fish in those waters. But they were in a minority. As Jean-Paul Sartre more or less said, life under the Occupation was intolerable, but somehow one got used to it. Sartre's opinions fluctuated during this period, but he lived much as did Picasso, of whom Jean Cocteau said, in his usual nasty way in the entry for 19 September 1944 of his journal (in which he refers mainly to society events and his little physical ailments), "All extreme regimes, in literature as in politics, have adopted Picasso. It is odd, these days, to see him praised as 'un pur de la Résistance' . . . Picasso has no opinion. He would think it unworthy of himself to have one."[13]

Picasso had never seen war, not World War I, which the French call "The Great War," and he probably knew nothing about it, soldiers having had no desire, when they finally got a leave, to talk about the horror, butchery, and bloody sacrifices in the trenches, knowing well that no one behind the lines would believe them anyway. He did not experience the Spanish Civil War, nor even, when he was going back and forth between Paris and Royan, the exodus of people terrified by memories of atrocities the German uhlans had committed in the northeastern provinces during the 1914 war. For a man of his generation and age, his experience of death was very limited. In 1895, he had seen his sister Conchita dead, but had he seen her die? (Death is so quick and sudden in diphtheria and children were kept away from such scenes.) He had seen the painter Wiegels, his neighbor, dead at the

FIG. 2

Pablo Picasso, *Crucifixion,* 21 October 1932. Pen and ink on paper, 10 × 13 in. (25.5 × 33 cm). Musée Picasso, Paris. M.P. 1085.

Bateau-Lavoir in 1908 (he hung himself). He had certainly seen his loved mistress ("ma jolie") Eva very ill in 1915, but was he there when she was dying in the clinic? He had seen Guillaume Apollinaire dead, though not dying. That same evening, looking into his shaving mirror, he drew a self-portrait[14] that was stricken but not despondent, his forehead wrinkled, his mouth set and drawn, and death in his eyes – a sort of death mask, but a death mask searching for pain, misery, and emotion *in the mirror.* Guilt stifles real sadness. Picasso's relationship with Apollinaire had been rather hectic, and it is important to recall that Apollinaire died of the "Spanish" flu, and that Picasso was superstitious.

It seems that Picasso could feel what he called his "emotions"[15] only through the intermediary of a mirror. It was a real mirror, in this case, but otherwise he discovered his feelings in the mirror of other peoples' eyes or faces, or at least what he projected there, even into those bodies at rest or convulsed – in short, through the intermediary of his painting. Simplifying excessively, it could be said that he did not feel and had no consciousness of what he felt, but that through an acrobatic leap he painted it in others. That is what Jaime Sabartés expresses by saying that in a portrait one can immediately see the mood of the artist and of the model at the very moment when the portrait was made.[16] Picasso told Christian Zervos that painting allowed him to "evacuate" an excess of emotion. [17] This can mean he must have painted what he *saw* then, but he *saw* through his *emotion,* the projection of his own violence: "she" sleeps all the time meant that he wanted to sleep and could sleep curled up in the maternal lap. "She" cries, "she" has fits of hysteria or anger, meant that he himself was suffering and angry, and so on.

Many men like war. Even Apollinaire, who was rather "feminine," could say "Ah, Dieu! que la guerre est jolie."[18] Little boys play at war. Up to that time, in any case, it was women who hated war, which meant waiting, anxiety, shredding linen for bandages, fear for husbands, brothers, fathers, and sons – all experienced passively, in solitude. But in real life, Picasso was afraid of all physical violence. His own violence passed directly, without his becoming aware of it, into what he called painting (which means art in general). He probably never even boxed anyone's ears. He complained but he did not hit; a little authority would probably have made his life, and those of others, easier, but his vengeance consisted in sulking; fortunately for him and for those around him, as well as for us who can see the superb paintings produced during his periods of crisis, his vengeance consisted in the violence in his painting.

The war in Spain certainly disturbed him, but probably without his really feeling it: it was far away. The Occupation was something else to endure, but like Sartre, he got along somehow. Practically, he managed well, protected as he was by André-Louis Dubois even after he left the Sûreté nationale, Maurice Toesca, and the Spanish ambassador Lequerica.[19] He was protected by Arno Breker as well, and in general by the German embassy.[20]

The Germans considered Paris to be a sort of shop window that would demonstrate to the world their love for art.[21] Museums were partly reopened, the Paris Opera was flourishing, artists were pampered, and Picasso was the most famous of them

all. It is said that he refused the supply of coal offered by the German ambassador, but his cellar was full of coal (of course, the studio in the rue des Grands-Augustins was hard to heat, but everyone was cold, everyone had chilblains, and Picasso managed to keep warm enough). He sold pictures (to the Germans, obviously, but he did not have to know that) through the intermediary of the Galerie Louis Carré, and through various runners; he sold enough to live comfortably. He took part in small exhibitions held in various galleries. He managed, probably through Breker, who admired his sculpture, to have cast in bronze the big Boisgeloup heads, the *Death's Head* (cat. no. 54), and the *Cats,* at the very moment when the Germans were pulling down statues all over Paris in order to melt them down for the bronze.[22] He was able to get thick beefsteaks. When he later said to someone that it was dangerous for him to go from the rue des Grands-Augustins to the Bibliothèque Nationale, which was ten minutes' walk away, he was forgetting that children were managing to go to school, and that the texts by Reventos that he said he had copied there at that time were in fact copied between 9 and 14 February 1947. The fat sketchbook known as Carnet X (dating between 1941 and 1963) in which he copied these texts makes the dates clear.

This is not to attack Picasso, but only the legends around him. Why should he be a hero? An artist is an artist; it is not the same profession. All Picasso wanted was not to be compromised, to go on living and painting peacefully. Germans came to visit him, which was useful for his security, but he never appeared with them in public. Heller, however, saw him at the Opera (Picasso, who hated music!), at a performance of *Jeanne au bûcher.*[23] Everyone has seen photos of the Opera house during the war, the good seats entirely filled with Germans. For the "decent" people who experienced the Occupation as a kind of Lent, this may have been a little too much. It is true Picasso was a friend of Paul Eluard and Robert Desnos (on the other side of the barricade), but Eluard's Resistance was relatively theoretical, certainly poetical. Desnos, who lived near the rue Guénégaud, just a short distance from

Picasso, and who managed with his wife Youki always to keep open house in his attic, was arrested in February 1944 for actual resistance. Malicious gossips claimed at the time that Picasso had called Robert an idiot;[24] that having been warned, he should have escaped over the rooftops. (But Youki had gone out, and Desnos was afraid that she might be arrested in his stead.) In any case, Youki made it her business to have *Contrée* published, a book for which Picasso had done an etching (*Seated Woman,* 23 December 1943; cat. no. 72). A letter from her dated 21 May 1944 begs Picasso to agree to deliver this etching, which apparently he was then refusing to do. Perhaps he didn't like Youki, but it is also likely that participating in the publication of a book of poems by someone who had been deported for taking part in the Resistance would have been compromising at the very moment when the Germans, at bay, were at their most savage. Who knows?

The Occupation was intolerable; people barely survived. Some have called it a time of purgatory, in the sense that in Purgatory time does not count, nor does hope; all is gloomy, dark, and cold. One might also describe this period as a long winter that lasted four years, in the sense that winter means that Nature is dead. This cold drove people into themselves, into a total silence. People lived under the leaden lid of a stormy, icy sky. Except for bicycles and the Germans' big cars streets were empty, the intersections full of boards covered with German Gothic lettering. Curfew, glacial winter, and fear were the only items on the menu. You never knew what might happen to those you loved. No one talked. Parents forbade their children to tell their classmates what happened at home; silence and suspicion were the watchwords. For a "mirror-being" like Picasso, a fearful, worried person who could not endure "emotion," it was, though he probably did not realize it, a psychological ordeal that could not fail to lend a certain tone to his painting.

Those of Picasso's works done between 1939 and 1942 are probably the most powerful, obviously with some failures, but the most beautiful. It is interesting to note that the most eloquent, beautiful, and strongest are always triggered by an event,

"a catastrophe." For, if he was afraid, it was because day after day he woke up in fear of a *catastrophe* that he could not, of course, name, something experienced in early childhood and definitively buried. A current event, not necessarily a catastrophic one, was enough to bring back to life the poisoned and enduring splinter. This is true for many people, as one realizes if one listens to them with a "benevolent and evenly suspended" attention.[25] In Picasso's case, the catalyst was nearly always either the reactions of a child who was present (consider the role of little Raymonde's so-called sexual curiosity in the evolution of the *Demoiselles*), or else the emotions of others, those who were close to him.[26]

To show this, let us move completely out of the overloaded period of the Occupation. It is only in 1950–51 that this seventy-year-old man understood what his mother's pregnancy had meant for him and what was still lingering in his unconscious, as it would be for any child. It must be remembered that what we find as perfectly normal and even amusing today in little children was seen as a great sin at the end of the nineteenth century. In this case, the child desired the magical disappearance of the baby, who took up all the room when he was sitting on his mother's lap, and who was going to replace him (then he would probably be thrown in the trash can, replaced like a broken toy by a new one).

Although this was relived by him through little Claude's crises of anxiety and concern when his sister Paloma was about to be born, Picasso was referring only to himself in his sculptures of a pregnant *Goat* with an empty belly, a *Pregnant Woman* with an empty belly and empty breasts (made out of empty milk pitchers!), and especially the pregnant *Female Monkey* with that enormous, empty belly (Claude's property, because the head is made out of the bodies of two little cars that belonged to him).[27] As much as he can, the little monkey, who is really a little child, clings desperately to the maternal lap from which he is going to be evicted, from which he has already been evicted since he can no longer even put his arms around his mother's neck. This extended example attempts to give a sense of how things worked through Picasso's hand and eye, if not in his head. For I am convinced that he had no rational consciousness of these feelings.

Although at the time of the Spanish Civil War and the Occupation, Picasso lacked a child-mirror, he had another mirror, like himself somewhat inclined toward catastrophe: Dora Maar. Dora Maar reacted intensely to all the news, followed it closely, and belonged to a relatively well-informed intellectual milieu. She was, like Picasso, melancholic and high strung. He had only to watch her reactions to know what his were, although hers were stronger and dramatized. Nevertheless, it would not make sense to regard his terrified, terrifying, hard, nasty, cruel, spying "women of the war" as avatars of Dora Maar. He saw these women with his X-ray eyes (like Proust's)[28] in the streets, cafés, and metro, through the distorting mirror of his own passion, anger, mistrust, hatred, and rage – that is, they are his projections. These women could express themselves, whereas he, a Latin man who owed it to himself to be "macho" in the good sense of the word, could not show his feelings.

Strangely, this expression of personal suffering begins in September 1939 (in reality, as far as suffering per se is concerned, from 19 April 1939 onward), and fades at the worst time in the war, 14 July 1942, with the first version of *Man with a Lamb.* Then, in 1943, he creates many haggard women like the one of 6 July,[29] or clearly mad women like the one of 16 August,[30] but he also sketches the tender, attentive mother of *First Steps* (cat. no. 67),[31] who is unknown earlier, and the little boy who peacefully plays with his rattle-penis under the kind protection of a couple of pigeons/parents.[32] Why? Everything is going as badly as it can, and yet, Picasso feels better. Is it that the war and the Occupation are only a climate or an atmosphere (to use Arletty's expression),[33] the pressure and insecurity of which exacerbate a purely private crisis? "Picasso has no opinion!" And yet his work evokes the war, the catastrophe, more than any other. Here we have a conundrum.

Already in 1937, it is said, the artist was racking his imagination about the mural he had been commissioned to do for the Spanish Pavilion at the Paris World's Fair. And then Guernica happened, and the work bloomed almost overnight, like a moonflower.

Picasso, a true Spaniard from Málaga, and then from Barcelona, was incapable of seeing the Basque country as Spanish. All Spaniards in the south detest the Basques, though it is not quite clear why. They are nasty, dirty, and so on, they say. Picasso, however, had never seen the Basque country. To paint *Guernica,* he had to think about the villages of his youth that he knew and loved, devastated by the bombardment – Horta, seen first on his trip to Manuel Pallarés's home in 1898, and Gosol, visited in 1906. But the chaos he painted, the unimaginable, end-of-the-world turmoil, could only have been suggested to him by an entirely internalized memory of the only real cataclysm he had ever experienced – at the age of three, the earthquake in Málaga.[34] The horse and the bull in *Guernica* are the Spain of the corrida, not of the Basque country. As a child, Picasso was very sensitive, skinny, a little sickly, extremely high-strung, and full of imagination. A photograph made when he was four years old, and another when he was seven, show large, sad, passionate, deep eyes, already X-ray eyes, in a thin, pale face.[35] He looks like Proust when he was a child, a resemblance increased by the stiff, black shock of hair that covers his head like a cap.

The Málaga earthquake recurred in his nightmares, for he often spoke about it to Sabartés, who is an extremely precious source of truth about Picasso (here the historicity of things is of little importance; the fantasies are all that count for human beings). From the child's point of view, the heaving and burning earth cracked its shell and projected its anger outside. In the child, the same rage and pressure that were almost impossible to express made his soul, head, and heart crack open. Another child was going to be born (in fact Lola, his sister, was born shortly after the beginning of the earthquake) and the earth's fire erupted to punish him for his anxious hatred. In short, the catastrophe was all his "fault." He had caused this immense internal and external catastrophe that later made him shut his eyes to subsequent real catastrophes, which were nothing compared to that one. Because, all was his fault. Rage had created both earthquake and his own unconscious hatred that could kill the people he loved best.

The other catastrophe was the one evoked by the *Demoiselles* and by the drawings on some sketchbook pages[36] where a little toddler of about two, no doubt awakened by "the noise," tries to slip inside the curtain of "the parents' bedroom" to look. For the rest of his life this other "catastrophe" caused him to see embraces as veritable battles, hand-to-hand combat. Love and war were the same thing. Which one of the parents is going to kill the other behind the curtain? Who am I going to kill when I love? It would be better to drive them away beforehand, as it would be better not to fall asleep, so that the parents do not kill each other while one sleeps. Then, sleep late in the morning, while everyone else is up; sleep or daydream in a bed that is still somehow the maternal lap. Do nothing, remain rolled up against her, since that is what she wants, that is what will assure her of the perfect dependency (the safety pin) of her baby, who is in fact chained by the tentacles of an octopus, the octopuses that he painted and drew in the form of Marie-Thérèse, the woman he probably loved most.

Obviously, all this remained totally unconscious. Fortunately for the child, on the night of the earthquake his father carried him away wrapped in a shawl, held tight against him, protected from the fury of the earth and the boy's immense rage-guilt-terror. Then, in La Coruña, the father at first substituted for the mother by taking the child to school, reassuring him, and coming to pick him up (the boy was afraid of being left at school, and like all children who have a fear of leaving home, he was afraid of another "catastrophe"; he had to keep watch). The father later gave him a way to achieve his own independence. He provided pencils, brushes, lessons, then teachers and good training; he was truly a coach, instilling professional habits and respect for tools in his son, and the reason why, later on, Picasso could say that one had to master technique so fully that one could then and

only then forget it altogether. John Richardson says that Picasso, at the same time that he loved his father, hated him (passim). This is arguable, as the father appears everywhere, such as in the cubist compositions of men at table, the sculptors of the Vollard Suite, and in the character of Degas in his late work. It was a dispassionate relationship, with few disagreements. Of course they had a few conflicts as when, for example, the adolescent was wasting time running around at night in Barcelona.[37] However, these disputes allowed the young artist to work through his Oedipus complex in anger, but also in the security of affection.

Picasso's mother, who was very young when he was born, considered him, her firstborn and only son, to be a sort of messiah, for whom she had a passionate, possessive but distant, almost shy, love, at least after his earliest infancy. She was plump (a mark of beauty at the time), agile, vivacious, merry – a true Andalusian. Playing an active role in a big household, she probably was unable to provide him with the times of rest and evenly suspended attention that allow a baby, and then the adult that he is to become, to be alone-in-the-presence-of-someone and, so, to be able to live with other people as well as to be creative.[38] Picasso seems to seek this silent, restful presence/absence of the model in almost half the prints in the Vollard Suite, to cite only one example. A baby is ferocious when he is hungry, and later on feels quasi-sexual need, but he also wants calm and unintrusive affection. For little Pablo, as for any small child, his mother must have been the very image of beauty, of everything a woman should be. Later, of course, she became rather bossy, by character and by necessity: her husband, often away, was also depressed.

By moving to Paris, Picasso chose exile, the classic solution for those who are too attached to their mothers. She wrote to him constantly, probably to tell him about her life in Barcelona, since in reality they had little to say to each other, nor did she understand her son very well, either. These letters, boxes and boxes of them preserved in the Musée Picasso, are not accessible to the public, even to a privileged public, but only to Picasso's heirs. Thus, on the bedroom wall of Marie-Thérèse's daughter

Maya is a photocopied and enlarged extract from a letter dating from when Picasso was settling in Paris. His mother, naïvely, longs for the time when "he used to come and say goodnight to her in her room" after having run around town chasing girls until the wee hours. This comment recalls Proust's Narrator's good-night kiss from his mother, but upside-down.[39] Did she ask him to tell her about his escapades and love affairs, in order to erase them? She was a "good-enough mother" but intrusive.[40] In any case, she did not let go of her son (cf. the "octopuses"), who loved her passionately, but often hated her (the one does not go without the other, and it is not for nothing that "passion" means passionate love as well as the Passion of Christ).

Picasso, like Hermann Broch's *Virgil* and like Apollinaire, always somehow lived in what Broch, following the Goethe of the second part of Faust, called "the kingdom," "the intermediate space of the Mothers": "Oh! the weakness of the mother, who is only birth and knows nothing about re-birth, who doesn't want to know anything about it."[41] This kingdom is that of art, and poetry. But there has to be a father who keeps one from languishing there, from wallowing there in a dream, without doing anything, without being reborn. And Picasso had had the good luck to have, on and off, a good father, who let him develop the necessary distance for transforming his fascinated, voyeur's eyes into X-ray eyes, a seer's eyes. For a "seer" also makes use of projection, and even projective identification.

In *Guernica,* it is his mother that Picasso "sees" in the form of Marie-Thérèse, weeping over the still-unborn baby of the earthquake; and then, on 1 July 1937, he throws himself into his great *Weeping Woman* (fig. 3, cat. no. 9), which he will work through in seven states (the number seven was always magical for Picasso).[42] Hieratic, tragic, dignified, she is a *mater dolorosa,* so typical of Spanish painting and sculpture, including her tears. Yes, Picasso told Malraux, it was Dora Maar, adding that he "felt" that "women are machines for suffering."[43] Poor Dora Maar's tears and these "machines for suffering" have caused much ink to flow, especially among feminists. However, here we have a hodgepodge of images: Mary Magdalen, the only

woman described weeping at Christ's feet; the tale of the Italian statuette in plaster of paris that Picasso's father had "broken" in order to give her a veil, and, as tears, glass pearls, thus "Hispanicizing" her in the very manner that his son would later practice in his art; in addition, his mother had written him that her face was covered with soot and her eyes weeping and full of tears because of the convents and churches that were burning in Barcelona.[44] In the sixth state, Picasso darkened, "covered with soot" his *Weeping Woman*'s face, then he "cleaned it up" in the seventh state, working with his scraper on the dense drypoint lines as if in a mezzotint, and bringing out the modeling of the eyes, the cheekbones, and the tears. Picasso's mother had then taken vows that gave her admission to a sort of lay sisterhood (as is done, or was, in Spain, among bourgeois or noble women). These women continued to lead secular lives but

FIG. 3
Pablo Picasso, *Weeping Woman,* 1 July 1937, state VII. Etching, aquatint, drypoint, scraper on copper on paper, 27 ¼ in. × 19 ½ in. (69.2 × 49.5 cm). Cat. no. 9.

were buried in the habits of the orders they had chosen. It is well known how the Republicans lined up skeletons of nuns in open coffins on the steps of the convents in Barcelona (the Spanish Republicans were not fond of the clergy, and for good reason, but went a little too far). In the panic of the civil war, Picasso's mother, a very old lady at the time, must have dreaded to imagine herself thus violated in her eternal repose, and she must have written about it to her son in a tearful letter. Finally, the Museo Nazionale Romano has a Greco-Roman head of Medusa with closed eyes (fig. 4), which Picasso probably never saw when he was there in 1917. The woman, shown in profile, the snakes represented by lovely wavy hair, is very beautiful. A close look reveals, under these eyes hollowed out by death, the cheek creased by tears. So the dying Medusa had wept like a female deer; at least the Greco-Roman sculptor thought so.

FIG. 4
Greco-Roman, *Head of Medusa*, stone. Museo Nazionale Romano, Rome.

And why not a passionate dreamer like Picasso? For him, his mother – and thus all women – was somehow part Medusa, and in his boyish fits of exasperation and fury, he must have killed her phantasmatically, like any child who was even a little bit sensitive, or nervous as they said then. My last spice added to the sauce of the *Weeping Woman* is purely imaginative, but it might finish the dish.

The two little Weeping Women of 4 July 1937 (cat. nos. 10–11)[45] are already no longer dignified, mourning figures, but rather women in fits of hysterical rage and suffering who shred their handkerchiefs with their teeth. It is they who we encounter again in the drawings after *Guernica,* up until October. The images are of Medusa, or rather the Erinyes, which amounts more or less to the same thing, except in time: one comes before, and the others after the murder, realized or dreamed, which are nearly equivalent in the guilt of the child who continues to live in each of us.

On 13 January 1939, Picasso's mother really died. Very old, she still had been quite active. During the taking of Barcelona, which was still bloodier than the fighting of 1936, she was magisterially directing a house full of children, including her own grandchildren and probably others as well. Like a proper nineteenth-century Spanish woman, that day she was getting dressed at dawn behind the door of the armoire (the children all slept in her bedroom). She probably lost her balance while putting on her skirt, fell, broke her spine, and died a few hours later. It was clearly impossible for Picasso to go to Barcelona. He had to visualize the abstract event of a distant death. Probably without knowing what he was doing, he nevertheless did it. The offspring was the *Woman with a Tambourine,* from the second half of January (figs. 5–6, cat. nos. 25–26)[46] and the two works entitled *Woman in an Armchair,* one done on 19 April and the other a little later on an undated copper plate.[47] The physical effort required by working on copper – and probably the friendly atmosphere of the Lacourière workshop – allowed him more easily to "evacuate," to root out an anxiety of which he probably knew nothing except a sense of oppression – one might almost

FIG. 5
Pablo Picasso, *Woman with a Tambourine,* January 1939, state I.
Aquatint and scraper on copper on paper, 25 ⅞ × 20 in. (65.8 × 51 cm).
Cat. no. 25.

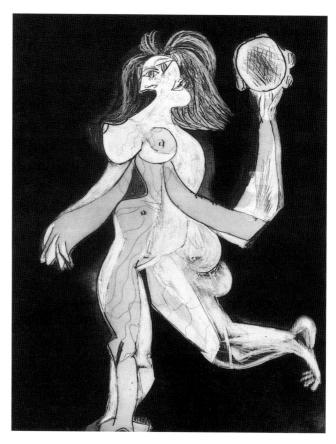

FIG. 6
Pablo Picasso, *Woman with a Tambourine,* January 1939, state V(B).
Aquatint and scraper on copper on paper, 25 ⅞ × 20 in. (65.8 × 51 cm).
Cat. no. 26.

say a sense of "occupation" in the sense in which France was "occupied."

What is interesting in the *Woman with a Tambourine* is that she does not become beautiful and balanced (the woman *and* the composition) until the fifth state, or at least the fourth. The first state is a riddle. The figure has the upper body of a bacchante, but her lower body shows the unstable equilibrium that makes one think of the quest for balance in bathers and dancers by Degas.[48] Picasso's source was a monotype reworked by Degas with pastel (whence, perhaps, Picasso's broad, furious lines grained with aquatint, which resemble pastel in the first state): *After the Bath*[49] (fig. 7). The whole lower part of the body, the dropped hand, the shadows, the phantom of the chair, the curtain, the hunched back, the shape of the breast in profile, and the buttocks are all there. Of course, the woman is reversed by printing from the copper plate, and moreover she is seen from

the front and not from the back, but such emendations are common in Picasso. If one adds to this the foot flattened out by the quest for balance, frequent in Degas's dancers, our maenad also begins by being, referentially, a "Woman at her Toilette," but one that cannot (without the support of the back of the chair in the Degas) keep her balance, which is rare for Picasso. Moreover, he persists, through relentless work (adding scrapings and aquatint), in keeping her in this crazy position for two additional states. Then, in the fourth state, he gives up and borrows from Poussin, that master of balance, the thrown-back leg of the bacchante in his *Bacchanal before a Herm* in the National Gallery in London (fig. 8). Poussin's maenad functions very well here, the hand holding the bunch of grapes becoming the lowered hand in the etching, the flying hair corresponding to the bacchante's wild locks. Time had gone by, and Barcelona had perhaps already fallen. In any case, Picasso's bacchante became the evocation (according to Picasso) of the fighting in the streets, and hand-to-hand combat. And yet, Degas remains: Picasso's bold stroke, scraping out the thrown-back leg of his figure crudely and furiously against the background of aquatint, corresponds exactly to the way in which Degas worked with a rag out of an inked background on his "dark" monotypes.

But why did Picasso persist in trying to make this woman, who can only fall, stand up? Certainly, it was, unconsciously, because of the way in which his mother died.[50] As for the bacchante, she is once again a young, joyous evocation of his mother, dancing for her fascinated firstborn son who will ever after be obsessed by the fact that she *had*

danced this dance of love/death (according to Picasso's private mythology) with/for another person, his father, an act that "dismembered" Picasso psychologically, like Pentheus. How much pain exists in all that, but what a beautiful image!

Then there were also the two sad and sinister women in an armchair (figs. 9–10).[51] The first is the before and the other the after. The first from 19 April shows us a heavy woman who nonetheless somewhat resembles Dora Maar (always the Proustian mixture of two persons), sadly pensive, horrified by what is happening in the street, worried about "the children," but keeping her feet on the ground, in the true sense of the word (fig. 9). The second, which Picasso labored over, going through six states, begins by being phantomlike, then, through scraping and burin work, takes on a ravaged, terrifying face (fig. 10). Her hands cling to the arms of the chair but her legs hang in front; she seems not to have any control over her feet, which

FIG. 7
Edgar Degas, *After the Bath,* ca. 1883–84. Pastel on monotype, 20⅛ × 12⅞ in. (52 × 32 cm). Private collection.

FIG. 8
Nicolas Poussin, *Bacchanal before a Herm* (detail), ca. 1632–33. Oil on canvas, 39⅜ × 56⅛ in. (100 × 142.6 cm). The National Gallery, London.

drag on the floor, showing the soles of her shoes. Probably Picasso had learned or imagined that when his mother fell, they had carried her in an armchair, and she must have lost the use of her legs because her back was broken. "Old age and death," is how Picasso described the meaning of the chair. But additionally, the most simplistic interpretation of dreams assumes, rightly, that a woman in an armchair is a woman in the arms of a man. So we come back to it again, to the fantasy of love/struggle to the death, since this broken woman is dying.

A period of not thinking about his mother's death followed. Picasso was very busy with the "total book" he and Vollard had planned, and political events were moving quickly. It is only in the relative calm of Royan that he begins, in September 1939, to mourn her.

From this point of view, the first Royan sketchbook is extremely instructive.[52] The Erinyes are beginning to harass the son who had, as a child, committed matricide in his head or at least in his angry heart.[53] The reason is given by the work alluded to in Picasso's drawing,[54] Goya's *Dream of Lies and Inconstancy* (figs. 11–12);[55] the inconstancy and lies of the mother who returned to the father and who loved other children, and the inconstancy of the son who has led his own life and loved other women. There is also the inconstancy of the mother[56] who is already the great *Woman Dressing Her Hair* of June 1940 (see page 22, fig. 8),[57] concerned only with herself and her beauty (a theme recurrent in Picasso), but not with her son.

Finally, we have the cruelty and possessiveness

FIG. 9 [above]
Pablo Picasso, *Woman in an Armchair,* 19 April 1939, state II. Etching, aquatint, scraper, and burin on copper on paper, 11 ¹¹/₁₆ × 9 ⁵/₁₆ in. (29.8 × 23.7 cm). Musée Picasso, Paris. M.P. 2809.

FIG. 10 [right]
Pablo Picasso, *Woman in an Armchair,* January–June 1939, state VI. Etching, aquatint, scraper, and burin on copper on paper, 13 ½ × 8 ¾ in. (34.2 × 22.2 cm). Musée Picasso, Paris. M.P. 2813.

FIG. 11
Pablo Picasso, *Sketch of Nudes,* October 1939. Pencil on paper, 8 ½ × 6 ¹¹⁄₁₆ in. (21.7 × 17 cm). Musée Picasso, Paris. M.P. 1990-111, folio 96R.

FIG. 12
Francisco de Goya, *Dream of Lies and Inconstancy,* from *Los Caprichos,* 1797–98. Etching and aquatint on paper, 7 ¹⁄₁₆ × 4 ¹¹⁄₁₆ in. (18 × 12 cm).

of the mother, who visibly intrudes, as seen in a series of drawings from the same Royan sketchbook (figs. 13–15; see also page 24, fig. 11).[58] It is a real, everyday, banal scene, like the one in Proust where Françoise kills a chicken, screaming "filthy beast!"[59] But, why did the writer and the artist chose these scenes from among countless others? The first image is anecdotal. In the kitchen (buffet, radio), the maid is seated on the inevitable chair, her shoulders covered with a little crocheted shawl and a hat on her head (women wore hats at that time, and all during the Occupation). She holds on her lap, on a newspaper, one of the sheep's heads, skinned but whole (eyes, gory flesh, and all), that Picasso used to give to his Afghan hound, Kazbek. He painted these

heads at least twice in that period, red and bloody.

The second image is savage (fig. 14). A hand thrusts a cutlass into the head, which has to be cut up. Then the woman loses her own identity (her head) (see page 24, fig. 11), but she holds the blood-soaked sheep's head in a way that sends a chill down the spine – from underneath, with two of her fat fingers sticking out, one from the eye socket and the other from the mouth (fig. 15). A drawing of the hands alone makes clear this position of the right hand. This woman with her "mantel" is at the same time a Virgin with Child and a Pietà holding Christ's dead body on her lap. It is a nightmarish image, which nonetheless will not be followed by an exact picture,[60] but rather by women-death's-heads, women-sheep's-heads. In

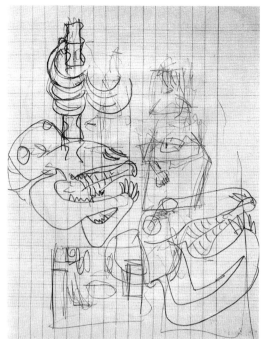

Picasso's own case it was the mother who was dead, but the son, as a result, felt himself to be half-dead, and also, in fantasies, the roles are often reversed. The fingers traversing the brain and putting out the eye are a clear sign that as a child this man had felt his mother to be intruding.

Who had killed whom in that lovemaking/fight? The artist's mourning had begun – who knows why? – without his ever thinking about it, but with extreme violence. It was to endure, in its Erinyes phase[61] – and the Erinyes all became women painted, usually in an armchair, whether one sees it or not – until one finds the sheep once again, but alive and cuddled by a bearded shepherd-father in the drawings for *Man with a Lamb* in July 1942. It is the lost lamb, but found again.[62]

There are few men in the work done between the *Garbage Man* of January 1940[63] and the early studies for *Man with a Lamb* (beginning 14 July 1942). The *Garbage Man* seems to be a pious hope; he disposes of garbage, from which, however– Picasso's sculpture shows this–good things may be salvaged. As for *Man with a Lamb* (cat. no. 66), he is at once the father (he often has a beard) who saves the son (the Málaga earthquake), and the son to whom the mother has entrusted the lamb and thus life, the Son who is "the Resurrection and the Life,"

FIG. 13 [above left]
Pablo Picasso, *Sketch of a Woman Holding a Sheep's Skull*, October 1939. Pencil on paper, 8½ × 6 11/16 in. (21.7 × 17 cm). Musée Picasso, Paris. M.P. 1990-111, folio 49R.

FIG. 14 [above right]
Pablo Picasso, *Sketch of a Sheep's Skull*, October 1939. Pencil on paper, 8½ × 6 11/16 in. (21.7 × 17 cm). Musée Picasso, Paris. M.P. 1990-111, folio 50R.

FIG. 15 [bottom right]
Pablo Picasso, *Sketch of a Sheep's Skull*, October 1939. Pencil on paper, 8½ × 6 11/16 in. (21.7 × 17 cm). Musée Picasso, Paris. M.P. 1990-111, folio 53R.

in short the "re-birth" of Hermann Broch's *Virgil.* Mourning, Picasso's war, is coming to an end.

As usual, all this begins in the prints, in particular the forgiveness – Picasso forgiving his mother, and forgiving also Lola, his sister, for having been born and for having been, in fact if not in truth, the child and then the adult to whom the mother paid the most attention, to whom she was the closest. It is of interest that the print that I have called, for lack of a better name, *Paris, 14 July 1942* (fig. 16, cat. nos. 57–58),[64] which is more a document than a marvel, shows us a whole group, a family bearing various kinds of food, doves, eggs, fish, and bread. A little girl leads a goat and a very old lady, who except for her small size in no way looks like the artist's mother, carries a lamb rolled up in her shawl. They seem to be bringing all this to the man with flowers, bearded like the man with a lamb, who is wearing shorts (as Picasso often also did), and whose left hand supports a dish that resembles a palette.

Brassaï recounts that a proof of this print was displayed in the rue des Grands-Augustins and that Jaime Sabartés had told him it was the beginning of *Man with a Lamb.*[65] The man, he said, is going to take the lamb from the arms of the old woman and keep it. And in fact the first sketches for the great sculpture were made on 15 July. This was the darkest

time in the war and the Occupation. But Picasso had more or less buried his Erinyes, and the benevolent Eumenides could replace them, or rather, the former could be transformed into the latter.[66] Perhaps he simply had rediscovered among his papers the photograph that was later returned to the Vilato family (into which Lola had married) by the Musée Picasso (fig. 17).[67] It represents the artist's mother at the age of eighty, visiting the Tibidabo fun fair around 1935–36, with the whole Vilato family of parents and children. The group's rhythm is comparable to that of the group in the print but without the food. The little girl in the photograph wears a huge straw hat but does not carry a plate (or a hat) full of flowers; the woman with the doves in the print has a mass of long hair that frames her face as Lola's hat frames hers, at the right in the photo; and (according to Xavier Vilato) some members of the family are more recognizable in that print than in the photograph, although disguised. From this point, the Good Shepherd can arrive, and as well the mother of the *First Steps* (cat. no. 67) (i.e., the print seems to be a source of the figure of *Man with a Lamb* and of a meaning of tenderness and generosity in *First Steps*).

But before we come to that point, we must consider Picasso's war-women, who are sinister, hard, rigid, malevolent, sly, and ferocious. They

FIG. 16
Pablo Picasso, *Paris, 14 July 1942,* 14 July 1942, state V (positive). Etching, scraper, and burin on copper on paper, 17 ¾ × 25 ¼ in. (45.2 × 64.1 cm.) Cat. no. 57.

FIG. 17
Picasso's mother (second from left) with the Vilato family at a fair in Tibidabo, Barcelona, ca. 1935–36. Picasso's sister, Lola Vilato, stands at the far right.

look one straight in the eyes (a raking gaze in these faces distorted by the paintbrush). They snigger cruelly. They are spies, informers, birds of prey, with stiff crow feathers in their hats. Picasso projects on them almost all the bad feelings that come to him en masse in the first years of mourning, and in the mourning for a mother who was loved too much yet at the same time hated for making her little child suffer and be angry at her, mortally angry. He had suffered a thousand deaths and had hated to death. All bad memories must be expelled so that the good ones can finally surface —Erinyes and then Eumenides.

One has only to look at these women-of-war: women in armchairs (real or virtual), women who suffer and who cause others to suffer — the hardness of the woman in a greenish yellow that sets teeth on edge, with her bloody lips (cat. no. 56);[68] the stiff, falsely resigned look of the other, gray and blue, with a cardboard flower in her hat, and once again, that bloody mouth (cat. no. 44);[69] another one, from 5 June 1941, who looks as though she had been crushed by a steamroller;[70] the sort of human beast, from 13 June 1941, all dressed up, with an enormous phallic nose and a ridiculous little hat;[71] the sinister one, all white and gray, fat, shapeless, with her malevolent proud smile, from 1 August 1941.[72] And already, by 16 October 1939, a weeping woman exists with potatolike face.[73]

One might mention any number of others, these superb paintings of horrible and malevolent women, but the worst are the ones from 26 June and 27 July 1941 (figs. 18–19).[74] The first, who is squinting (cf. the leucoma on the eye of the 1903 *Celestine*), looks at you with a false and gluttonous smile. The other, with a grotesque basket of flowers on her head, looks at you obliquely, out of the corner of her eye, ready to denounce. She is wickedness itself.

Poor Picasso! No doubt he was a little bit paranoid during those years! But what beautiful paintings he made out of that real but imagined persecution. There is also the new version of Ingres's *Odalisque with Slave,* which had been lovingly rendered in drypoint in 1933 (*Flute-player and Sleeping Woman*[75]), and who reappears in a jail-like

FIG. 18
Pablo Picasso, *Seated Woman with a Hat,* 26 June 1941. Oil on canvas, 28¾ × 23 in. (73 × 58.4 cm). Private collection. Courtesy Cahiers d'Art, Paris.

and angular guise in *L'Aubade* (see page 30, fig. 16), where we find the doubled woman, one dreaming and one thinking about making love (the musician). But in this state of persecution, suffering, and deformation, is sex really a possibility?

Even the magnificent *Still Life with Blood Sausage* (cat. no. 42) speaks of persecution.[76] There is nothing "dead" about it except the conventional word in the title (*nature morte*). In reality, it is probably the only self-portrait painted during that period, perhaps made when thinking about the about-to-be-shot Christ figure in *Third of May, 1808,* because of the similarity between the triangular light that here escapes from the suspended bulb and the one that lit, triangularly, Goya's man with his outstretched arms. In any case, it is an inner portrait of Picasso's fantasies and anxieties, which may be indicated by the monochromatic, grayish brown color scheme. But in this portrait the mother is a participant, so that it is more a portrait of their relation to each other, as was present in the psyof

FIG. 19
Pablo Picasso, *Seated Woman with a Hat,* 27 July 1941. Oil on canvas,
36 ¼ × 28 ¾ in. (92.1 × 73 cm). Private collection. Courtesy Cahiers d'Art, Paris.

the artist on 10 May 1941. The subject has nothing to do with shortages and restrictions. It offers, in wartime, a feast fit for kings, centered on a kitchen table. For Picasso, everything happens in the kitchen, the place where one lives (see *The Charnel House,* cat no. 82). These yards of rolled-up blood sausage are, of course, an allusion to the maternal belly, the sausage being a pig's intestine that has been washed clean, filled with blood, and boiled.[77] The two artichokes allude to the hearts (as in "artichoke hearts") of the mother, who loved other people, and the son, who did not remain eternally faithful to his mother. The drawer with its knives and forks is clearly a mouth full of devouring teeth, the baby's teeth chewing on the breast.

Who has ever thought of arranging these instruments this way in a drawer? It is contrary to simple good sense. The cutlass, to cut the sausage, and if possible the umbilical cord, is still there, not yet used. The wedge of camembert, a sixth of the whole, may allude to the prediction Max Jacob

made to Picasso: decline at age sixty, death at sixty-eight (in 1941, he was precisely sixty years old). The newspaper, moreover, is necessarily full of bad news in 1941; it is in the obituary column that deaths are announced, including that of his mother, and soon his own. As for the bottle of white wine (Picasso drank only water), it contains a liquid, but what? Milk? Or perhaps the vinegar that was offered to Christ when he was thirsty? Lastly, in the center of the "belly" of the roll of sausage, there is something bizarre, a small triangular vessel containing three kinds of marbles that form something like an ace of clubs – the triangulation of father, mother, and child, the "seeds" that we find in the middle of the open belly of the *Small Pregnant Woman* from 1948.[78] A superb painting, one of the most eloquent of this period, it is hardly a riddle.

From all this rubble, Picasso is going to manage, in 1943, to reconstitute an effigy of his mother: a bronze head with a hairstyle from 1900 (the little bun perched high up), stuck onto a dressmaker's wooden dummy from the era of corsets, with an arm and hand from the Easter Island, a gift from Pierre Loeb and one of the artist's treasures (cat. no. 73). All this is put together in such a way that one sees the "collage."[79] As a joke, Picasso later put a painter's smock on his sculpture and attached to its hand a palette and brushes, showing in this way that if his father was indeed the manner of his work, it was his mother who was the inspiration, through The Others (women, of course). Mourning, and also passion, were over, and the art was affected by it, for the artist always did his best painting only when he was in a crisis, whatever it was. But perhaps after 1944 he was happier, because he was more indifferent, more cynical. The passion, and the Passion, were over for him. His war was over. He was no longer "occupied"! And "there was fun sometimes in Hell, wasn't there?" as Kipling puts it about the war in the trenches in 1917.[80]

Circumventing Picasso:
Jean Paulhan and His Artists

Michèle C. Cone

During the Occupation, Georges Braque, Jean Fautrier, Jean Dubuffet, and Chaim Soutine had in common the patronage of Jean Paulhan (1884–1968), one of the few figures of the Parisian prewar intellectual community to remain influential during the war and for several years afterwards.[1] Paulhan (fig. 1) either wrote about these artists, proselytized on their behalf, or bought their work. Unlike the *Bleu Blanc Rouge* painters, who thought they were creating a non-decadent avant-garde, and the *Between-the-Jew-and-the-Pompier* contingent of romantic realists supported by the anti-Semitic critic Lucien Rebatet,[2] the artists that Paulhan admired assumed their "decadent" vanguardism despite the prevailing antidecadence rhetoric in the official art press.

Although the subject of death and decay was unwelcome in a country allegedly going through national renovation under Marshal Pétain, it frequently appeared in the work of Paulhan's favorites. And, at a moment when an expressive *matière* denoted decay, decadence, obscenity, and Jewishness in art, it continued to be used by the artists who interested Paulhan. However, with respect to *matière* – the autonomous language of paint and of other materials of painting – Paulhan

felt that his artists also parted from Picasso. "[*Matière*] is in Rembrandt (not in Bosch): it is in Soutine or Rouault . . . It is in Fautrier ([but] not in Picasso who makes admirable colored drawings. . . .)" Paulhan wrote to Fautrier in 1943.[3] Put in more flattering words, whereas in Picasso's wartime skulls, death often has the look, form, and feel of dry bones, death images tend to be spectral in Braque and Dubuffet, and viscous in Fautrier and Soutine.[4]

In the context of the rampage against decadence by Vichyites and collaborationist critics, and of the reverence in which Picasso was held by enemies of Vichy and of the Third Reich, Paulhan's opinions revealed a singularly independent turn of mind. But then, Paulhan was used to assuming difficult positions. In his role as editor of the prestigious *Nouvelle revue française* (NRF), which he took over in 1925, he often had to critique the writings of famous authors who thought they were beyond reproach. He managed to remain a friend of the painter André Lhote while assailing his art. On the intellectual plane, Paulhan fit in with groups that hated each other: he was close to the surrealists in the early twenties and to Georges Bataille and his colleagues of the Collège de Sociologie in the late thirties. During the Occupation, he contributed to

Resistance publications while also playing artistic mentor to Nazi officials stationed in Paris.

Caught in the unoccupied zone near Carcassonne after the invasion and partition of France, Paulhan — who had been associated with leftist causes — had difficulty obtaining a pass to return to occupied Paris. The negotiations with the Vichy government that made it possible for him to return home, like those which enabled so-called degenerate artists also caught in the unoccupied zone to return safely to Paris after the Armistice, remain something of a mystery. A French official at the prefecture, André-Louis Dubois, has taken credit for "protecting" Picasso during the Occupation.[5] In the case of vanguard artists who were French nationals and not Jewish, the issue of degeneracy turned out to be more serious in the eyes of Vichyites and French critics than of the Nazis. "Let them degenerate if they want to, all the better for us," Hitler told Albert Speer upon hearing that there was degenerate art on view at the 1943 Paris Salon d'Automne.[6] Early on, Pierre Drieu la Rochelle, a French mouthpiece for the Nazis and Paulhan's new colleague at the NRF, had exceptionally exonerated Braque from the onus of decadence in the cultural weekly *Comoedia*.[7] "Your Braque piece in *Comoedia* is excellent," was how Paulhan expressed gratitude to the man who made it possible for Braque to work in peace.[8]

Braque and the old-time NRF editor had met in 1935, long after Paulhan bought his first Braque, a 1912 collage. The friendship intensified after the Armistice when Paulhan decided to write his thoughts on Braque for publication, and started to spend many hours at the artist's studio watching him work and hearing him talk. The first version of what was to become *Braque le patron* came out in *Comoedia* 31 October 1942.[9] "Am I still a friend of Picasso? I wrote on Braque," Paulhan answered the poet Jean Grenier who had queried him on that subject.[10]

Meanwhile, the book with text by Paulhan and lithographs by Braque was taking shape at

[page 98]
Pablo Picasso
Girl Asleep at a Table (Intérieur à la femme endormie) (detail)
18 December 1936. Cat no. 1.

FIG. 1
Jean Dubuffet, *Portrait of Jean Paulhan,* 1945. Ink on paper, 14⅞ × 12⁹⁄₁₆ in. (38 × 32 cm). Musée des Arts Décoratifs, Paris. Donation Jean Dubuffet.

the atelier of Fernand Mourlot: "I will always remember seeing Braque during the Occupation arrive at the atelier rue Chabrol on a prehistoric bicycle; he was magnificent, an impressive stature, with a remarkable head, pale eyes and white hair," recalled Mourlot in his memoirs.[11] Paulhan came too, to look things over and to correct Braque's grammar, for in the initial project the artist's thoughts were to be included verbatim at the end of the Paulhan text.[12]

Although Braque was hardly a discovery in 1940, Paulhan befriended the famed cubist at a critical time in the artist's development — the start of a new phase of sometimes monumentally sized paintings depicting abruptly cut-off views of painterly, somewhat abstract interiors with still lifes — a hairbrush, washbowl, and water jug on a table in *The Wash Stand* (1942–44; The Phillips Collection, Washington, D.C.); a grill, a fish, a platter, a large fork and sieve on a kitchen table in *Kitchen Table with Grill* (1943–44; private collection, Switzerland); a coal scuttle, stove, palette, waste basket, and heavy table in the workplace of an artist in *The Stove* (fig. 2), and sometimes the black silhouettes of female or male sitters such as *Patience* (1942; private collection, Geneva). Paulhan in fact

FIG. 2
Georges Braque, *The Stove,* 1942. Oil and sand on canvas, 57⅜ × 34 in. (145.7 × 86.4 cm). Yale University Art Gallery, New Haven, Connecticut. Gift of Paul Rosenberg and Company in memory of Paul Rosenberg.

became the owner of one of the tall, narrow kitchen paintings and received as a gift one of Braque's still lifes with black fish. He also acquired a sketch of an interior with two female figures.[13] In February 1942, Paulhan wrote to his friend the novelist Marcel Jouhandeau: "Yesterday [I went to] Braque. His latest canvases are marvelous. What serenity, what presence, I remain enchanted."[14]

Referred to as examples of Braque's "late works"

by the organizers of the 1997 exhibition at the Royal Academy in London, paintings by this artist dating from after 1938 probably influenced the works of the *Bleu Blanc Rouge* painters, whose first group exhibition took place in early 1943. Similarities with the work of Braque are seen in the penchant of Edouard Pignon and Maurice Estève in particular for somewhat abstract interiors with a plain still-life motif arranged on a table, the pervasively silent mood, the occasional view out of a window with a female presence inside the room, and everything compressed within a shallow pictorial space (fig. 3). But the 1943 paintings of these *Bleu Blanc Rouge* painters are more conventional in subject matter and in form.

They include no bathroom paraphernalia, no camouflaged "forms which have no literal meaning whatsoever."[15] There is

FIG. 3
Edouard Pignon, *Seated Woman at a Table,* 1942. Dimensions unknown. Formerly Jacques Bazaine Collection, Paris.

MICHÈLE C. CONE 101

none of the "metamorphic" confusion that Braque said was fundamental to what he sought to express and that Paulhan admired in art and poetry.[16] And, they display a far less painterly *matière*. Furthermore, the *Bleu Blanc Rouge* painters' use of mostly primary colors gives their paintings cheerful connotations totally at odds with Braque's more muted palette. Indeed, as pointed out by John Golding, "whereas the earlier paintings [of Braque] were characterized by an air of serenity and a quiet, restrained splendour, [his] wartime pictures tend to be austere, at times even tragic in their implications."[17]

In conveying confinement, the cold of unheated interiors in the winter, the heightened importance of food, and also in a recourse to a palette dominated by grays, black, dark blues, and browns, paintings by Braque are closer to Picasso's output during the same years than to the *Bleu Blanc Rouge* painters. But in the treatment of the death image, Braque and Picasso part ways. Like Picasso, Braque painted a number of skulls during the Occupation years, but he later denied their symbolic connotations, insisting to John Richardson that what fascinated him in painting a skull next to a rosary was "the tactile quality of the rosary and the formal problems of mass and composition posed by the skull."[18]

There is indeed a striking difference in the skull image by Braque and by Picasso. For one thing, Braque did not make skull sculptures, but only

paintings where a skull form is present. For another, Braque's painted skulls are far less assertive than Picasso's; they glance to the side rather than confront the viewer directly, and they have a ghostly, evanescent quality, not the dry and bony texture of skeletons (figs. 4–5). And most telling, when seen in profile, a palette image can transmute into both a skull and an amoeba (*The Stove*; *Large Interior with Palette* [1942; The Menil Collection, Houston]; *Still Life with Palette* [1943; The Saint Louis Art Museum]). Thus, rather than expressing fear of the finality of death or insisting on a dichotomy between death and life, these works suggest that there might be a continuum between the end and the beginning of life.

Paulhan, who favored Braque's *matière* over Picasso's and who liked Braque far more than he did Picasso (Paulhan and Braque apparently shared an interest in Tibetan Buddhism), wrote of his preference from the point of view of a Frenchman who believes in national characteristics. He appreciated Braque's lack of brashness and attributed to him a typically French understanding of the materials of his craft: "Picasso makes so much noise that one loves Braque first for his discretion, then for his silence, and finally because one imagines that he knows so much more than the other . . . ," he wrote Jouhandeau in 1932, three years before meeting Braque in person.[19] He reiterated his preference to Jouhandeau in 1939: "The Braques are remarkable . . . It greatly surpasses Picasso . . . I think that what I like in him [Braque] . . . is the patience, the fine touch of the French artisan . . . One is never more keenly aware of the Cocteau side of Picasso than in front of a Braque."[20]

In 1943, the Galerie de France offered an aperçu of Braque's early works, soon after which twenty-two recent paintings and nine pieces of sculpture were featured at the 1943 Salon d'Automne. While the *Je suis partout* critic, Lucien Rebatet, sneered at "the resurgence of an old world that clings to the debris of its past, both anarchical and academic,"[21] positive reports on visits to the artist's studio filled the pages of the more moderate cultural weekly *Comoedia*. From Marguerite Bouvier we learn that Braque was a fanatic of the Greek author Hesiod.

From the painter Jean Bazaine (one of the *Bleu Blanc Rouge* painters) we hear that Braque liked comparing himself to a gardener among his trees: "I prune, I clip, I command."[22] Braque emerged from the war untainted, although he confided to the printmaker Mourlot that he might have gone on the propaganda trip organized for French artists by the Nazis "had they liked his paintings."[23]

Overall, the Paris to which Braque and many other artists returned after the Armistice had a very strange atmosphere. No exhibition could open without first being visited by a Nazi censor. In galleries and in museums, art by Jewish artists was kept definitely out of sight. The surrealists were

rarely on display, either. New names signed the columns of an aryanized art press, and at the *Nouvelle revue française,* Paulhan had to share power with the pro-Nazi appointee, Drieu la Rochelle. The gallery scene was also transformed. Paul Rosenberg, whose gallery had represented Braque, had left for the United States. Galleries owned by Jews were aryanized – handed over to collaborationist owners, or fictitiously sold so that the true owners could remain silent partners. Galerie Louise Leiris owned by Daniel-Henry Kahnweiler was in that category, as was the Galerie René Drouin owned by Leo Castelli.[24]

It was at Galerie Drouin that Jean Fautrier was launched in October–November 1943. "I convinced René Drouin to give Fautrier a major exhibition," Paulhan wrote to a friend on 29 September 1943. "He [Drouin] has, on place Vendôme, the most beautiful gallery in all of Paris."[25] Paulhan took many friends on studio visits to Fautrier's atelier at 216, boulevard Raspail, including resisters and collaborators, pro- and anti-Semites, and even the Nazi official, Gerhard Heller, who would remember Paulhan as "my mentor in modern art."[26] Paulhan wrote the catalogue essay for the 1943 Drouin exhibition, the first version of a longer text entitled *Fautrier l'enragé.*[27] He also published an article on the artist in *Comoedia* (13 November 1943).

To this day, Fautrier (1898–1964) is best known for his Hostage series of paintings started in 1943 and exhibited in 1945, which unveiled a new process – the building up of a tactile relief on which the artist could then draw or paint, a new vision anticipating *l'art informel,*[28] and a resonant subject matter – the routine Nazi roundup and killing of hostages in retaliation for the assassination of one of their men. (For a while, fearing arrest, Fautrier lived in hiding at Châtenay-Malabry outside Paris,

FIG. 6
Jean Fautrier, *Rabbit Skins,* 1927. Oil on canvas. 51½ × 38⅛ in. (131 × 97 cm). Marie-José Lefort Collection, London.

FIG. 7 [right]
Jean Fautrier, *Open Corpse,* 1928. Oil on canvas, 45⅝ × 28¾ in. (116 × 73 cm). Musée des Beaux-Arts, Dijon, France.

from the mid-twenties, but also in mostly black paintings like *Black Flowers* (1926; Limmer Gallery, Freiburg), *Still Life with Pear* (1928; private collection, Germany), and *Nude* (1926; Limmer Gallery, Freiburg). Like Soutine, whom it is tempting to compare to the Fautrier of *Rabbit Skins,* the French-born artist had stayed away from the whole episode of cubism. Indeed, his late twenties and early thirties demoiselles (*Young Women* [1929; Marie-José Lefort Collection, London]) had more to do with "precultural representation"[30] than with the cubist distortions of Picasso's *Demoiselles d'Avignon* (see page 44, fig. 7).

Present in the Drouin selection was the painting that began Paulhan's Fautrier binge, *Open Corpse* (fig. 7), a human body in frontal view, open as for an autopsy, its guts a zigzagging line within a dark

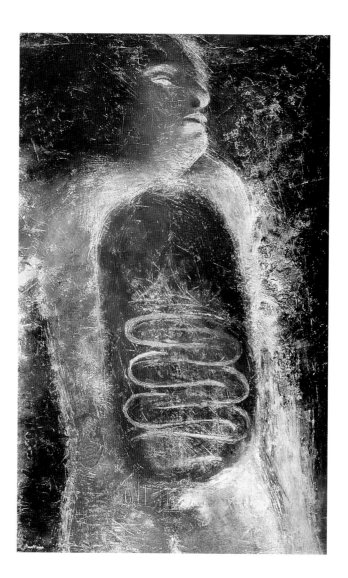

within earshot of woods where the Nazis came to finish off their victims by gunshot.)

This view of Fautrier's career — revised by a retrospective exhibition at the Musée d'Art Moderne de la Ville de Paris in 1989 — obliterates some twenty years of his painting production prior to 1943 and omits the important exhibitions of his art at Galerie Visconti in 1924, at Georges Bernheim in 1928, and at the NRF gallery in 1934. The wartime Drouin retrospective showed both old and new work by an artist then in transition.

Among the early paintings on view were two still lifes of a decomposing boar, and *Rabbit Skins* (fig. 6),[29] a luminous painting showing five dead hares dangling in graceful abandon from the end of a string in a dark, cavelike space. A delicate, sometimes furry texture and soft contours predominate, not only in black-on-black still lifes of dead animals oval. "This cadaver that has just been broken open for an autopsy, resembles some marching condottiere,"[31] Paulhan remarked, discovering in an ambiguous overlay of two states of being the sense of metamorphosis that he also valued in Braque's late works. Paulhan, who had seen death closely during World War I and become fascinated with morbid images, hung *Open Corpse* in the dining room of the home on rue des Arènes that he shared with his wife, and to which he brought his writer friends.

The list of works for the Galerie Drouin show indicated a hiatus in Fautrier's production between 1932 and 1938 (when the artist left Paris and became a nightclub owner and instructor in a ski resort), and a reprise in 1938 of fruit and flower paintings, still black with blurred contours, such as *Fruit in a Bowl and Flowers* (1939; Michael Werner Gallery, Cologne). In 1940–41, Fautrier was going to give up oil and canvas, as he began to layer absorbent paper mixed with paste in lieu of a simple prepared canvas base.[32] In *The Rabbit* (1941; Limmer Gallery, Freiburg) and *The Fish* (1943; private collection, Paris) – two works that have been traced back to the Galerie Drouin 1943 retrospective[33] – contrasts of light and dark are disconnected from the outlined skeleton of the depicted objects. Graffiti-like, gestural short markings identify the subject matter. The catalogue list also included several landscapes from 1943 as well as two paintings of heads dated 1943. In addition, it showed five pieces of sculpture (including four heads from 1942–43), a number of unidentified drawings from 1942–43, and three sets of book illustrations.

It would thus appear that a number of works in the style of the Hostage paintings might have been seen in the 1943 exhibition, though – no doubt for safety reasons – none bore a title that risked offending the Nazi censors. More intriguing than the subject matter at that point was the change in surface quality from flat to impastoed, as if a fragment of Soutine's raised and heavily textured surfaces were being analyzed in close-up view (fig. 8).

Fautrier not only exhibited art that was flagrantly "decadent" by the standards of his enemies, he illustrated the poems of Resistance friends, and helped a Jewish artist survive. A letter from Paulhan – who had taken an interest in a Jewish painter named Benn [Rabinowicz] – reveals that in 1943 Fautrier spent 3,000 francs for a work by Benn.[34] Soon after this letter Paulhan thanked Fautrier for a precious gift. "I don't think that our friends in [internment?]camps could have received anything better or more nourishing."[35]

Not surprisingly, Fautrier's exhibition aroused the passion of Lucien Rebatet, the pro-Nazi critic of *Je suis partout*: "If you want an aperçu of *dementia praecox*, go see [Fautrier's] mauve or yellow landscapes, his pink apples . . . These kilos of paint . . . What debauchery, for Gods sake! What a waste of canvas which could have been more usefully employed for making sheets or baby diapers."[36] Rebatet favored watercolor, the medium most antithetical to Fautrier's raised impastoed surface, and, among contemporary watercolorists, praised romantic realists Roland Oudot and Maurice

FIG. 8
Jean Fautrier, *The Hostage,* 1944. Oil and pigments on paper laid down on canvas, 25⅛ × 21¼ in. (64 × 54 cm). Courtesy Galerie Daniel Malingue, Paris.

Brianchon, whose Between-the-Jew-and-the-Pompier aesthetics combined escapist themes, refined taste, harmony and moderation, and a Bonnardian lightness of touch (fig. 9).

At a time when thick painterly *matière* was abhorred by all major French critics as un-French, degenerate, and, in the words of Jean-Marc Campagne, the critic at *Les Nouveaux Temps,* typical of Jewish art,[37] Fautrier's use of it daringly flaunted the acceptable. In inventing an original way to address artistic and racial issues, Fautrier was exceptional among French artists. And, in pushing the issue of *matière* beyond Soutine's viscous surfaces, he was making visible the link between Soutine and postwar *art informel.*[38]

Although Fautrier and Soutine were near contemporaries (Soutine was born in 1893 and Fautrier in 1898), may have lived at La Ruche during the same years, and while the dealer Paul Guillaume bought paintings by the two of them,[39] no evidence exists that they knew each other. A portrait by Fautrier of Soutine's first dealer, Leopold Zborowski, is the sole evidence of a possible personal link.[40] Furthermore, everything in their backgrounds and personalities would have separated them. Soutine's father was a poor Jewish clothes mender in a small Lithuanian village from which young Chaim had run away in order to pursue his goal of becoming an artist. Fautrier had a wealthy French mother who uprooted her son to London at age ten, letting him study at the best London art schools. One was short and pudgy, the other a natural athlete.

In a well-known photograph, Fautrier displays the ascetic face of Marcel Duchamp, distorted by an Antonin Artaud grimace. Sensual lips on a chubby face characterize Soutine's physiognomy in a 1938 photo portrait. "Handsome, elegant, nervous, he startled, intimidated, fascinated, was either adored or hated, yet felt forever alone on his mountains," is how one female admirer remembered Fautrier.[41] For her part, Soutine's companion in the late thirties, Gerda Groth, better known as Mlle Garde,[42] found Soutine singularly lacking in seduction. He was also, she discovered, incapable of creating a particular atmosphere around him.

FIG. 9
Maurice Brianchon, *Bois de Boulogne,* 1942. Dimensions unknown. Present location unknown.

"He settled in a lodging without changing a thing, as if he were provisionally camping there."[43]

Yet far apart as they might be, they shared a strange ambivalence — attraction and repulsion — toward decaying flesh and viscous matter that was totally foreign to Picasso's fear of death syndrome and images of dry, bony skulls. Something in their past experience — memory of the shtetl for one, trench life in World War I for the other — seemed to have familiarized them with gory sights to such an extent that they could contemplate death from a perversely formal viewpoint. Indeed, Fautrier's most powerful works — both his early representations of the dead hare, dead boar, and human corpse, and his World War II Hostage images — bring to mind Elie Faure writing of Soutine's *Carcass of Beef* of 1928: "It is in dead flesh that he finds his most erotic pleasures."[44]

Paulhan was himself very much aware of a Fautrier/Soutine connection. Explaining his initial reticence toward Fautrier to the critic Marcel Arland, he wrote to him in 1941: "I never slighted Fautrier. At the same time, I found him estimable, brilliant — and yet he did not interest me very much. I said to myself: he is obviously gifted and what else? Neither the ardor of Soutine, nor the faith of Rouault."[45] The Soutine reference remained in the foreground even after Paulhan overcame his doubts about Fautrier. In a letter of 28 June 1943 written to Marcel Jouhandeau, he said, "I would like some day to take you to Fautrier. I don't think that, other than [André] Masson (and maybe Soutine), there is a greater painter today."[46] And to his friend Henri Pourrat, in a letter of 24 August 1943, he noted, "He [Fautrier] is with Soutine the greatest of painters among the young: a thousand feet above [Roland] Oudot, [Maurice] Brianchon and the others."[47]

In fact, Paulhan coveted owning a Soutine long before he went on his Fautrier binge, and it is likely that Paulhan turned to Fautrier's strangely morbid paintings in part because of their affinity with Soutine's sensibility. "I have often dreamt about [owning] a Soutine," he wrote to the paraplegic poet Joë Bousquet, a conduit to the surrealists and to Jewish artists during the war, asking him to find one or two works by Soutine "at 15 no more than 20,000 francs."[48] We do not know if Paulhan's wishes were fulfilled at that time, and if so, what painting or paintings Paulhan bought. What we do know is that with the exception of

FIG. 10
Chaim Soutine, *Young Girl at Fence,* ca. 1940. Oil on canvas, 33⅞ × 25⅞ in. (86 × 65.4 cm).

Maternity (1942; Madeleine Castaing Collection, Paris), showing a seated mother holding the limp body of a child on her lap, "in his last phase, the years of Vichy France, Soutine's focusing image was not death, dying or the depiction of life," as Maurice Tuchman has pointed out in his recent contribution to the Soutine catalogue raisonné.[49]

The last paintings, although steeped in the French countryside and in the observation of French country people, evoke the artist's nostalgia for another place and time, as if the roots he had so diligently repressed had surged back to the surface. Mlle Garde was a witness to this change: "One day, watching me cry, Soutine asked me the reason. I told him I was nostalgic for my parents, and I added, 'How can you not think about yours without sadness?' He immediately wrote a letter to Lithuania and awaited an answer every day."[50]

It might well be the world of Soutine's youth that he depicts in *Maternity,* in the portrait of a little girl in a pensive pose leaning on a balustrade entitled *Young Girl at Fence* (fig. 10), in *Thérèse by the River* (ca. 1942; private collection, Paris), in *Grandmother and Child* (ca. 1943; private collection), showing a white-haired older woman dressed in black who smiles at the child holding her hand – paintings with the quality of Proustian memory. They look as if Soutine had posed French models but painted them as characters from the shtetl. Even *Return from School after the Storm* (fig. 11), with its dark blue-green trees rising in an empty plain and children shuffling along a dirt path, speaks of walks through windblown Russian steppes rather than the French countryside.

The nostalgia present in Soutine's last paintings – the distant memory of friendly faces and familiar sights – is hardly surprising. The small village in occupied France where he stayed in hiding during the war could easily merge in his mind and in his art with the village in distant Lithuania where he was born and raised. Furthermore, the persecution of Jews in his country of adoption, occupied France, could well remind him of his early encounter with racial persecution in his native village in Lithuania.

Indeed, no sooner was the Armistice signed by Marshal Pétain in June 1940 than the first anti-Jewish measures were instituted. More and more ignominious obstructions were put in place in the occupied zone, affecting the daily life of Jews, both foreign and French ones. On an early morning in July 1942, the Vélodrome d'Hiver roundup took place. Thousands of Jews were awakened by the French police, told to take a few personal things, and put on buses headed for the Vél d'Hiv sports stadium. After a few nights and days spent at the open stadium, most of them were transferred to the Drancy internment camp outside Paris, the antechamber of Auschwitz.[51] As of June 1942, Jews were forced to wear the yellow star to make them more easily identifiable for arrest.[52] Routine roundups took place, in the course of which men were asked to lower their trousers for signs of circumcision, then taken away.

Aged forty-six in 1939, Soutine was at the peak of his career, the years of starvation in Montparnasse behind him. He lived comfortably in the Villa Seurat (some claiming that he was sympathetic to the right-wing Action française), his medical and

emotional problems were attended to by his devoted companion, Mlle Garde, and his ego nurtured by Madeleine Castaing, his major collector at that point. Suddenly his foreignness and then his Jewishness boomeranged back at him, transforming his everyday life into a permanent nightmare. In September 1939, when the war broke out, he was at Civry near Avallon with Mlle Garde, visiting an art dealer. As Soutine was a Russian and Garde a German national, they were told by French officials – the then-French government feared the presence of traitors among foreigners – that they could not return to Paris, and must remain at Civry in *résidence surveillée*. They escaped and went back to Soutine's atelier in Paris.

In May 1940, when German nationals were isolated from the rest of the population, again as potential traitors – Mlle Garde was sent to Gurs, the ignominious internment camp in the Pyrenees that, under the Vichy government, became a way station for Auschwitz. (Among the lucky ones, she was not deported, but never saw Soutine again.) In a panic after her disappearance, Soutine turned to Madeleine Castaing. From the June Armistice signed by Marshal Pétain's anti-Semitic government until his transport to the Junot hospital in Paris in August 1943, Soutine stayed in hiding around the village of Champigny – in the care of a new companion, Marie-Berthe Aurenche (Max Ernst's former mistress).

When hardly anyone dared to mention his name, much less buy his work, the Castaings continued to collect it to the very end of his life.[53] On 9 August 1943, he died during an operation for his stomach ulcers. Mlle Garde, by then living in hiding in Paris, reported, "Two days later, I followed the funeral to Montparnasse Cemetery. There were very few people, for most of Soutine's friends, and the painters of Montparnasse, had to remain in hiding. However, Jean Cocteau, Picasso, and Michonz followed the funeral procession."[54]

Paulhan never established a personal relationship with Soutine the way he did with Braque, Fautrier, and Jean Dubuffet, explaining to Bousquet that "I could have met him but there was a time when I found it more proper not to see the painters that the

FIG. 11
Chaim Soutine, *Return from School after the Storm,* ca. 1939. Oil on canvas, 17 × 19½ in. (43.2 × 49.5 cm). The Phillips Collection, Washington, D.C.

NRF talked about. It was a bit stupid."[55] Paulhan's meeting with Dubuffet occurred in the last months of the Occupation, when the outcome of the war in favor of the Allies seemed assured. "I have discovered another brilliant painter whose name is Dubuffet; in a minuscule atelier on the rue Lhomond he paints puppets, and metro scenes. Otherwise, wine merchant (wholesale) and friend of [Georges] Limbour," he wrote to Jouhandeau in March 1944.[56]

Born in 1901, and slightly younger than Fautrier and Soutine, Dubuffet belonged with their generation. Like Fautrier, Dubuffet had given up painting during the thirties for a more lucrative activity. He resumed his vocation in 1942, "resolved to devote two or three years (with enough money to live on for that length of time) to making paintings for my own use and without worrying about whether or not they were susceptible to being approved by anybody."[57]

FIG. 12
Anonymous, "The Marshal Speaking in Front of a Microphone." From an exhibition of children's drawings at Musée Galliéra, Paris, 1942. Dimensions unknown. Present location unknown.

As with Fautrier, more attention has been paid to Dubuffet's postwar art in relation to *l'art informel* than to the work that came before. Overlooked in particular are the May–June 1944 "messages" scribbled in an awkward hand on messy newspaper print, which simulated the anonymous graffiti used by lovers, the deranged, and resisters to communicate. Sentences like "The key is under the shutter," "I think of you," "Thank you very much my health is excellent," "Georges arrives tomorrow morning," "Emile has left," are also reminiscent of messages scribbled in prison or heard over the BBC radio during the war.

Typical of the Vichy years are also colorful oil paintings and drawings based on children's art, made at a time when the art of children was much celebrated and even shown in museums. But whereas the children's drawings on view at the Paris Musée Galliéra paid homage to Marshal Pétain (fig. 12), Dubuffet's works concentrated on scenes of the wartime everyday, filled with expressive, toylike figures. In these works, sad-looking people stand in a crowded subway car (fig. 13), go about their business on foot on a city street, play jazz, bicycle on an open road, and milk cows. All these "puppets from the city and the country" (the title of the series) – Hoffmanesque automatons – operated in the odd terrain of plastic naïveté overlaid with mature emotion. Dubuffet noted that

> *I liked the kind of painting that children make, and aimed at nothing more than to make equivalent ones, for my sole pleasure. I believed that paintings deprived of technique like those made by children, effortlessly and quickly, can be as effective, even more effective than paintings produced in the cultural circuit, and that they can also be carriers of unexpected bonuses offering novel overtures to thought.*[58]

One such painting, *View of Paris: Everyone at the Windows* (fig. 14), depicted an old building façade with little white stick figures standing on the window sills, the arched windows suggesting an alignment of tombstones. Made the day after the poet Max Jacob's memorial, it was given to

FIG. 13
Jean Dubuffet, *Metro*, 1943. Oil on canvas, 64 × 51¼ in. (162.6 × 130.2 cm). Courtesy PaceWildenstein, New York.

Paulhan. (Both Dubuffet and Paulhan had been friends of the dead poet.) According to the artist, it was inspired by "the wall of ghosts that surged in [my] mind during the ceremony"[59] that he and Paulhan had attended.

René Drouin, at the urging of Paulhan, included Dubuffet in two group exhibits at his gallery – *The Nude* in May 1944 (with *Seated Woman in Front of Blinds* [May 1943; C. Renault Collection, Paris]) and *Twenty-One Landscapes* in July 1944 (with *Grassy and Earthy Landscape* [February 1944; private collection, Zurich]). The critic Georges Limbour, a longtime friend, expressed his admiration in the soon-to-become-defunct *Comoedia* on 8 July 1944. The critic Gaston Diehl, who had championed the *Bleu Blanc Rouge* painters and might have responded positively to the cheerful look if not the less than cheerful content of Dubuffet's works, called his art "a dangerous joke"("une facétie dangereuse") in

the about-to-disappear newspaper *Aujourd'hui* on 17 July 1944. This comment was not going to deter Drouin from giving Dubuffet a one-man show at his gallery in October 1944, for which Paulhan wrote the catalogue introduction in the form of a letter to the artist.

One might well ask what criteria allowed Paulhan, the famed editor and discoverer of literary talent, to switch so easily from new authors to new artists. As the critic André Berne-Joffroy conceded, "One cannot forget that his strange lucidity – so suddenly displayed in the realm of painting soon after 1940 – was sustained by the very same qualities he had cultivated with *extraordinary* care in literature . . . on the basis, it is true, of exceptional talent."[60] Indeed, his beginnings as an art "critic" coincided with the publication in 1941 of *Les Fleurs de Tarbes,* a summation of his views after fifteen years as arbiter of contemporary literature and poetry in Paris.

In this pessimistic and disorienting text – offered as a series of glimpses rather than a demonstration – creativity is shown to be at a near impasse. Everything has been said "and in the end every word becomes suspect if it has been used before."[61] What is left to explore is the very *matière* of language, its texture dissociated from sentences, from words, and even from letters.[62] Paulhan's commitment to *matière* in painting would seem to have derived from the priority that he assigned to *matière* in literature. But no sooner had he laid down his demand for a *literature de la matière* (that would be obviously incomprehensible) than he declared the cliché, the banal, the *lieu commun* – which he intuitively disliked – to be a necessity of literature if language were to recover both its adhesion to the world and its communicability.

The idea of the commonplace also partook of his judgments on art, as when he said of Braque in *Braque le patron* that

What I meant to say also is that Braque's painting is banal. No doubt fantastic but ordinary. Fantastic – when one thinks about it – as it is to have one nose and two eyes, and the nose precisely between the two eyes.[63]

As John Culbert pointed out with regard to Paulhan's writings, "one of the dominant traits of Paulhan's work is the refusal to settle differences."[64] In order to interest Paulhan the critic, a work — whether of literature or of art — must waver on the cusp of the accessibly seductive and the repulsively difficult, always risking failure like a high-wire act. It was thus hardly surprising to read Paulhan saying of Fautrier's wartime painting that it was very close to insult and to filth.[65]

But Paulhan did not suddenly become an authority on new art. He himself had mentors. One of them was Henri Michaux, the Belgian surrealist poet/painter and contributor to NRF who had "long tried to interest Paulhan in a new possible orientation in painting."[66] Michaux had traveled to the Far East and become fascinated by Tibetan Buddhism. The Buddhist view of dying as a process of metamorphosis between two states of being, which Paulhan may have discovered himself when he lived in Madagascar from 1908 to 1910, probably influenced his fearless affinity for morbid images as much as death's routine presence at the front lines during World War I had when he fought with the Zouaves. But more important was Michaux's discovery in China of a new approach to making art: "[I]n Chinese painting, images are there and yet they're absent. Like delicate phantoms that haven't been summoned by desire."[67] In Michaux's description, we recognize traits that applied to the art that Paulhan admired.

This being said, at a time when the romantic realists Oudot and Brianchon were being celebrated in the pages of the Fascist sheet *Je suis partout*, and the *Bleu Blanc Rouge* painters Jean Bazaine, Edouard Pignon, André Fougeron, Maurice Estève, and Alfred Manessier were claiming attention as the new French vanguard, Paulhan's support of Fautrier, Dubuffet, and Soutine showed unusual courage. Small wonder Rebatet called him "an Aryan ashamed of his foreskin and of his baptism" in the pages of *Je suis partout*.[68] And yet, considering his support of Braque and circumventing of Picasso, who was as engaged against fascism as he was, Paulhan's choices seem to have been more personal than ideologically motivated.

FIG. 14
Jean Dubuffet, *View of Paris: Everyone at the Windows,* 23 March 1944. Oil on canvas, 35 × 45 ⅝ in. (89 × 116 cm). Private collection, Paris.

Reports from the Home Fronts: Some Skirmishes over Picasso's Reputation

Michael FitzGerald

Accounts of life in Paris following the Liberation sometimes give the impression that Picasso ranked with the Louvre as a symbol of French culture. Magazine and newspaper reporters who had followed the Allied invasion across France and were experienced hands at delivering breaking accounts of the latest military assaults suddenly focused their skills on this single artist, a sixty-four-year-old man who wasn't a French citizen and had received no official recognition from the nation's cultural establishment. The war correspondent for the *San Francisco Chronicle,* Peter D. Whitney, filed one of the first celebrations. Under a boldface headline, "Picasso Is Safe," the article proclaimed the artist "the world's greatest painter" and proceeded to print Picasso's account of the Occupation.[1]

Nor was this phenomenon limited to journalists, whose attention might be explained by a desire for an assignment that did not require dodging mortar shells, diving into muddy foxholes, or sleeping on rocky ground. Picasso's studio on the rue des Grands-Augustins became such a popular destination for furloughed GIs that Thursday mornings were set aside for men and women in uniform to see where Picasso lived and to have the chance to

examine a few of the many paintings he had made during the years of isolation (fig.1). Picasso bantered about these sessions with his friend, the photographer Brassaï, "Yes, it's an invasion! Paris is liberated, but me, I was and I remain besieged."[2]

Unlike earlier phases of his career, this round of celebrity was not sparked by controversy over his most recent work. Except for a small number of pictures that may have hung unceremoniously in a few Parisian galleries or in a friend's home, Picasso's wartime art was hardly seen outside his studio until the Salon d'Automne opened in October. Even then, the paintings themselves prompted less debate than did the political implications of his recent affiliation with the Communist Party and longstanding animosity over his repudiation of academic standards. As Picasso explained to Whitney, "I have not painted the war because I am not the kind of a painter who goes out like a photographer for something to depict. But I have no doubt that the war is in these paintings I have done. Later on perhaps the historians will find them and show that my style changed under the war's influence." Nonetheless, the *Chronicle*'s editors chose the phrase "War in his art" to run boldface under a photograph of the artist.

FIG. 1
Allied soldiers in Picasso's studio after the Liberation, September 1944.
Photograph by Robert Capa.

While other essays in this volume will take Picasso's suggestion and explore the often subtle ways in which the experience of the war may be reflected in the art, this essay examines the development of his public reputation, from the beginning of the war to its conclusion, through published commentary, trade in art, and exhibitions in galleries and museums. Disconnecting Picasso's art from contemporaneous discussions and presentations affecting his reputation seems appropriate, because the war largely cut off both the artist and his work from interested audiences. Despite the near blackout, controversies over his art continued, in part fed by rumors. And, in the absence of significant new information, events that occurred immediately before and after the war – rather than activities during the Occupation – shaped the argument. While generated by the exceptional conditions of that time, the "disembodiment" created between the artist and his public image was far from unique. It represents a problem that increasingly has confronted artists and other public figures of this century, as the professions of journalism and public relations have

separated individual and image to satisfy burgeoning popular fascination with celebrity.

Preceding the war, two crucial events occurred in Picasso's career – the international tour of *Guernica* and the retrospective exhibition organized by the Museum of Modern Art. After first presenting *Guernica* (pages 40–41, fig. 1) in the Spanish Pavilion of the Paris World's Fair in 1937, Picasso allowed the mural to travel to London and the United States as a fundraising promotion for the Republicans (fig. 2).[3] It arrived in London in October 1938 and New York in May 1939, followed by appearances in many cities across America. Perhaps even more than the initial presentation in Paris, these showings highlighted the political content of the painting and Picasso's willingness for it to be used for propaganda. This emphasis intensified as the months passed and the Nazis' military campaigns expanded from Spain to Czechoslovakia and Poland.

In New York during summer 1939, *Guernica* certainly struck prominent critics as more than a statement about events in Picasso's homeland, by then already two years in the past. Henry McBride, a longtime defender of the avant-garde, wrote that "we shall regard *Guernica* as the most concrete and powerful statement of the hatreds generated by these political wars of the present."[4] Elizabeth McCausland, a critic deeply committed to political action as well as to Picasso's art, saw the painting not only as an unequivocal statement of his public opposition to Franco, but also as a rejuvenation of his art after he had, in the previous few years, "arrived at the nadir of personal revolt and spiritual defiance."[5]

This shift of focus from Picasso as an extreme individualist and aesthetic innovator to an artist of deep political commitment carried into the Modern's retrospective, which opened in September 1939, the first month of the European war. In February, *Time* had already set the stage, passing from describing Picasso as possessing "probably the greatest painting virtuosity in the world" to highlighting his response to the civil war. "The two works which have put him in the news since 1936 have been public, polemical jobs: his

[page 112]
Pablo Picasso
Skull and Pitcher (detail)
10 March 1945. Cat. no. 79.

big, lacerating mural, *Guernica,* for the Spanish government pavilion at the Paris exposition of 1937, and a series of hairy-nightmare etchings entitled *Dream and Lie of Franco*"[6] (cat. no. 2). Reviewing the exhibition, McCausland returned to *Guernica* and praised Picasso for having "turned his gaze outward, away from the depths of subjective experience to the tragedies of social experience."[7] And, like many publications, the *Nation* singled out *Guernica* as the culmination of Picasso's achievement, calling it the "supreme glory of his life."[8]

This focus on the painting certainly flowed from publicity generated by the tour, but it also reflected Alfred Barr's organization of the exhibition. By including not only the painting but fifty related works, he created a mini-exhibit within the full retrospective. And by showing only a few, relatively minor pieces from the two years following the completion of *Guernica,* he implied that this most recent work was less significant.

Moreover, because the beginning of the war prevented the return of *Guernica,* as well as many other loans, the mural remained in the Modern's possession (at Picasso's request). After traveling to nine American cities, many works in the exhibition were retained by the museum for safekeeping, and

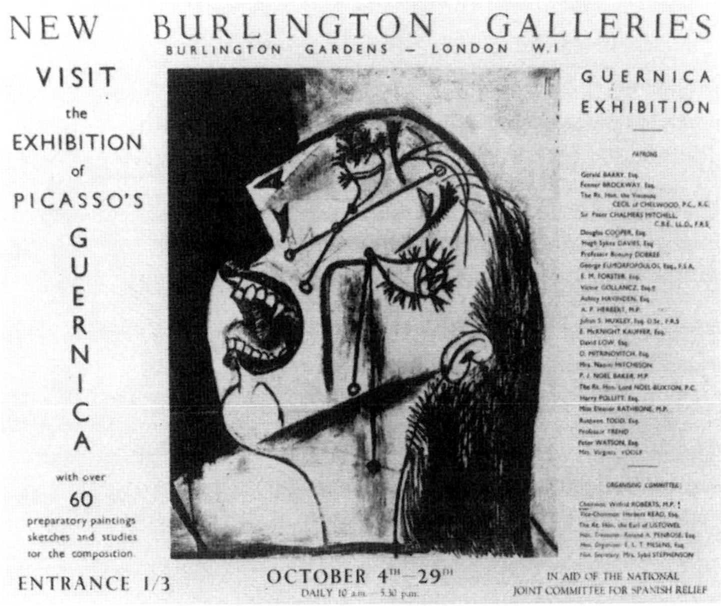

Guernica, in particular, was regularly brought out to serve as a symbol of opposition to not just Franco but Hitler as well. In August 1943, the Modern reinstalled the painting and issued a press release that explicitly linked the destruction of the Basque town to recent events across Europe. Noting that Guernica had been destroyed by the German Luftwaffe, the release continued,

> *this destruction of a defenseless town was an experiment by the German Luftwaffe in the psychological effect on the surrounding population of obliteration by air power of a hallowed center of a people's culture and religion. The Germans considered the experiment (with its horrible mutilation and destruction of hundreds of human beings as well as cultural treasures and landmarks) an unqualified success. Reportedly it was written up in German military journals as an advance in the technique of total war. The technique was later employed against parts of Warsaw, Rotterdam, and in England at Plymouth, Coventry, and the national shrine of Canterbury; while London's great Cathedral of St. Paul's was saved as though by a miracle when all around it was laid low by bombs.*[9]

The press release then recounted a report that seemed to show Picasso using the mural to condemn the Nazis' activities outside Spain. "There is a story that after the fall of Paris, Otto Abetz, Hitler's agent in the city, visited Picasso's studio, where the artist was still living. He saw a study sketch of the mural on Picasso's wall and asked the artist, "Did you do that?" "No," Picasso replied, "you did." This may be the first publication of this frequently told story, a tale that made the rounds in many variations during and after the war, sometimes substituting a stream of unidentified officers for Abetz or postcard reproductions of the painting (given as souvenirs to uncomprehending Nazis) for the sketch.

Before America entered the war, the Modern began to promote its activities as part of the opposition to Hitler's "prejudice about art," particularly post-impressionist and twentieth-century artists. In the months after Pearl Harbor, the museum greatly accelerated these efforts to make contemporary art

FIG. 2
Announcement of the exhibition of *Guernica,* 4–29 October 1938, New Burlington Galleries, London.

a weapon against the country's enemies. The most extensive manifestation was *The Road to Victory* (June 1942), a "procession of photographs of the nation at war," organized by Edward Steichen, and an exhibition that served as a model for Steichen's later and far more popular *Family of Man.* Yet the museum placed most of its emphasis on less literal projects. The fall 1942 *Bulletin* claimed that

> **THE MUSEUM COLLECTION is a symbol** *of one of the four freedoms for which we are fighting –* **the freedom of expression**. *Composed of painting, sculpture, architecture, photography, films and industrial design from 25 countries it is* **art that Hitler hates** *because it is* **modern**, *progressive, challenging; because it is* **international**, *leading to understanding and tolerance among nations; because it is* **free**, *the free expression of free men.*[10]

Having already judged Picasso the greatest artist of the twentieth century, Barr placed him at the head of this offensive.

The problem, or the advantage, was that no one knew what Picasso was doing. With his decision to return to Paris after the Nazis' conquest of France rather than accept invitations to flee to America, Picasso slipped into obscurity. For the first time in his career since the creation of cubism made him a public figure, he was not regularly observed by working journalists. A few articles appeared in the

FIG. 3
A corner of the Galerie Louise Leiris, Paris, between 1944 and 1946, showing recent paintings by Picasso.

American press, but these were based on old information. In 1942, Meric Callery, a sculptor and collector who had been a friend of Picasso's through the thirties, recounted for *Art News* "the last time I saw Picasso," but her story ended in 1940 with good wishes – "And there in that stricken Paris he still is . . . Our thoughts go out to him and worry over him."[11] Rumors that Picasso had sold out to the Nazis, or, alternatively, had been thrown into a concentration camp, circulated without convincing serious observers.

Exhibitions of his art were presented in America, but they were stuck in time, because most of his work in the country had been shipped over for the retrospective. Besides the Modern's own efforts, Picasso's longtime dealer, Paul Rosenberg, organized several shows at the New York gallery he opened after he fled from France. But these consisted of stock pictures from the twenties and thirties he had lent to the exhibition, plus a few others he had sent to the 1939 World's Fair. Pierre Matisse provided another venue for the works in New York. Reviews were respectful of these familiar, increasingly classic paintings, but discussed them in exclusively stylistic terms, far removed from the reality of current events.[12]

In Paris, the situation obviously was much worse. Predictably, the collaborationist press ridiculed Picasso. If these pieces easily could be dismissed as slander, denunciations by some respected artists, particularly Maurice de Vlaminck, were startling, especially since Picasso had no way to respond to them in print.[13] Throughout the Occupation, no one-man exhibition of his work occurred in France. Whether it was officially banned is not entirely clear. Certainly, the Nazis considered his art degenerate, and claims have been made that Franco's minister requested a prohibition. On the other hand, individual dealers may have chosen not to risk the retaliation that might well have resulted from the announcement of a show. Whatever the case, very few, if any, contemporary works by Picasso were exhibited in Paris during the war. After all, Rosenberg had left the country, and Daniel-Henry Kahnweiler was hiding in the countryside while his daughter-in-law,

FIG. 4
Pablo Picasso, *Portrait of Martin Fabiani*, 28 July 1943. Pencil on paper, 20⅛ × 12⅝ in. (51.1 × 32.1 cm). Private collection.

Louise Leiris, maneuvered to prevent the Nazis from taking possession of their gallery. Although she secured title in 1941, it would have been foolhardy to mount a display. As a photograph in Harriet and Sidney Janis's book illustrates, however, Leiris did buy wartime paintings from Picasso around the time of the Liberation, several of them among his most powerful (fig. 3).[14]

With Picasso's traditional dealers out of the action or lying low, two new arrivals played a small role in buying and promoting his work. The most problematic was Martin Fabiani, who had taken over Ambroise Vollard's stock and publishing business after his death in 1939 (fig. 4). By continuing with plans to publish an edition of the comte de Buffon's *Histoire naturelle* with illustrations by Picasso (1942), Fabiani ingratiated himself and was rewarded by a group of pencil portraits, which

Picasso drew on 28 July 1943.[15] Unlike the portraits of Paul Rosenberg and his family that Picasso made in 1918, this batch does not mark the beginning of a long relationship. Fabiani was far more interested in the market for old-master, impressionist and post-impressionist art, where the profits were much greater and a booming market thrived during the war. To capitalize on it, of course, he had to deal with the Nazis and their agents, and he had to be willing to accept items that were probably illegally confiscated or coerced from their owners. Apparently Fabiani had few scruples. His shady dealings did touch Picasso through trades or purchases, although little precise documentation of their transactions is known to exist.[16]

The second new arrival, Louis Carré (fig. 5), proved more substantial. In a small way, Carré had begun working with Picasso during the year or two before the war.[17] Since the artist's agreement with Rosenberg was limited to *première vue*, Picasso could sell to other dealers the paintings Rosenberg did not select. In the late thirties, Carré bought a few and discussed with Picasso his not very successful efforts to sell them in New York. When Rosenberg and Kahnweiler withdrew, Carré pursued a more substantial relationship, and Picasso responded. His first two exhibitions after the war were held at the Galerie Louis Carré. Moreover, during the Occupation, Carré mounted some exhibitions of avant-garde art, particularly a show of Matisse drawings in November 1941. Most twentieth-century artists, including Matisse, were not prohibited from exhibiting by the Nazis, but Carré seems not to have organized a show of Picasso's work at this time.[18]

FIG. 5
Installation view of an exhibition of recent paintings by Picasso at the Galerie Louis Carré, Paris, June 1945.

In general, Picasso had little reason to sell his work during the war. He had plenty of money to cover living expenses, and potential buyers had access only to French francs (or, possibly, German scrip). Measured against the U.S. dollar or the Swiss franc, the French franc's abysmal value on the open market made it far more desirable to hold paintings for future sale than to build up a stock of dubious currency.[19]

Thus, it seems that the works by Picasso on public view in Paris during the Occupation were almost entirely resale items – works that were offered at auction or in galleries by private collectors or dealers.[20] The number was small and, as in New York, the works were almost certainly not current, having previously passed from Picasso to another owner. Only on one occasion does it appear that Picasso himself presented a work, probably a recent one. This was a charity auction to raise funds for indigent artists, an event that received attention in the Parisian press, but which did not appear to rouse the authorities to action.[21]

Throughout the Occupation, Picasso kept largely to himself and his circle of friends, confining his movements to the neighborhood of his Grands-Augustins studio and the apartment he provided for Marie-Thérèse Walter on the boulevard Henri-IV. Despite sharing the very real physical deprivations most Parisians endured during this period and regular, intrusive visits from the Nazis, Picasso worked productively in his studio. Soon after the Liberation, he gave James Lord a rosy account of the time. "All he [Picasso] wanted in life was to be free to keep on working. By an irony, he added, the war years had been the most peaceful of his career. Denounced as degenerate and subversive, forbidden to exhibit, he had been left in peace to work as he pleased." Certainly, Picasso's experience was more harried than this retrospective comment implies, but it does capture the tremendous reduction in public attention that resulted from the blackout and the advantage he took of it.

Meanwhile, concerned people across Paris and around the world waited for news of Picasso's activities. Probably no one listened more attentively and with greater devotion than Alfred Barr.[22]

When Picasso once again became a center of media attention in the weeks following the Liberation, Barr labored to gather all the published accounts, canvas mutual friends, and even question Picasso. Barr was not only eager to catch up with Picasso's recent activities, he also wanted to know whether the direct political engagement evident in Picasso's prewar art had continued, all in preparation for an updated version of his 1939 catalogue, the book that would become the basic text on Picasso for decades, *Picasso: Fifty Years of His Art*. He published a preliminary account of his findings in the *Museum of Modern Art Bulletin* for January 1945, "Picasso 1940–1944: A Digest with Notes."

In this admittedly provisional analysis, Barr affirmed Picasso's unique importance on two fronts. Highlighting the Nazis' condemnation of Picasso's art, Barr cited *Dream and Lie of Franco* and *Guernica* to confirm the political significance of his work. (Barr had so far seen only a small number of the wartime works, mainly in reproduction.) Barr also found patriotic value in the artist's life during the Occupation. "He was not allowed to exhibit publicly and he made no overt gestures but his very existence in Paris encouraged the Resistance artists, poets and intellectuals who gathered in his studio or about his café table." He then cited Gladys Delmas, "a young American who lived through the occupation period in Paris": "Picasso's presence here during the occupation became of tremendous occult importance . . . his work has become a sort of banner of the Resistance Movement."[23]

Indeed, Barr's double-barreled praise largely reflected the opinion of respected publications. In late October, the *New York Times Magazine* had reported a similar status:

Today Picasso stands out as the standard-bearer of the artistic movement. In the first place, his attitude during the occupation has won general admiration. He steadfastly refused to fall for propaganda wiles as did too many French painters and sculptors. He neither exhibited his works in Paris under German auspices nor accepted junketing tours through the Reich under the plea that "art has no country." And when the German authorities offered him coal with which to heat his studio he replied that he preferred to freeze – like most Parisians. For these reasons – and others – Picasso occupies the place of honor in the Autumn Salon.[24]

As a matter of future interest, the *Times* reported without comment Picasso's recent affiliation with the Communist Party and his remark that he "prefers not to discuss this matter."

The difference between Barr's account and that of the *Times* and most other publications is the claim that Picasso was more than a symbol of intellectual independence to Resistance members, that they actually gathered in his studio and around him at cafés. Christian Zervos, who had served in the Resistance, immediately fired off a letter of correction.[25] "I have just read the note you have published on Picasso-as-Resistance worker in the Bulletin of the Museum. For the love of Picasso, do not include these notes in a book on the artist." Going on to criticize the sources as "bad journalism," Zervos declared emphatically that Picasso had not been active in the Resistance: "The participation of Picasso in the Resistance is false. Picasso simply kept his dignity during the Occupation the way millions of people did here. But he never got involved in the Resistance. Realize that his work itself is the greatest form of resistance."

No doubt startled by the vehemence of Zervos's denial, Barr sought to question Picasso directly. Through a friend, James Plaut, who had been director of the Museum of Contemporary Art in Boston and was then an Office of Strategic Services (OSS) officer leading the American investigation of Nazi art looting, Barr submitted a list of written queries about various matters to Picasso's secretary, Jaime Sabartés, who supposedly showed them to Picasso and noted his replies.[26] When Plaut sent Barr the responses in October 1945, he described the process and his concerns about the results:

I enclose herewith the Picasso material. The circumstances under which it was obtained were the anticipated ones. P. has kept himself incommunicado for the past month, and has been in Paris only sporadically.

. . . I laid it on thick with S. [Sabartés] who responded well to blandishments (augmented by cigars, soap and chocolate!). Even he, if one is to believe him, has seen P. very seldom of late . . . S. obtained answers to all questions which, in his words, P. considered relevant. I feel that they are, in some degree, evasive and unsatisfactory but – on the whole – they are rather more detailed and informative than I had expected.

Coming from a seasoned interrogator accustomed to grilling Nazi officials and collaborationist dealers, this ultimately positive judgment deserves respect – especially since Picasso answered "no" to Barr's question about whether the Resistance forces had met in his studio.

When Barr prepared the final text for *Fifty Years,* he largely adhered to Zervos's position. Introducing his discussion with Picasso's refusal of offers of sanctuary in America and noting that press accounts of his activities during the Occupation have been "embellished by journalistic legend," he nonetheless asserted Picasso's great symbolic importance and recounted the episode, observed by John Groth, of Picasso's being solicited by Eluard to be the first artist to inscribe a book for presentation to de Gaulle.

Picasso, unlike his friends Paul Eluard and another ex-Surrealist poet Louis Aragon, had taken no active part in the underground Resistance movement, yet, as has been indicated, Picasso's presence in Paris while the Germans were there had gradually taken on an aura of great symbolic importance. His attitude had been passive but it had been implacable and uncompromising and had created a legend which had probably been more effective than if he himself had joined the F.F.I. [Forces françaises de l' intérieur] and gone underground.[27]

Barr must have been well aware that nothing in Picasso's past suggested that he would have taken this extreme course.

If Barr revised his characterization of Picasso's life during the Occupation, he pressed further the assertion that Picasso's art engaged the politics of

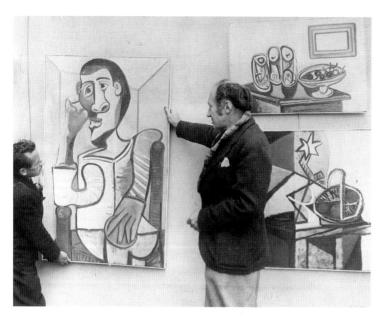

FIG. 6
Workers hanging pictures by Picasso at the Salon d'Automne,
Paris, October 1944.

his time. Calling the *Charnel House* (cat. no. 82) "Picasso's most important postwar composition," Barr presented it as the answer to those who doubted the seriousness of his art, or sought to explain it exclusively in terms of formal issues. Lamenting that the painting was not finished in time to be included in the Victoria and Albert exhibition in December 1945 of Picasso's and Matisse's wartime work, Barr offered it as the proof of Picasso's intentions:

> *The* Charnel House *might have sobered those who found Picasso's distortions an outrageous effrontery; it might have embarrassed those defenders who, ignoring the psychological tensions of his recent art, still tried to seek refuge in the esthetic of form and color so dogmatically popularized in the 1920s; and it might have stilled those who demanded that Picasso deal more directly and explicitly with the state of the world.*[28]

Barr then gave his interpretation of how Picasso's art was relevant: "The *Guernica* was a modern Laocoon, a Calvary, a doom picture. Its symbols transcend the fate of the little Basque city to prophesy Rotterdam and London, Kharkov and Berlin, Milan and Nagasaki – our dark age. In the *Charnel House* there are no symbols and, perhaps, no prophecy. Its figures are facts – the famished, waxen cadavers of Buchenwald, Dachau and Belsen."[29]

When the wartime paintings were first shown, at the Salon d'Automne from October to November 1944, their specific content seems to have been submerged in the outcry by academics and anti-communists over the decision to show anything by Picasso in an official setting (figs. 6–7). At the Victoria and Albert exhibition of works by Picasso and Matisse, the focus of criticism was, again, primarily the reputations of the artists rather than the specific work on view. It was not until the following summer, when Carré held an exhibition at his gallery, that the paintings themselves were seriously examined in the press.[30] *Art News* reported a widespread belief: they were not shocking or even particularly surprising to those who knew Picasso's earlier work. "To Picasso's American audience, familiar at best with work of the late 'thirties, these oils may not indicate any very radical departure."[31] Of course, everyone except a small circle of friends had been in the dark about the recent work. As critics became more familiar with it, they began to identify elements of style and subject matter that seemed to reflect the experience of the war. More than any other published source, Harriet and Sidney Janis's book probably attuned audiences to these possibilities, even though the Janises emphasized formal innovation over social content. By 1947, *Art News* reviewed one of the dealer Samuel Kootz's exhibitions in New York with the summary comment, "Here is the now famous war style of violently abstracted sailors, skulls, and tomato plants."[32]

Kootz's appearance is indicative of the state of the Picasso market in the early postwar years. Despite Picasso's considerable productivity during the war and a lack of buyers that had resulted in a large stock of paintings, there was not a continuous outpouring of exhibitions once peace arrived. After the celebratory exhibitions at the Salon d'Automne and the Victoria and Albert Museum, relatively few of Picasso's pictures were on view in Paris or New York. The 1945 exhibition at Carré's gallery included twenty-one of the wartime paintings, a few of which contained relatively obvious references to the war. The following summer, Carré held another show. Although it began with the great prewar canvas *Night Fishing at Antibes* (cat. no. 31),

FIG. 7
Visitors in the Picasso exhibition at the Salon d'Automne, Paris, October 1944. Photograph by Robert Doisneau.

the selection was dominated by the pastoral work that Picasso had done in spring 1946. This was Picasso's last exhibition with Carré, and no other dealers immediately stepped in to take his place. Picasso's ties with Paul Rosenberg had been permanently severed by the war, and Kahnweiler was cautious about picking up the contract. As Françoise Gilot recounted, Picasso used the free-spending Kootz to goad Carré and Kahnweiler toward greater commitments.[33]

The exhibitions Kootz presented from 1947 to 1948 were high on hype but low on paintings – both numbers and quality.[34] By 1947, Kahnweiler had concluded a deal to represent Picasso's work, yet he did not hold an exhibition of the paintings until May 1953.[35] So, during the late forties and early fifties, Picasso's work was not widely shown. Even when they were available, the wartime pictures, in particular, seem not to have been in great demand by buyers. This is one reason why Sally and Victor Ganz were able to buy important paintings for fairly low prices. To cite only one example, in 1948 they bought *Still Life with Blood Sausage* (cat. no. 42) from Kahnweiler for $5,000; Leiris had bought it from Picasso at least several years earlier (it appears in a photo of the gallery; see fig. 3).[36]

But if Picasso's work was not widely seen during these years, his name was more frequently in the press. When Picasso declared his adherence to the Communist Party in October 1944, most critics accepted his explanation that he was expressing an admiration for the party's leadership in the Resistance, a role that was widely admired at the time. Despite Picasso's denial that his work was programmatic, left-leaning critics, such as McCausland, and reporters, such as Jerome Seckler, saw an affirmation of the political involvement Picasso had shown with *Guernica,* and sought to identify it in his current work.[37] Certainly, Picasso's standing as a man of culture grew through the late forties. In 1947, *Life* went so far as to assert that "the only person in France who can compare with Picasso as a subject of conversation is Charles de Gaulle."[38]

Increasingly, this notoriety rested on Picasso's association with the party. The most prominent events were his participation in the first Congress of Intellectuals for Peace in Wroclaw, Poland, in August 1948, the Party Conference held in Paris in April 1949, and the Second World Peace Conference held in Sheffield, England, in October 1950. By that year, opinion in America and in France was tinged with disrespect. The *New York Times* ran an article ridiculing both his allegiance to the party and the drawings of doves he had provided as emblems of world peace. And the newspaper buttressed its account by relating the lambasting he had received in segments of the French press.[39] A few years later, even Alfred Barr admitted privately his disgust with Picasso's political activities. After his promotion of Picasso as a force against dictatorship, Barr must have been deeply disappointed by the artist's willingness to make a portrait of Stalin in 1953 and paint the openly propagandistic *Massacre in Korea* (1951).[40]

To a considerable extent, the blackout of Picasso's art that began with the Occupation continued through most of the postwar decade and left a vacuum of expectations that was filled by assumptions about the man, not the artist. By the mid-fifties, he would grow tired of the farce, drop his public involvement in politics, and withdraw into a personal world of art.[41] But during the previous fifteen years, he had been, in a sense, besieged.

Guide to the Use of the Catalogue Section

In the catalogue entries accompanying each plate:

For the dimensions of paintings, drawings, and prints, height precedes width.

For the dimensions of sculptures, height precedes width precedes depth.

For prints, the dimensions given are for the plate.

Dimensions, in general, are supplied by the owner.

Inscriptions are supplied by the owner or gleaned from literature on the work. It has not been possible to directly examine each work, and must therefore be accepted that certain inscriptions may be misquoted or omitted.

Abbreviated bibliographic references refer to the following list of selected bibliographic sources:

Baer

Baer, Brigitte. *Catalogue raisonné de l'oeuvre gravé et des monotypes, 1935–1945.* Vol. 3 (1986) of Bernhard Geiser and Brigitte Baer. *Picasso: Peintre-graveur.* 7 vols. and addendum. Bern: Editions Kornfeld, 1986–96.

Boggs

Boggs, Jean Sutherland, ed. *Picasso & Things: The Still Lifes of Picasso.* Exh. cat. Cleveland: The Cleveland Museum of Art, 1992.

Cowling/Golding

Cowling, Elizabeth, and John Golding. *Picasso: Sculptor/Painter.* Exh. cat. London: The Tate Gallery, 1994.

Gohr

Gohr, Siegfried, ed. *Picasso im Zweiten Weltkrieg: 1939 bis 1945.* Exh. cat. Cologne: Museum Ludwig, 1988.

Janis

Janis, Harriet, and Sidney Janis. *Picasso: The Recent Years, 1939–1946.* Garden City, N.Y.: Doubleday, 1946.

Léal

Léal, Brigitte. *Musée Picasso: Carnets. Catalogue des dessins.* 2 vols. Paris: Editions de la Réunion des Musées Nationaux, 1996.

Musée Picasso I

Musée Picasso: Catalogue sommaire des collections. Peintures, papiers collés, tableaux-reliefs, sculptures, céramiques. Paris: Editions de la Réunion des Musées Nationaux, 1985.

Musée Picasso II

Richet, Michèle. *Musée Picasso: Catalogue sommaire des collections. Dessins, aquarelles, gouaches, pastels.* Paris: Editions de la Réunion des Musées Nationaux, 1987.

Rubin

Rubin, William, ed. *Pablo Picasso: A Retrospective.* Exh. cat. New York: The Museum of Modern Art, 1980.

Picasso dation

Picasso: Une nouvelle dation. Exh. cat. Paris: Réunion des Musées Nationaux - Grand Palais, 1990.

Spies

Spies, Werner. *Die Zeit nach Guernica 1937–1973.* Exh. cat. Berlin: Nationalgalerie Staatliche Museen, 1992.

Spies/Piot

Spies, Werner, and Christine Piot. *Picasso: Das plastische Werk.* Stuttgart: Gerd Hatje Verlag, 1983.

Ullmann

Ullmann, Ludwig. *Picasso und der Krieg.* Bielefeld: Karl Kerber Verlag, 1993.

Zervos

Zervos, Christian. *Pablo Picasso.* 33 vols. Paris: Editions Cahiers d'Art, 1932–78.

1

Girl Asleep at a Table (Intérieur à la femme endormie)

18 December 1936
Oil on canvas, 38 ¼ × 51 ¼ in. (97 × 130 cm)
Signed and dated at lower left: *18D. XXXVI. Picasso*
The Metropolitan Museum of Art, New York, The Mr. and
  Mrs. Klaus Perls Collection, 1997
Photograph © 1996 The Metropolitan Museum of Art, New York

Zervos VIII, 309 (as "Le Poète")

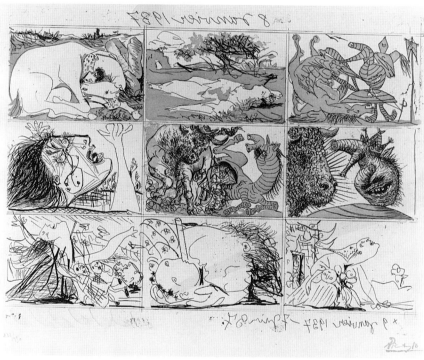

2

Dream and Lie of Franco (Sueño y mentira de Franco)

8–9 January and 7 June 1937
Etching, sugar-lift acquatint, and scraper on copper on paper,
12 ½ × 16 ⅝ in. (31.7 × 42.2 cm) each
Stamped signature at lower right; numbered at lower left: *132/850*;
   dated in the plates: *8 Janvier 1937* and *9 Janvier 1937–7 Juin 37*
Fine Arts Museums of San Francisco, Achenbach Foundation for Graphic Arts

Baer, cat. nos. 615–616; Gohr, 225; Rubin, 340; Spies, 14; Ullmann, figs. 86–87

3

Figure

28 January 1937
Pencil on paper, 15 ¹³⁄₁₆ × 12 ⅜ in. (40.2 × 31.5 cm)
Signed and dated at lower right: *28-1-37. Picasso*
Private collection, courtesy Guillermo de Osma Gallery, Madrid

Gohr, 95 (as "Modepuppe und Ertrinkende"); Ullmann, fig. 89
  (as "Modepuppe und Ertrinkende"); Zervos VIII, 323

4

Study for Guernica *(Head of a Horse)*

2 May 1937
Oil on canvas, 25 ⅜ × 36 ³⁄₁₆ in. (65 × 92 cm)
Dated at upper left: *2 Mai 37*
Museo Nacional Centro de Arte Reina Sofia, Madrid

Gohr, 176; Spies, cat. no. 2; Ullmann, fig 118; Zervos IX, 11 (as "3 mai 1937")

5

Study for Guernica

9 May 1937
Pencil on paper, 9 ⅝ × 17 ¹⁵⁄₁₆ in. (24.5 × 45.5 cm)
Museo Nacional Centro de Arte Reina Sofia, Madrid

Spies, cat. no. 1; Zervos IX, 18

6

Study for Guernica *(Mother and Dead Child)*

28 May 1937
Crayon, gouache, and collage on paper, 9 ¹/₁₆ × 11 ⁷/₁₆ in. (23 × 29 cm)
Dated lower left: *28 Mai/37*
Museo Nacional Centro de Arte Reina Sofía, Madrid

Ullmann, pl. II; Zervos IX, 37

7 [right]

Weeping Woman with Handkerchief

26 June 1937
Oil on canvas, 21 ⅝ × 18 ⅛ in. (55 × 46 cm)
Signed and inscribed along top edge: *à mon ami Zervos Picasso*
Los Angeles County Museum of Art, gift of Mr. and
  Mrs. Thomas Mitchell

Spies, cat. no. 15; Ullmann, pl. XI; Zervos IX, 51 (as "22 juin 1937")

8

Weeping Woman

1 July 1937
State III
Etching, aquatint, drypoint, scraper on copper on paper,
  27 ¼ × 19 ½ in. (69.2 × 49.5 cm)
Signed at lower left: *Picasso*; numbered at lower right: *3/15*;
  dated in the plate at lower right: *1ᵉʳ juillet 37*
Gecht Family Collection, Chicago

Baer, cat. no. 623 III; Ullmann, fig. 155

9

Weeping Woman

1 July 1937
State VII
Etching, aquatint, drypoint, scraper on copper on paper,
  27 ¼ × 19 ½ in. (69.2 × 49.5 cm)
Signed at lower right: *Picasso*; numbered at lower left: *13/15*;
  dated in the plate at lower right: *1ᵉʳ juillet 37*
National Gallery of Canada, Ottawa

Baer, cat. no. 623 VII

10

Weeping Woman (I)

4 July 1937
Drypoint and aquatint on paper, 13 ⅝ × 9 ⅝ in. (34.5 × 24.6 cm)
Dated in the margin at upper right: *4 juillet 37 (I)*; and in the
 plate at upper right: *4 juillet 37. (I)*
Private collection

Baer, cat. no. 625 A; Ullmann, fig. 158

11

Weeping Woman (II)

4 July 1937
Drypoint and aquatint on paper, 13 ⅝ × 9 ⅞ in. (34.7 × 25 cm)
Dated in the margin at upper left: *4 juillet 37 (II)*; and in the
 plate at upper left: *4 juillet 37. (II)*
Private collection

Baer, cat. no. 626 A; Ullmann, fig. 159

12

Combat in the Arena

10 October 1937
State IV
Drypoint, scraper, and burin on copper on paper, 15 ½ × 19 ½ in.
 (39.6 × 49.5 cm)
Signed and numbered at lower left: *33/50 Picasso*; dated in the
 plate at lower right: *10 Octobre 37*
Galerie Louise Leiris, Paris

Baer, cat. no. 629 IV(B)

13

The Supplicant

18 December 1937
Gouache and india ink on wood panel,
  9 ⁷⁄₁₆ × 7 ¼ in. (24 × 18.5 cm)
Dated at lower left: *18 D 37.*
Musée Picasso, Paris

Musée Picasso I, M.P. 168; Rubin, 345; Spies,
  cat. no. 17; Ullmann, pl. XIV

14 [right]

Weeping Woman

1937
Oil on canvas, 21 ⅝ × 18 ⅛ in. (55 × 46 cm)
National Gallery of Victoria, Melbourne
Purchased by donors of the Art Foundation of
  Victoria with the assistance of Jack and Genia
  Liberman family, Founder Benefactor, 1986

Spies, cat. no. 14; Ullmann, pl. XII (as "18.10.1937")

135

15

The Cock

29 March 1938
Pastel on paper, 30 ½ × 21 ¾ in. (77.5 × 55 cm)
Signed and dated at lower right: *Picasso/29.3.38.*
Private collection

Rubin, 354; Zervos IX, 113

16

Reclining Nude

17 May 1938
Oil on canvas, 35⅜ × 46⅝ in. (90 × 118.5 cm)
Dated on the stretcher: *17.5.38.*
Private collection

Ullmann, pl. XV (as "Okt.–Nov. 1938"); Zervos IX, 218 (as "Automne 1938")

San Francisco only

17

Woman Sacrificing a Goat

20 June (?) 1938
Graphite on paper, 9 ½ × 17 ⅞ in. (24.2 × 45.5 cm)
Drawing on reverse dated: *20.6.38*
Musée Picasso, Paris

Musée Picasso II, M.P. 1205(v); Spies, cat. no. 18; Ullmann, fig. 176;
  Zervos IX, 116 (as "20 juin 1938")

San Francisco only

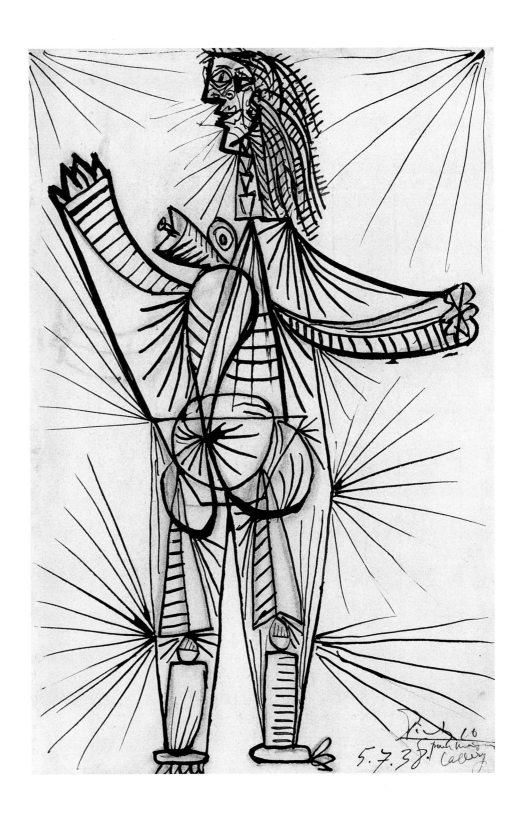

18

Woman Standing with Arms Spread

5 July 1938
Pen and india ink over charcoal, 12 × 8 ¹⁄₁₆ in. (30.5 × 20.5 cm)
Signed, dated, and dedicated at lower right: *Picasso/pour
  Madame Callery/5.7.38*
Galerie Rosengart, Lucerne

Zervos IX, 178

19

Bathers with Crab

10 July 1938
India ink and gouache on paper, 14 ⅜ × 19 ⅞ in. (36.5 × 50.5 cm)
Dated at upper left: *10.7.38.*
Musée Picasso, Paris

Musée Picasso II, M.P. 1207; Spies, cat. no. 25; Zervos IX, 172

New York only

20

Three Figures

10 August 1938
Pen and ink on paper, 17 ½ × 26 ⅝ in. (44.5 × 67.5 cm)
Signed and dated at lower left: *10 Août 38 Picasso*
Private collection

Zervos IX, 200

21

Seated Woman

29 August 1938
Oil on canvas, 25⅝ × 19¾ in. (65.1 × 50.2 cm)
Dated at bottom center: *29 At 38*; signed at lower right: *Picasso*
Private collection

Rubin, 358; Zervos IX, 211

22

Man with a Straw Hat and an Ice Cream Cone

30 August 1938
Oil on canvas, 24 × 18 ⅛ in. (61 × 46 cm)
Dated at bottom center: *30 A 38*
Musée Picasso, Paris

Musée Picasso I, M.P. 174; Rubin, 360; Zervos IX, 205

23

Still Life with Palette, Candlestick, and Head of a Minotaur

4 November 1938
Oil on canvas, 29 × 35 ½ in. (73.7 × 90.2 cm)
Signed at lower left: *Picasso*; dated on reverse below center: *4.11.38*
The National Museum of Modern Art, Kyoto

Boggs, cat. no. 100; Ullmann, pl. XVIII; Zervos IX, 235

24

Still Life with Candle, Palette, and Black Bull's Head

19 November 1938
Oil on canvas, 38 ⅛ × 51 ³⁄₁₆ in. (97 × 130 cm)
Signed at upper right: *Picasso*; dated on stretcher: *19 Novembre 38*
Menard Art Museum, Aichi, Japan

Zervos IX, 240

25

Woman with a Tambourine

Second half of January 1939
State I
Aquatint and scraper on copper on paper, 26 ¼ × 20 ³⁄₁₆ in.
  (66.5 × 51.2 cm)
Collection E.W.K., Bern

Baer, cat. no. 646 I (as "Début 1939"); Gohr, 66, cat. no. 61; Ullmann, fig. 186

26

Woman with a Tambourine

Second half of January 1939
State V(B)
Aquatint and scraper on copper on paper, 26 ³⁄₁₆ × 20 ³⁄₁₆ in.
 (66.5 × 51.2 cm)
Signed and annotated: *Picasso bon à tirer*
Private collection

Baer, cat. no. 646 V(B) (as "Début 1939"); Gohr, 57, cat. no. 61

27

Bull's Skull, Fruit, and Pitcher

29 January 1939
Oil on canvas, 25 ⅝ × 36 ¼ in. (65 × 92 cm)
Signed and dated at bottom center: *29.1.39. Picasso*
The Cleveland Museum of Art, Leonard C. Hanna, Jr., Fund 1985.57

Boggs, cat. no. 102; Ullmann, pl. XX; Zervos IX, 238

28

Head of a Woman (Dora Maar)

28 March 1939
Oil on wood panel, 23 ⁹⁄₁₆ × 17 ¾ in. (59.8 × 45.1 cm)
Signed and dated at lower right: *Picasso/39*; dated on reverse: *28.3.39*
Solomon R. Guggenheim Museum, New York, Thannhauser
  Collection, gift, Hilde Thannhauser, 1978

29

Head of a Woman

1 April 1939
Oil on canvas, 36¼ × 28¾ in. (92 × 73 cm)
Collection of Mrs. Lindy Bergman

Cowling/Golding, cat. no. 111; Janis, pl. 53; Rubin, 362; Ullmann, pl. XXI; Zervos IX, 282

30

Cat Seizing a Bird

22 April 1939
Oil on canvas, 31⅞ × 39⅜ in. (81 × 100 cm)
Dated at upper left: *22–4.39.*; dated on the stretcher: *22.4.39.*
Musée Picasso, Paris

Musée Picasso I, M.P. 178; Spies, cat. no. 65; Zervos IX, 296

31

Night Fishing at Antibes

August 1939
Oil on canvas, 81 × 136 in. (205.8 × 345.4 cm)
The Museum of Modern Art, New York, Mrs. Simon Guggenheim
  Fund
© 1998 The Museum of Modern Art, New York

Janis, pl. 5; Rubin, 365; Ullmann, fig. 190; Zervos IX, 316

32

Seated Man and Woman at Her Toilette

20 September 1939
Gouache and india ink on paper, 8 ¼ × 10 ⅝ in. (21 × 27 cm)
Dated at upper left: *20 Septembre/39.*; dated on reverse:
  Royan/20 Septembre/39/(I)
Musée Picasso, Paris

Musée Picasso II, M.P. 1221; Spies, cat. no. 41; Zervos IX, 331
  (as "22 septembre 1939")

San Francisco only

33

Standing Nude and Seated Woman

25 September 1939
Oil on canvas, 16 ⅛ × 13 in. (41 × 33 cm)
Signed and dated at lower left: *25.9.39. Picasso*
Private collection, courtesy Guggenheim, Asher Associates Inc.

Ullmann, fig. 223 (as "Herbst 1935")

34

Sheep's Skull

1 October 1939
Oil and india ink on paper, 18 ³⁄₁₆ × 25 ⅝ in. (46.2 × 65 cm)
Dated at lower right: *1ᵉʳ Octobre/39.*
Musée Picasso, Paris

Boggs, cat. no. 103; Musée Picasso II, M.P. 1223; Picasso dation, 54; Zervos IX, 348

New York only

35

Flayed Head of a Sheep

4 October 1939
Oil on canvas, 19 ⅝ × 24 in. (50 × 61 cm)
Dated at lower right: *4.10.39.*; dated on reverse: *Royan, 4.10.39*
Musée des Beaux-Arts, Lyon (on deposit from the Musée Picasso,
  Paris)

Boggs, cat. no. 104; Janis, pl. 103; Picasso dation, cat. no. 17; Zervos IX, 351

New York only

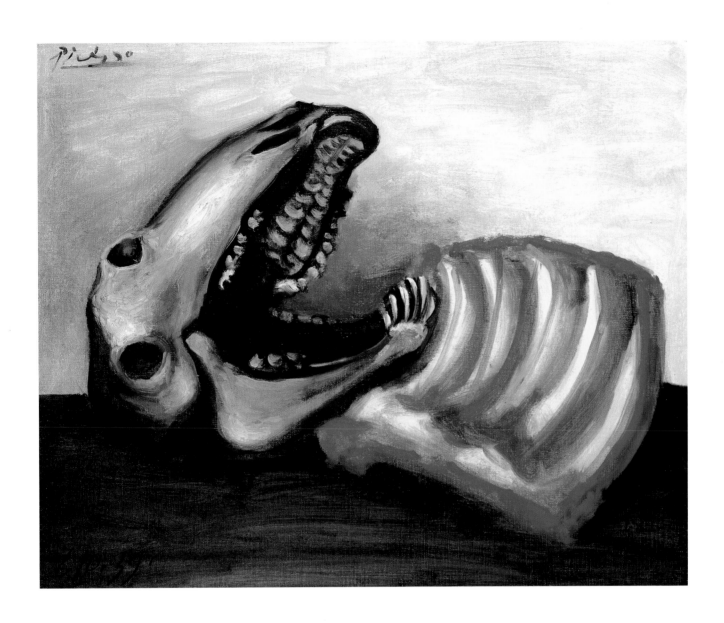

36

Still Life with Sheep's Skull

6 October 1939
Oil on canvas, 19¾ × 24 in. (50.2 × 61 cm)
Signed at upper left: *Picasso*
Mr. and Mrs. Marcos Micha

Boggs, fig. 104b; Spies, cat. no. 54; Ullmann, pl. XXII; Zervos X, 122

37

Three Skulls of Sheep

17 October 1939
Oil on canvas, 25⅝ × 35 in. (65 × 89 cm)
Dated at middle right: *Royan 17.10.39.*
Marina Picasso Collection (Inv. 12961), courtesy Galerie Jan Krugier,
    Ditesheim & Cie, Geneva

Boggs, cat. no. 105; Picasso dation, 54; Ullmann, pl. XXIII; Zervos IX, 349

38

Woman with a Green Hat

29 October 1939
Oil on canvas, 25⅝ × 19¾ in. (65.1 × 50.2 cm)
Signed and dated at lower left: *Picasso/29.10.39*
The Phillips Collection, Washington D.C., gift of the
  Carey Walker Foundation, 1994

160

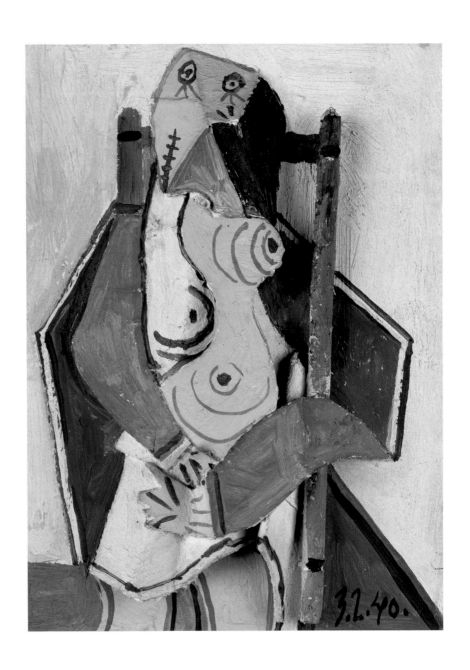

39 [left]

Head of a Bearded Man

7 January 1940
Gouache on paper, 18⅛ × 14¹⁵⁄₁₆ in. (46 × 38 cm)
Signed at upper right: *Picasso*; dated at
  lower left: *7-1-40.*
Galerie Cazeau-Béraudière, Paris

Zervos X, 194

New York only

40

Seated Woman

3 February 1940
Oil, cardboard, and wood on cardboard box, 6⅛ × 4½ in.
  (15.5 × 11.5 cm)
Dated at lower right: *3.2.40.*; annotated on stretcher on
  reverse: *Ce bas-relief peint est bien de la main de Pablo
  Picasso/Paul Eluard/12.1.52*
Sammlung Berggruen

41

Head of a Woman

2 March 1940
Oil on paper mounted on canvas, 25 ¼ × 18 ⅛ in. (64 × 46 cm)
Signed and dated at upper right: *2.3.40./Picasso*
Private collection, Zurich

Janis, pl. 98 (as "February 3, 1940"); Zervos X, 299

42 [right]

Still Life with Blood Sausage

10 May 1941
Oil on canvas, 36 ½ × 25 ⅞ in. (92.7 × 65.8 cm)
Signed at lower left: *Picasso*
Collection of Tony and Gail Ganz

Boggs, cat. no. 107; Janis, pl. 60; Ullmann, pl. XXVIII; Zervos XI, 112

San Francisco only

43

Head of a Woman

25 May 1941
Oil on canvas, 21 ⅜ × 15 in. (55 × 38 cm)
Signed on reverse: *Picasso*
Národní Galerie, Prague

Ullmann, fig. 258; Zervos XI, 143

44 [right]

Woman in a Gray Hat Seated in an Armchair

26 June 1941
Oil on canvas, 36 ¼ × 28 ¾ in. (92 × 73 cm)
Private collection

Zervos XI, 199

45 [left]

Woman Seated in an Armchair

4 October 1941
Oil on canvas, 39⅜ × 31⅞ in. (100 × 81 cm)
Signed and dated at upper right: *4.Octobre./41./Picasso*
Henie-Onstad Art Centre, Hövikodden, Norway

Gohr, cat. no. 10; Spies, cat. no. 55; Ullmann, pl. XXXVIII; Zervos XI, 319

46

Woman Seated in an Armchair

12 October 1941
Oil on canvas, 31¾ × 25⅝ in. (80.7 × 65 cm)
Signed at lower left: *Picasso*
Kunstsammlung Nordrhein-Westfalen, Düsseldorf

Spies, cat. no. 63; Zervos XI, 340

48

Still Life with a Pigeon

13 November 1941
Oil on canvas, 23 ⅝ × 28 ¾ in. (60 × 73 cm)
Signed at upper left: *Picasso*; dated on stretcher: *13.11.41*
Nagasaki Prefectural Art Museum

Gohr, cat. no. 12; Janis, pl. 57 (as "1942"); Ullmann, pl. XXXII

47 [left]

Bust of a Woman

15 October 1941
Oil on canvas, 45 ⅝ × 35 in. (116 × 89 cm)
Dated on reverse: *15.10.41*
Private collection

Ullmann, fig. 278; Zervos XI, 338

San Francisco only

49

Nude

28 November 1941
Ink on paper, 15⅞ × 12 in. (40.5 × 30.5 cm)
Signed and dated at lower right: *Picasso/28.11.41.*
The Solomon R. Guggenheim Museum, New York

50 [right]

Head of a Woman

November 1941
Oil on newspaper, 23⅝ × 16⅞ in. (60 × 43 cm)
Musée Picasso, Paris

Picasso dation, cat. no. 69; Ullmann, fig. 262 (as "4.11.1941")

New York only

51

Reclining Nude

16 December 1941
Watercolor and ink on paper, 11 ¹³⁄₁₆ × 15 ¾ in. (30 × 41 cm)
Signed and dated at upper right: *16.12.41./Picasso*
Private collection, courtesy Guggenheim, Asher Associates Inc.

Ullmann, pl. XLIV; Zervos XI, 365

52 [right]

Face (Visage)

1941
Charcoal on newspaper, 23 ⅝ × 17 ⅛ in. (60 × 43.5 cm)
Marina Picasso Collection (Inv. 12961), courtesy Galerie Jan
Krugier, Ditesheim & Cie, Geneva

Picasso dation, 156; Ullmann, fig. 263; Zervos XI, 290

53

Two Nude Women

1941 (recto)
Gouache and ink on paper
Signed at lower right: *Picasso*

Head of a Woman

1941 (verso)
Ink on paper
Signed at lower right: *Picasso*

11 ⅝ × 15 ¾ in. (29.5 × 40 cm)
Private collection

54

Death's Head

1941 (?)
Bronze and copper, 9 ⅞ × 8 ¼ × 12 ⅝ in. (25 × 21 × 32 cm)
Musée Picasso, Paris

Boggs, cat. no. 114 (as "1943"); Cowling/Golding, cat. no. 102; Gohr, 89, 118
   (as "1943"); Janis, pl. 130; Musée Picasso I, M.P. 326 (as "1943"); Rubin, 373;
   Spies/Piot, cat. no. 219. II (as "1943"); Ullmann, figs. 191 and 320 (as "1943")

55 [left]

Still Life with Steer's Skull and Table

6 April 1942
Oil on canvas, 46⅛ × 35 in. (117 × 89 cm)
Signed at upper right: *Picasso*; dated at lower right: *6.4.42.*
Pinacoteca di Brera, Milan, gift of Emilio and Maria Jesi

Boggs, fig. 108b; Cowling/Golding, cat. no. 112; Janis, pl. 102 (as "3 April
  1942"); Spies, cat. no. 58; Ullmann, pl. XXXVI; Zervos XII, 35

56

Woman in a Hat Seated in an Armchair

23 April 1942
Oil on canvas, 31⅞ × 25⅝ in. (81 × 65 cm)
Dated at upper right: *23.4.42*
Private collection

Zervos XII, 43

<table>
<tr><td>57 [top]</td><td>58</td></tr>
</table>

57 [top]	58
Paris, 14 July 1942	*Paris, 14 July 1942*
14 July 1942	14 July 1942
State V (positive)	State V (negative)
Etching, scraper, and burin on zinc on paper,	Etching, scraper, and burin on zinc on paper,
17 ¾ × 25 ¼ in. (45.2 × 64.1 cm)	17 ¾ × 25 ¼ in. (45.2 × 64.1 cm)
Dated in the plate at lower left: *Paris 14 juillet 42*	Dated in the plate at lower left: *Paris 14 juillet 42*
Collection E.W.K., Bern	Collection E.W.K., Bern
Baer, cat. no. 682 V (B); Gohr, 74, cat. no. 71; Ullmann, fig. 323 (as "Bukolische Szene")	Baer, cat. no. 682 V (Bb); Gohr, cat. no. 71

59

Man with a Lamb

19 July 1942
India ink on paper, 26⅜ × 8¾ in. (67 × 22.3 cm)
Dated at upper left: *19 juillet 42.*
Private collection

Zervos XII, 88

60

Woman in Gray (Paris)

6 August 1942
Oil on panel
39 ¼ × 31 ⅞ in. (99.7 × 81 cm)
Signed at upper left: *Picasso*
The Alex Hillman Family Foundation Collection

New York only

61 [right]

Woman with an Artichoke

1942
Oil on canvas, 76 ¾ × 51 ¼ in. (195 × 130 cm)
Signed at lower right: *Picasso*
Museum Ludwig, Ludwig Collection, Cologne

Gohr, cat. no. 20; Janis, pl. 77; Rubin, 368; Ullmann, pl. XLII; Zervos XII, 1

Not included in exhibition

62

Still Life with Basket of Fruit

1942
Oil on canvas, 28 ¾ × 36 ¼ in. (73 × 92 cm)
Signed at lower right: *Picasso*
Art Depot, Sweden

Gohr, 181 (as "1941"); Ullmann, fig. 246 (as "August 1942"); Zervos XII, 110

63

Flower Vase on a Table

1942
Oil on canvas, 38 ⅟₁₆ × 51 ¼ in. (96.8 × 130.2 cm)
Signed at bottom center: *Picasso*
The University of Iowa Museum of Art,
  gift of Owen and Leone Elliott

64

Study for Man with a Lamb: *The Lamb*

26 March 1943
India ink on paper, 19⅞ × 26 in. (50.5 × 66 cm)
Dated at lower left: *26 Mars 43*
Musée Picasso, Paris

Musée Picasso II, M.P. 1317; Rubin, 376; Spies, cat. no. 73;
  Ullmann, fig. 330; Zervos XII, 299

San Francisco only

65

Study for Man with a Lamb

27–29 March 1943
Ink and ink wash on paper, 26 × 19 ⅝ in. (66 × 50 cm)
Dated at lower right: *29 Mars 43/27 Mars 43*
Musée Picasso, Paris

Musée Picasso II, M.P. 1318; Spies, cat. no. 76; Zervos XII, 298 (as "29 Mars 1943")

New York only

66 [left]

Man with a Lamb

Ca. March 1943
Bronze
87 ½ × 30 ¾ × 30 ¾ in. (222.5 × 78 × 78 cm)
Marked on rear of base: *No. 1 Cire Perdue/C. Valsuani*
Philadelphia Museum of Art, gift of R. Sturgis and
  Marion B. F. Ingersoll

Cowling/Golding, cat. no. 105 (as "February–March 1943"); Gohr, 117;
  Janis, pl. 131; Musée Picasso I, M.P. 331 (as "February or March 1943");
  Rubin, 377 (as "1944"); Spies, cat. no. 79 (as "February 1943"); Spies/Piot,
  cat. no. 280. II (as "1944"); Ullmann, figs. 335–336 (as "February 1943")

67

First Steps

21 May 1943
Oil on canvas, 51 ¼ × 38 ¼ in. (130.2 × 97.1 cm)
Signed at upper right: *Picasso*
Yale University Art Gallery, New Haven, gift
  of Stephen C. Clark

Gohr, cat. no. 23 (as "6 Juli 1943"); Janis, pl. 105; Rubin,
  375; Ullmann, fig. 315; Zervos XIII, 36

68

Buffet at the Catalan

30 May 1943
Oil on canvas, 31⅞ × 39⅜ in. (81 × 100 cm)
Signed at upper right: *Picasso*
Staatsgalerie Stuttgart

Gohr, cat. no. 26; Ullmann, pl. XXIX; Zervos XIII, 26

69

Head of a Woman

3 June 1943
Oil on paper on canvas, 26 ⅛ × 20 ⅛ in. (66.3 × 51.1 cm)
Signed at lower left: *Picasso*; dated at upper left: *3 juin 43/IX*
The Menil Collection, Houston

70 [left]

Atelier Window

3 July 1943
Oil on canvas, 51⅝ × 38 in. (130 × 96.5 cm)
Signed and dedicated at lower left: *A Mary et Leigh Block /
    leur ami / Picasso*
The Israel Museum, Jerusalem, gift of Mary and Leigh Block
    to the America-Israel Cultural Foundation

Janis, pl. 22; Spies, cat. no. 85; Ullmann, fig. 242; Zervos XIII, 68

71

Still Life with Skull and Pitcher

15 August 1943
Oil on canvas, 19¾ × 24 in. (50 × 61 cm)
Signed and dated at lower right: *Picasso 15 At 43*
Courtesy Michael Werner Gallery, New York and Cologne

Ullmann, pl. XXXVII; Zervos XIII, 90

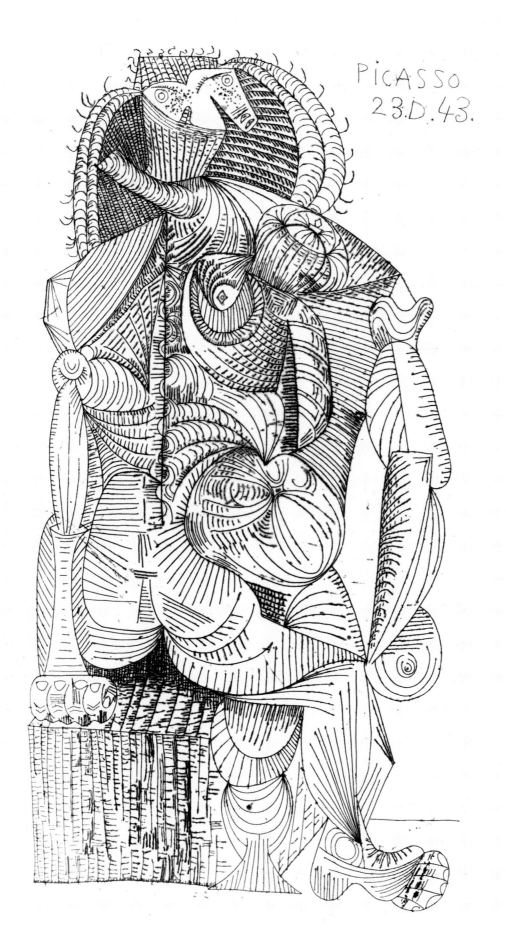

PiCASSO
23.D.43.

192

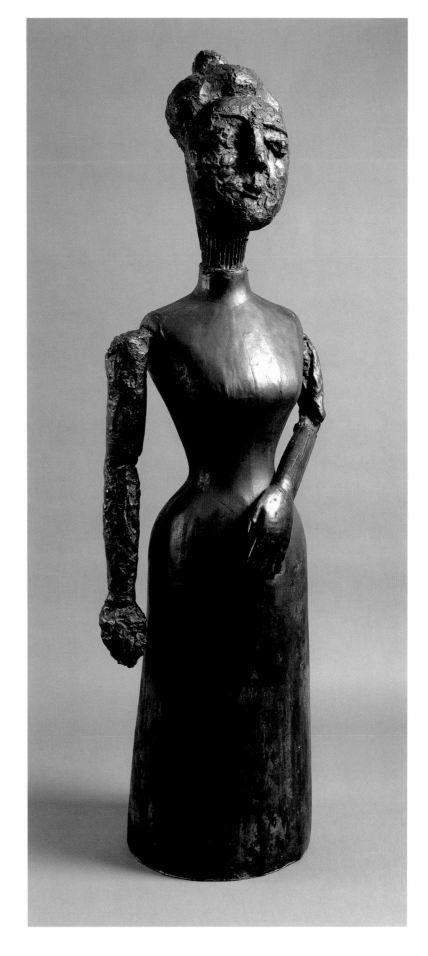

72 [left]

Seated Woman (frontispiece for Contrée)

23 December 1943
Robert Desnos, *Contrée* (Paris, 1944)
Etching, 9⅝ × 5⅜ in. (24.5 × 13.1 cm)
Signed and dated in the plate at upper right:
  Picasso/23.D.43
Fine Arts Museums of San Francisco, Achenbach
  Foundation for Graphic Art

Baer, cat. no. 689; Ullmann, fig. 274

73

Woman in a Long Dress

1943
Bronze, 63½ × 21½ × 18 in. (161.3 × 54.6 × 45.7 cm)
Private collection

Cowling/Golding, cat. no. 104; Janis, pl. 130; Spies/Piot, cat. no. 238. II

San Francisco only

75

Reclining Nude and Woman Washing Her Feet

18 April 1944
Oil on canvas, 38 × 51 in. (97 × 130 cm)
Signed at lower right: *Picasso*; dated on reverse: *18 avril/44*
Private collection, New York

Janis, pl. 11 (as "August 18, 1944"); Zervos XIII, 273 (as "August 18, 1944")

74

The Reaper (Le Faucheur)

1943
Bronze, 20 ⅛ × 13 ⅛ × 7 ¹¹⁄₁₆ in. (51 × 33.5 × 19.5 cm)
Marked on left side of base: *CIRE PERDUE PARIS E. ROBECCHI*
Musée Picasso, Paris

Picasso dation, cat. no. 49; Spies/Piot, cat. no. 234; Ullmann, fig. 322

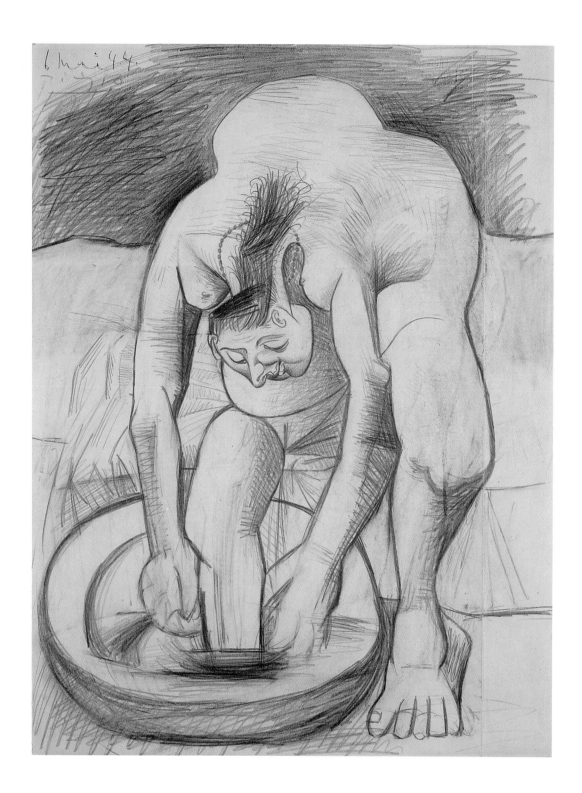

76

Woman Washing Her Foot

6 May 1944
Graphite with incised line on cream wove paper, 20 × 15 ⅛ in.
  (50.7 × 38.6 cm)
Signed and dated at upper left: *6 Mai 44/Picasso*
The Art Institute of Chicago, bequest of Curt Valentin
Photograph © The Art Institute of Chicago. All rights reserved.

Ullmann, fig. 272; Zervos XIII, 291

77 [right]

Cock of the Liberation

23 November 1944
Oil on canvas, 39 ½ × 31 ¾ in. (100.3 × 80.7 cm)
Signed and dated at lower left: *Picasso/23.11.44.*
Milwaukee Art Museum, gift of Mr. and
  Mrs. Harry Lynde Bradley

Zervos XIV, 40

78

Pitcher and Candle

20 February 1945
Oil on canvas, 36¼ × 28¾ in. (92 × 73 cm)
Private collection

Zervos XIV, 70

79

Skull and Pitcher

10 March 1945
Oil on canvas, 28⅝ × 36⅛ in. (72.7 × 91.8 cm)
Signed at lower right: *Picasso*; dated on the reverse: *10.3.45*
The Menil Collection, Houston

Boggs, fig. 119a; Gohr, 124; Spies, cat. no. 89; Ullmann, pl. XLVIII; Zervos XIV, 87

80

Still Life with Skull, Leeks, and Pitcher

14 March 1945
Oil on canvas, 29 × 45⅞ in. (73.6 × 116.6 cm)
Dated at upper left: *14.3.45.*; signed at lower right: *Picasso*
Fine Arts Museums of San Francisco, museum purchase,
    Whitney Warren, Jr., Fund, in memory of Mrs. Adolph B.
    Spreckels, Grover A. Magnin Bequest Fund, Roscoe and
    Margaret Oakes Income Fund, and bequest of Mr. and Mrs.
    Frederick J. Hellman by exchange

Boggs, fig. 119b; Janis, pl. 65; Zervos XIV, 99

81

Skulls

19 March 1945
Ink, ink wash, and charcoal on paper, 19⅞ × 26 in. (50.5 × 66 cm)
Dated at lower left center: *19.3.45.*
Musée Picasso, Paris

Picasso dation, M.P. 1990-78

San Francisco only

82

The Charnel House

1945 (with additional work in 1946)
Oil and charcoal on canvas, 78 ⅝ × 98 ½ in. (199.8 × 250.1 cm)
Signed and dated at lower left: *Picasso/45*
The Museum of Modern Art, New York, Mrs. Sam A. Lewisohn
  Bequest (by exchange) and Mrs. Marya Bernard Fund, in
  memory of her husband Dr. Bernard Bernard, and
  anonymous funds, 1971
© 1998 The Museum of Modern Art, New York

Boggs, fig. 118b; Gohr, 87, 96; Janis, pl. 16 (as "1944–"); Rubin, 389
  (as "[1944]–1945"); Spies, cat. no. 91; Ullmann, fig. 349 (as "end
  1944/Summer 1945"); Zervos XIV, 76

83

Monument to the Spanish Who Died for France
  (Monument aux Espagnols morts pour la France)

1945–47
Oil on canvas, 76 ¾ × 51 ¼ in. (195 × 130 cm)
Dedicated at bottom center: *AUX ESPAGNOLS MORTS POUR
  LA FRANCE*; dated on the stretcher: *31.1.47*
Museo Nacional Centro de Arte Reina Sofia, Madrid

Cowling/Golding, cat. no. 114; Rubin, 393; Ullmann, pl. XLVII

| | PICASSO | OTHERS |

JANUARY 1937

Having left the château of Boisgeloup in Gisors, Normandy, after separating from his wife Olga Khokhlova, Picasso again lives in Paris in his apartment at 23, rue La Boétie. Toward the end of 1936 he also had taken a studio in the dealer Ambroise Vollard's house at Le Tremblay-sur-Mauldre. He established Marie-Thérèse Walter there with their daughter Maya and, over the next few years, would pay them short visits.

Picasso participates in an exhibition organized at the Galerie du Front Populaire, 83, rue La Boétie, in support of the Republican forces in Spain. The exhibition *Braque, Matisse, Picasso* takes place at the Galerie Paul Rosenberg, 21, rue La Boétie.

With the help of Dora Maar, who soon after takes an apartment nearby in the rue de Savoie, Picasso finds a new studio at 7, rue des Grands-Augustins (6th arrondissement). He occupies the top two floors in a seventeenth-century house that before the Revolution was the Hôtel de Savoie-Carignan. Traditionally the house is identified as Balzac's site for his *chef-d'oeuvre inconnu.* Before Picasso's occupancy, the actor Jean-Louis Barrault used the upper floor as a rehearsal hall, and the lower floor continued to be used by a weaving shop. Picasso also now rents a small annex studio on the same street that he uses to store sculptures.

1 – Picasso, with Dora Maar and his son Paulo, visits Max Jacob at the Benedictine abbey at St.-Benoît-sur-Loire, where Jacob had lived since 1921. This is their last direct contact.

8-9 – Picasso etches the plates for the *Dream and Lie of Franco* (cat. no. 2). The etchings, with a separate sheet containing a poem by Picasso, are sold to benefit the Spanish Republic. All eighteen designs in the sequence are also printed separately as postcards for sale.

Around midmonth, a delegation from the Spanish Republican government, including the architect Josep Lluis Sert, designer of the Spanish Republican Pavilion for the 1937 World's Fair in Paris; the writer Louis Aragon; José Gaos, general commissioner of the Spanish Pavilion; Juan Larrea, poet and director of public information for the Spanish embassy; and Max Aub, the cultural delegate for the Spanish embassy, calls upon Picasso in the rue La Boétie to invite him to paint a mural for the Spanish Pavilion, originally scheduled to open on May Day.

In mid-January Jaime Sabartés moves out of Picasso's apartment, temporarily interrupting his service to Picasso as secretary and confidant.

[left]
Picasso in his studio in at 7, rue des Grands-Augustins, winter 1944-45. Photograph by Francis Lee.

[above]
The Spanish Pavilion at the World's Fair, Paris, summer 1937.

FEBRUARY 1937

7 - 8 – Málaga, Picasso's birthplace, falls to Franco's troops.

MARCH 1937

Picasso is included in the exhibition marking the Cinquantenaire of the Société des peintres-graveurs français at the Bibliothèque Nationale.

Picasso serves on the organization committee for the exhibition *L'Art catalan du Xe au XVe siècle,* presented at the Musée du Jeu de Paume from March through April.

8-18 – The Battle of Madrid is fought between Republican and Nationalist forces in Spain.

APRIL 1937

An exhibition entitled *Picasso, les debuts du cubisme* opens at the Galerie Pierre, 2, rue des Beaux-Arts.

1-30 – The exhibition *Recent Works of Picasso* at Rosenberg and Helft in London presents twenty-nine paintings from 1930 to 1934.

12-24 – The Valentine Gallery in New York shows drawings, gouaches, and pastels by Picasso.

26 – Nazi planes of the Condor Legion bomb Guernica, a Basque town of 7,000 inhabitants, for three hours on its Sunday market day, killing 1,654 and wounding 889. Accounts of the attack, including photographs, are carried over the next few days by the French newspapers *Ce Soir* and *L'Humanité,* providing the inspiration for Picasso's mural *Guernica.*

MAY 1937

1 – Working in his new studio, Picasso begins sketches for *Guernica,* producing more than fifty studies in all. By 11 May he outlines the composition on canvas. Dora photographs the painting at seven different stages over its approximately month-long period of development.

Toward the end of May, André Malraux and the Spanish photographer and essayist José Bergamín visit Picasso and see the almost finished *Guernica.* He is also visited by Roland Penrose with Henry Moore, and by Salvador Dalí.

24 – The World's Fair is inaugurated. By 26 November it has attracted over one million visitors. The various national pavilions contain 345 mural decorations by many prominent modern artists, including Fernand Léger, Robert Delaunay, Joan Miró, and Raoul Dufy.

JUNE 1937

An exhibition of early works by Picasso is presented at the Galerie Kate Perls, 13, rue de l'Abbaye.

Guernica is installed in the Spanish Pavilion by mid-June.

Jean Cassou publishes his monograph, *Picasso* (Paris: Editions Braun).

7 – Thirty-two works by Picasso are included in *Les Maîtres de l'art indépendant 1895-1937* at the Petit Palais, which runs until October. Among the works is *Les Demoiselles d'Avignon* (page 44, fig. 7) in its first official public exhibition.

[above]
Picasso working on *Guernica* in his studio, June 1937. Photograph by Dora Maar. Musée Picasso, Paris, Picasso Archives.

[left]
Guernica installed in the Spanish Pavilion at the World's Fair in Paris, summer 1937, with Alexander Calder's *Mercury Fountain* in the foreground. Photograph by Hugo Herdeg.

JULY 1937

1 – Picasso works through seven states to develop his large etching of the *Weeping Woman.*

12 – The Spanish Pavilion opens, three weeks late. In addition to *Guernica,* two cement sculptures by Picasso from the Boisgeloup period – *Head of a Woman* and *Woman with a Vase* – are exhibited outside the pavilion, as well as two Boisgeloup heads (one cement, one plaster), and a bronze nude on the third floor. The iron sculpture *La Montserrat* by Julio Gonzáles, the mural *The Reaper* (Le Faucheur) by Miró, and Alexander Calder's *Mercury Fountain* are also on view. Picasso's etching of the *Dream and Lie of Franco* is available on sale to benefit the Republican cause.

Despite criticisms of the painting from both the political left and right, *Guernica* attains immediate and widespread acclaim, with reproductions in *Life* (26 July), *Regards* (29 July), the first issue of *Verve,* and a special issue of *Cahiers d'Art* (vol. 12, nos. 4–5) including sixty-nine illustrations of works by Picasso and texts by Christian Zervos, Cassou, Georges Duthuit, Larrea, Amédée Ozenfant, Paul Eluard, Michel Leiris, and Bergamín.

Following the opening, Picasso departs for Mougins with Dora, staying at the Hôtel Vaste Horizon. Paul and Nusch Eluard, Penrose and Lee Miller, Man Ray, and Zervos are also there. The dealer Paul Rosenberg visits to select several paintings for sale.

18 – The *Springfield [Massachusetts] Republican* publishes a statement made by Picasso in May or June and issued at the time of an exhibition of Spanish war posters shown in New York under the auspices of the North American Committee to Aid Spanish Democracy. Speaking from his position as a Spanish artist, but also as director of the Museo National del Prado, an honorary title given him in 1936 by the Spanish Republican government, Picasso defends against recent attacks the record of the Republicans in protecting and preserving Spanish art treasures.

30 – Picasso is included in *Origines et développement de l'art international indépendant* at the Musée du Jeu de Paume. Until 31 October.

18 – In Munich Hitler inaugurates the Haus der Deutschen Kunst with the *Grosse Deutsche Ausstellung.*

19 – The exhibition *Entartete Kunst* is presented in Munich at the old Galeriegebäude. It would later travel to Berlin and other large cities in Germany and Austria, attracting major audiences. Until 30 November.

19 – Max Beckmann emigrates from Germany to Amsterdam.

28 – Lyonel Feininger emigrates from Germany to America.

AUGUST 1937

An exhibition of work by living French artists, entitled *Ausstellung Franzosischer Kunst der Gegenwart,* is organized by the Association française d'action artistique, part of the French Ministry for Foreign Affairs, for the Berlin Akademie der Kunste. Among the better-known artists included are Léger, Georges Braque, Henri Matisse, André Derain, Maurice de Vlaminck, and Aristide Maillol.

SEPTEMBER 1937

Toward the end of the month, Picasso returns to Paris.

Lázló Moholy-Nagy emigrates to the United States.

OCTOBER 1937

Picasso travels to Switzerland, where he visits Paul Klee in Bern. He sees Bernhard Geiser, who later catalogues his etchings, and reportedly conducts banking business in Geneva.

The first installation by the newly formed Musée d'Art Vivant opens at the Maison de la Culture in Paris, and includes works by Picasso.

14 – The *Carnegie International* exhibition opens in Pittsburgh, with Picasso included among the artists representing France.

26 – Picasso completes the painting *Weeping Woman* (Tate Gallery, London).

NOVEMBER 1937

The Conseil des musées nationaux rejects by a vote of nine to five a Picasso still-life painting, *Still Life with White Pitcher,* purchased at auction in June for 56,500 francs by the French government for the Musée du Jeu de Paume.

An exhibition *Picasso from 1901 to 1937* appears at the Valentine Gallery in New York.

1-20 – Jacques Seligman and Company, New York, presents *20 Years in the Evolution of Picasso, 1903–1923.*

5 – The sale at the Hôtel Drouot in Paris of the well-known collection amassed by the investment group Oeil Clair includes a cubist painting by Picasso.

9 – Picasso gathers with various artists and writers at the tomb of Guillaume Apollinaire in Père-Lachaise Cemetery for the annual commemoration of his death. This event continues through the war years. On this occasion, Picasso refuses to shake the hand of the Italian theorist Filippo Tomasso Marinetti, offering the rejoinder, "You forget that we are at war."

DECEMBER 1937

17 – The exhibition *L'Art cruel* at the Galerie Billiet in Paris includes works by Picasso and a catalogue preface by Cassou protesting the war in Spain. Until 6 January 1938.

19 – The *New York Times* publishes a statement by Picasso addressed to the American Artists' Congress in New York, expanding upon his statement of 18 July 1937 in the *Springfield Republican* and defending again the Spanish Republican government against propaganda claims that it has allowed the destruction of Spanish art treasures: "Artists who live and work with spiritual values cannot and should not remain indifferent to a conflict in which the highest values of humanity and civilization are at stake."

30 – The Galerie La Boétie in Paris shows works by Picasso in an exhibition organized with the Amis du front populaire to benefit children of Spain. Until 20 January 1938.

JANUARY 1938

The *Exposition internationale du surréalisme* at the Galerie Beaux-Arts, 140, rue du Faubourg Saint-Honoré, contains two paintings by Picasso.

Guernica is included in a large traveling exhibition of works by Picasso, Matisse, Braque, and Henri Laurens, opening at the Kunstnernes Hus in Oslo and moving to the Statens Museum fur Kunst in Copenhagen, Liljevalchs Konsthall in Stockholm, and Konsthallen in Göteborg, finally closing in April.

9 – Spanish Republican forces win an important battle for the city of Teruel in Aragon, but then lose the city again on 22 February.

FEBRUARY 1938

15 – Picasso completes *Woman with a Cock* (private collection, Switzerland).

MARCH 1938

11 – With the Anschluss, Germany annexes Austria; German troops enter Austria on 12 March.

16–18 – German and Italian planes bomb Barcelona, killing 1,300 and wounding 2,000.

APRIL 1938

Picasso and Sabartés meet unexpectedly in the street, and a reconciliation ensues. Picasso introduces his new dog Kazbek, who has replaced Elft (now retired to the château of Boisgeloup), and who figures in numerous works from the war years.

JUNE 1938

Picasso is included in an exhibition at the Galerie de Beaune in Paris, organized in memory of Apollinaire.

Picasso by Gertrude Stein (Paris: Librarie Floury) is published.

JULY 1938

Picasso returns to Mougins with Dora for the summer, staying again at the Hôtel Vaste Horizon with the Eluards. A young woman named Inés who works at the hotel will go to Paris in the autumn to work for Picasso as a housekeeper. She marries Gustave Susaier in 1940, has a son, and continues for years to work in Picasso's household, occasionally appearing in his art. Some authors place the date of their meeting a year or two earlier.

Picasso visits Matisse at Cimiez, above Nice.

Works by Picasso are included in an exhibition at the Galerie Jeanne Bucher in Paris, organized to benefit Spanish children.

Picasso's Afghan hound Kazbek in the rue des Grands-Augustins studio, 1944. Photograph by Brassaï.

SEPTEMBER 1938

Picasso returns to Paris. Shortly after, perhaps alarmed by preparations around Paris to protect the city from aerial bombardments, he goes to Le Tremblay-sur-Mauldre, joining Marie-Thérèse and Maya.

5 – French troops move into position along the Maginot line.

29 – The Munich Accord is signed by representatives of Britain, France, Germany, and Italy, supposedly guaranteeing "peace in our time," but sanctioning the transfer of Czech lands to Germany.

OCTOBER 1938

Picasso sojourns in Vézelay with the Zervoses.

4-29 – In an exhibition organized by Penrose, Herbert Read, and Edouard Mesens, *Guernica* is shown with more than sixty studies at the New Burlington Galleries in London under the auspices of the National Joint Committee for Spanish Relief. A pro-Franco exhibition of work by the Spanish artist Ignacio Zuloaga is held concurrently. Afterward, Picasso's works also are shown at the Whitechapel Gallery in London and in Manchester (but apparently not in Leeds or Liverpool, as commonly reported).

19 – The exhibition *Picasso and Matisse* appears at the Museum of Modern Art in Boston. Until 11 November.

The volunteer International Brigade fighting on the Republican side in Spain is disbanded.

Oskar Kokoschka and John Heartfield emigrate from Czechoslovakia to London.

NOVEMBER 1938

Picasso donates 100,000 francs to the Comité d'aide à l'Espagne for the purchase of milk for Spanish children.

The exhibition *Art français contemporain* at the Palais des Beaux-Arts contains a room dedicated to Picasso.

7-26 – A Picasso exhibition entitled *21 Paintings – 1908 to 1934* appears at the Valentine Gallery, New York.

9 – The Kristallnacht pogrom in Germany devastates Jewish businesses and synagogues.

DECEMBER 1938

Picasso is confined in bed by an attack of sciatica.

New issue of *Cahiers d'Art* is devoted to Picasso and El Greco, with an article on Picasso by Zervos, a poem ("A Pablo Picasso") by Eluard, and illustrations of 120 works from 1926 to 1938.

JANUARY 1939

Picasso works nearly every day for several months at Roger Lacourière's print workshop in the rue Foyatier in Montmartre, mostly on a long series of etchings reproducing his writings with marginalia added to each page. The intended book, which Vollard wanted to publish, is never completed.

13 – Picasso's mother dies in Barcelona. Because of the war, he is unable to attend the funeral.

17 – An exhibition at the Paul Rosenberg gallery in Paris features thirty-three works by Picasso from the past three years.

30 – Ten works by Picasso are included in *Figure Paintings* at the Marie Harriman Gallery in New York. Until 18 February.

26 – Barcelona surrenders to Franco. Picasso's nephews, Fin and Javier Vilato, have been fighting on the Republican side.

FEBRUARY 1939

Picasso's nephews flee Spain for Paris. Picasso consigns them to the Lacourière workshop to learn printing. Many other Spanish refugees pour into France, and many of them come to see Picasso.

MARCH 1939

Picasso: Recent Works is shown at Rosenberg and Helft in London, featuring thirty-two paintings.

Works by Picasso are included in the exhibition on *Les Ballets Russes de Diaghilev* at the Musée des Arts Décoratifs.

15 – Adolph Hitler enters Prague.

28 – Madrid falls to General Francisco Franco.

APRIL 1939

8 – Italy annexes Albania.

MAY 1939

The exhibition *Picasso in English Collections* appears at the London Gallery, London.

5-29 – *Guernica* and approximately sixty related studies are shown at the Valentine Gallery in New York under the auspices of the American Artists' Congress to benefit the Spanish Refugee Relief Campaign. They subsequently travel to the Stendahl Gallery in Los Angeles, the San Francisco Museum of Art, and the Arts Club of Chicago before returning to New York in November for the Picasso retrospective at the Museum of Modern Art.

22 – In Berlin, Italy and Germany sign a pact of cooperation.

JUNE 1939

In one wing of his Grands-Augustins studio, Picasso installs the engraving press that had belonged to Louis Fort and had recently been housed at the château of Boisgeloup. Other work is also undertaken at the studio, including the installation of central heating.

30 – The German government conducts a major sale of "entartete kunst" at the Galerie Fischer in Lucerne, Switzerland, selling around 300 paintings and 3,000 works on paper, including four works by Picasso that fetch prices among the highest in the entire auction. Until 4 July.

JULY 1939

8 – Picasso and Dora travel by Train Bleu to Antibes, where they rent an apartment that had been occupied by Man Ray.

By **19** – Marie-Thérèse and Maya relocate to Royan, a seaside city on the southern Atlantic Coast, presumably as a precaution owing to the increasing threats of war.

23 – Picasso hurries back to Paris for Vollard's funeral, which is held on the 28 July at the Basilique Sainte-Clotilde. Among those in attendance are Marc Chagall, Paul Valéry, Maurice Denis, Maillol, Georges Rouault, Dufy, and Derain.

29 – Picasso invites Sabartés to accompany him south. His chauffeur Marcel drives them, stopping the next morning in Fréus to attend a bullfight. After their arrival in Antibes, Picasso escorts Sabartés on a tour of towns along the coast. In his apartment, he converts one of two main rooms into a studio, attaching three unequal pieces of canvas directly to the walls and eventually using the largest for *Night Fishing at Antibes* (cat. no. 31).

22 – Vollard dies in a hospital in Versailles following an automobile accident.

AUGUST 1939

Inspired by scenes around the port of Antibes but also by concerns over war, Picasso completes *Night Fishing at Antibes.*

26 – With the announcement by the French government of general mobilization, Picasso decides to return to Paris, departing with Dora Maar and Sabartés by train and leaving Marcel to drive back with the summer's art work.

23 – The Soviets sign a nonaggression pact with Germany, leading the French government to ban the Communist Party. The USSR occupies part of Poland and other Baltic states.

SEPTEMBER 1939

3 – Picasso flees Paris in a car driven by Marcel, with Dora, Sabartés and his wife, and his dog Kazbek. (Sabartés supplies this date but elsewhere gives the departure date as 29 August; some authors give 1 September as the date.) They leave near midnight, drive all night, and arrive in Royan the following morning. Marie-Thérèse and Maya are living at the villa Gerbier de Joncs. Picasso and Dora Maar take rooms at the Hôtel du Tigre. He sets up a studio at Gerbier de Joncs and later, on 4 January, finds an apartment to rent for studio space in the villa Les Voiliers, located next to the Hôtel de Paris (later the headquarters of the German command) and offering a clear view of the sea.

7 – After a public announcement that all foreigners who had arrived in Royan after 25 August could not remain, Picasso returns by car to Paris with Sabartés and Marcel to obtain a residency permit, promptly leaving again for Royan on 8 September.

1 – Germany invades Poland.

3 – Britain and France declare war against Germany.

OCTOBER 1939

12-22 or **26** – According to some sources, Picasso makes a second trip back to Paris.

NOVEMBER 1939

12-26 – According to Sabartés, Picasso returns for the second time to Paris.

15 – The Museum of Modern Art in New York presents *Picasso: Forty Years of His Art,* containing 344 works. The exhibition would later travel in modified versions to the Art Institute of Chicago, City Art Museum in Saint Louis, Museum of Fine Arts in Boston, Cincinnati Art Museum, Cleveland Museum of Art, Isaac Delgado Museum of Art in New Orleans, Minneapolis Institute of Arts, and Carnegie Institute in Pittsburgh. After the close of the show, Picasso leaves the art in the United States, some of it then appearing in smaller traveling exhibitions. Until 7 January 1940.

30 – The USSR invades Finland.

DECEMBER 1939

5-21 – Picasso makes another trip to Paris with Sabartés.

JANUARY 1940

3 – Picasso meets Andrée Rolland and agrees to rent from her an apartment in the villa Les Voiliers for a studio. It is on the third floor with windows onto the sea. He occupies the apartment later in the month.

André Breton visits Royan from January to July.

FEBRUARY 1940

5-29 – Picasso returns to Paris. He and Miró visit Yvonne Zervos at her Galerie Mai at 12, rue Bonaparte.

MARCH 1940

15 – Picasso visits Paris again by himself, and stays two months. Until mid-May.

Drawings in a Royan sketchbook dated between 3 and 14 March show the development of *Woman Dressing Her Hair* (The Museum of Modern Art, New York).

APRIL 1940

11 – Breton writes to Picasso from Poitiers, thanking him for the offer of a painting that could be sold for living expenses, "mes seuls moyens de vivre d'ici peu de temps."

19 – An exhibition of gouaches and watercolors by Picasso takes place at the Galerie Mai. Until 18 May.

MAY 1940

7 – An exhibition *Peintres-Graveurs français* opens at the Bibliothèque Nationale, with works by Picasso.

Picasso meets Matisse in the street, and they share views on the sorry state of France's military. Picasso quips that the generals are from the Ecole des Beaux-Arts.

16 – Picasso departs Paris for Royan by train. Millions of refugees are fleeing southward in advance of the German invasion.

JUNE 1940

10 – Zervos writes to Picasso in Royan with news of the German advance. A soldier had reported to him that what the Germans did to Gisors "exceeds all imagination . . . the city is absolutely in ruins."

Germany invades Denmark and Norway.

10 – Beginning of the German aerial attack on the Netherlands and Belgium, followed immediately by invasion.

12 – German troops cross the border from Belgium into France.

28 – Belgium surrenders.

Jacques Lipchitz flees Paris for Toulouse; he emigrates to the U.S. in 1941. Miró leaves France for Palma de Mallorca.

3 – Germans bomb the Paris airports.

10 – Italy declares war on France and Great Britain; the French government abandons Paris.

12 – Daniel-Henry Kahnweiler and his wife flee Paris, taking up residence in Limousin near St.-Léonard-de-Noblat. Later, fearing the gestapo, they hide under false identity in the village of Lagupie in Gascony.

14 – German troops enter Paris.

16 – Paul Reynaud resigns as premier of France; Marshal Philippe Pétain replaces him. The French cabinet votes for peace with Germany.

[above]
Corner of Picasso's studio in the villa Les Voiliers, Royan, including on the wall the incomplete first version of *Head of a Bull,* 1940. Photograph by Pablo Picasso. Musée Picasso, Paris, Picasso Archives, gift of Sir Roland Penrose.

[left]
Picasso in his studio in Royan with *Woman Dressing Her Hair,* 1940.

19 – Picasso completes *Woman Dressing Her Hair,* the development of which coincided with the German march toward Paris. He is also producing some of his most grim and skull-like Heads of Women.

Picasso in his vault at the Banque Nationale pour le Commerce et l'Industrie, ca. 1940–44. Musée Picasso, Paris, Picasso Archives.

17 – Pétain announces on the radio that he had approached the enemy and called for an end to hostilities.

23 – Hitler visits Paris with Albert Speer and Arno Breker, among others.

25 – The Armistice of Rethondes is signed by Hitler and Pétain, dividing France into a German-occupied zone in the north and a free zone in the south controlled by Pétain's collaborationist government installed at Vichy on 10 July.

30 – Otto Abetz, soon to be appointed German ambassador to France, is charged with the "protection" of art belonging to the French state and Jewish individuals. The Einsatzstab Reichsleiter Rosenberg (ERR) is empowered to seize works for so-called scientific purposes.

JULY 1940

24 – Zervos writes to Picasso to inform him that the Spanish embassy posted announcements on the doors of his apartment in the rue La Boétie and studio in the rue des Grands-Augustins, placing both under its protection. He also tells Picasso that he is safeguarding certain of his sculptures for him.

AUGUST 1940

23 – According to Sabartés, Picasso departs Royan by car with Sabartés and Marcel to return permanently to Paris, arriving on 24 August. (Some sources give his departure date as 25 August.) Dora leaves at the same time by train, and Marie-Thérèse and Maya remain for the time being in Royan. Upon his return, Picasso lives in his apartment in the rue La Boétie and works in his studio in the rue des Grands-Augustins. The date he moves into the latter is not precisely known. Visitors were still calling on him in the rue La Boétie at the end of 1941, but he seems to have been more or less fully transferred by early 1942.

28 – Matisse arrives in Nice, having traveled from southwest France. In June he had canceled plans to emigrate to Rio de Janeiro. On 1 September, he writes to his son, Pierre, "if everyone who has any values leaves France, what remains of France?"

SEPTEMBER 1940

During the autumn, in Picasso's presence, German authorities examine his bank vault at the Banque Nationale pour le Commerce et l'Industrie, together with that of Matisse, who had moved to the south of France. Picasso is accompanied by the art dealer Pierre Colle.

Late in 1940 or early in 1941, Marie-Thérèse and Maya return to Paris from Royan, taking up residence in an apartment in the boulevard Henri-IV (4th arrondissement). They are joined there by Marie-Thérèse's mother. Typically, Picasso visits them on Thursdays, when there is no school, and Sundays. He continues to see his wife Olga, although they have been separated for many years. Their son Paulo spends the war years in Switzerland, where Bernhard Geiser helps look after him.

Italy attacks Egypt.

Rationing is instituted in Paris. The first anti-Semitic measures are enforced in the occupied zone. The Liste Otto is published, giving names of books and other publications withdrawn from sale, including works by political refugees and Jewish authors. A revised list is published in the summer of 1942.

26 – Walter Benjamin commits suicide after he is caught trying to cross from France into Spain.

27 – The Rome-Berlin-Tokyo pact is signed.

OCTOBER 1940

Italy attacks Greece.

Léger departs for the United States.

3 – The Statut des Juifs is passed by the Vichy government, authorizing the internment of Jews and stripping them of certain rights. It is announced in *Le Journal officiel* of 18 October.

NOVEMBER 1940

22 – Picasso is singled out among other modern artists in John Hemming Fry's *Art décadent sous le règne de la démocratie et du communisme* (Paris: Henri Colas), a Fascist attack on modern art in general and the purportedly degenerate influence of communism and the "mentalité juive."

3-5 – Confiscated art works are gathered at the Musée du Jeu de Paume for inspection by Reichsmarshal Göring, who makes a division of works for the German museums, ERR, Hitler, and his own collection.

DECEMBER 1940

Drawings by Picasso are included in an exhibition at the Galerie Jean Dufresne, 47, rue de Berri.

15 – The first edition of *Résistance* appears, a clandestine journal published by the Groupe du Musée de l'Homme.

JANUARY 1941

Georges Hugnet's small concrete poem *Pablo Picasso* is published in Paris.

14-17 – Picasso writes the script of his play *Le Désir attrapé par le queue* (Desire trapped by the tail), which was performed at a reading by friends in March 1944.

10 – The German-Soviet pact is renewed.

MARCH 1941

25 – After a period of refuge at the American-supported Villa Air-Bel at Marseilles with other writers and artists, Breton and his wife and daughter, Wilfredo Lam, the Victor Serges, and Claude Levi-Strauss all depart for Martinique by boat. André Masson and family would leave on 31 March.

APRIL 1941

6 – Germany invades Yugoslavia and Greece.

8 – A new law limiting certain economic activities by Jews in France forbids possession of telephones and attendance at public recreational and service establishments.

MAY 1941

13 – Otto Freundlich, who was living in St. Paul-de-Fenouillet, and who would later die after deportation, writes to Picasso asking him to pay five month's rent on his Paris studio so it would not be foreclosed.

The Chagalls leave from Marseilles for New York.

MAY 1941 [CONTINUED]

14 – The French police arrest over 3,000 foreign Jews around Paris. Within a year, 30,000 Jews would be interned in camps in the occupied zone.

JUNE 1941

An exhibition at the Musée de l'Orangerie of the private collection of Paul Jamot, recently donated to the state museums, includes works by Picasso.

After internment and escape, Max Ernst flees France across the Spanish border.

2 – A new Statut des Juifs is instituted.

22 – Germany invades the Soviet Union in Operation Barbarossa.

30 – The Vichy government breaks off diplomatic relations with Moscow.

JULY 1941

16 – Louise Leiris, sister-in-law of Kahnweiler, officially buys his gallery, then known as the Galerie Simon, in order to "aryanize" it. She had worked with Kahnweiler since 1920. The name is changed to Galerie Louise Leiris, where works by Picasso would continue to be handled during the war.

22 – A Vichy law is passed "to eliminate all Jewish influence in the national economy." Later modified by laws of 17 November 1941 and 25 June 1943, it requires the transfer of businesses, property, and securities to non-Jewish administrators within one year.

AUGUST 1941

30 – An article by Pierre Malo appears in the journal *Comoedia*, describing a visit to Picasso's studio where he saw, among other works, a sculpture of a death's head (probably the *Death's Head*, cat. no. 54).

20 – Raids in the 11th arrondissement result in the arrest of 4,300 Jews, 1,300 of them French; all are sent to the camp at Drancy outside Paris.

SEPTEMBER 1941

5 – A propagandistic exhibition entitled *Le Juif et la France* opens at the Palais Berlitz.

23 – In London, General Charles de Gaulle creates the Comité national de la France libre ("Free France").

The exhibition *Le Juif et la France* at the Palais Berlitz, Paris, 1941.

OCTOBER 1941

Picasso's friend and landlord from Royan, Andrée Rolland, visits him in Paris, and they cancel his lease on the Royan apartment. They meet at the apartment in the rue La Boétie and then lunch together with Dora at Le Catalan, a restaurant in the rue des Grands-Augustins frequented by Picasso and friends, who named it in reference to its genial owner, Monsieur Arnau, of French Catalonia.

French artists and their escorts departing for Germany, Gare de l'Est, Paris, October 1941: From the left: Charles Despiau (polka-dot bow tie), Othon Friesz (light-color overcoat), André Dunoyer de Segonzac (mustache), Maurice de Vlaminck (dark overcoat), Kees van Dongen (white beard), André Derain (behind and to the right of van Dongen).

From October to November, a tour to Germany for artists, accompanied by a journalist and an interpreter, is organized by the German Ministry of Propaganda. The participants include Henri Bouchard, Paul Landowski, and Louis Lejeune, all of the Académie des Beaux-Arts; the sculptors Charles Despiau and Paul Belmondo; and the painters Vlaminck, Derain, Kees van Dongen, Othon Friesz, André Dunoyer de Segonzac, Roland Oudot, Raymond Legueult, and Jean Janin. Maillol was excused due to his age, and Denis was able to avoid going.

11 – A law is passed allowing French bronze sculptures to be melted down to supply metal for the war effort.

22 – Louis Marcoussis dies in the village of Cusset, near Vichy.

24 – Delaunay dies in a hospital in Montpellier.

DECEMBER 1941

7 – The Japanese attack Pearl Harbor, drawing the United States into the war.

11 – Germany and Italy declare war on the United States.

JANUARY 1942

The second volume of Eluard's *Livre ouvert,* dedicated to Picasso, is published in Paris by *Cahiers d'Art.*

1 – Alberto Giacometti, having fled Paris, moves into a small hotel room in Geneva, where he spends the duration of the war.

29 – General Ernst von Schaumburg, the German commander in Paris, announces the deportation of 100 members of Communist and Jewish youth organizations, and the execution of six Communists and Jews. Many reprisals would follow.

FEBRUARY 1942

25 – Seven members of the Réseau du Musée de l'Homme, the Resistance organization, are executed.

A group exhibition at the Galerie Rive Gauche at 44, rue de Fleurus, contains works by Picasso. It continues through the end of the year. Picasso's *chef-d'oeuvre inconnu* is included in the exhibition *Le Livre français illustré* at the Galerie Friedland, and a public lecture on Picasso is presented by the youth group Jeune France on 20 or 21 March.

11 – Picasso meets Olga at his bank to discuss financial settlements. He would like her to move to Switzerland, where their son Paulo is living, but she refuses, claiming inadequate funds.

26 – At Dora's apartment, Picasso sees an incomplete portrait of her in charcoal by Jean Cocteau. He paints over the canvas his own *Portrait of Dora Maar* (private collection), eventually completing it on 9 October 1942 after numerous reworkings.

27 – Julio González dies after a long illness. Picasso attends the funeral at the parish church at Arcueil with Zervos and his Spanish friends Félix Fernández and Apelles Fenosa. He soon paints a series of memento-mori still lifes in González's memory. A few days after the funeral, Picasso remarks mysteriously to Fenosa, "I am the one who killed him."

The Communist Party leader Laurent Casanova, after escaping prison, lives in hiding in Paris. He would be given refuge in the apartment of Michel and Louise Leiris, where he meets Picasso.

3 – Allied bombing raids on the Renault factory on the outskirts of Paris kill over 600 people.

APRIL 1942

2 – Picasso writes a poem recording his distress over González's death and funeral.

10 – Picasso writes to Mme Rolland, asking her to send him the remaining contents of his studio in Les Voiliers in Royan. The German navy now occupies Royan, however, and she is not able to enter.

18 – Pierre Laval replaces François Darlan as prime minister under Pétain; he pursues policies of collaboration with Germany.

MAY 1942

2 – An exhibition opens at the Musée Saint-Pierre in Lyon that contains modern French art from private collections, including two paintings by Picasso.

4 – Picasso completes the large *L'Aubade* (Centre Georges Pompidou, Paris).

Marcel Duchamp sails from Marseilles to Casablanca and then makes his way to New York.

15 – Retrospective exhibition of the German sculptor Arno Breker appears at the Orangerie. The opening is attended by Cocteau, Derain, Despiau, van Dongen, Vlaminck, Maillol, and Segonzac; Cocteau writes a laudatory article for *Comoedia* ("Salut à Breker," issue of May 23). Until 31 July.

After the Breker opening, a Resistance group called Le Front national des arts is formed and publishes *L'Art français.* The artists André Fougeron, Edouard Pignon, André Marchand, Francis Grüber, Edouard Goerg, Jean Amblard, Jean-Claude Aujame, André Lhote, Maurice Denis, and Pierre Montagnac are active.

Arno Breker, Charles Despiau, Aristide Maillol, and Louis Hautecoeur, head of the fine arts department in the Ministry of Education and Youth, at the opening in Paris of the Arno Breker retrospective, May 1942.

22 – Eluard writes to Picasso to inform him of the analysis of his handwriting by a graphologist. Among other observations, the report indicated that Picasso "loves intensely and he kills what he loves."

26 – The dealer Martin Fabiani publishes le comte de Buffon's *Histoire naturelle* with illustrations prepared several years earlier by Picasso, a project first planned with Vollard but taken over by Fabiani when he acquired Vollard's business inventory.

29 – The first systematic deportations of foreign-born Jews to death camps in the east begin.

30 – In anti-Resistance measures, Jacques Decour, Georges Politzer, and Jacques Solomon are all executed. Decour had been the primary founder of the clandestine publication *Les Lettres françaises*, the first (delayed) issue of which appeared in September 1942.

JUNE 1942

A painting by Picasso sells at the Hôtel Drouot for the high price of 610,000 francs.

6 – Vlaminck's "Opinions libres . . . sur la peinture" is published in *Comoedia*, leveling a vitriolic ad hominum attack at Picasso under the pretense of an analysis of cubism. He finds Picasso guilty of having led French painting "into the most mortal impasse, into an indescribable confusion," and dangerously compares his work with the metaphysics of the Kabala and Talmud. This outburst is somewhat tepidly answered by Lhote in the 13 June issue of *Comoedia*. Vlaminck would reprise the article in his book *Portraits avant décès* (Paris: Flammarion).

By 7 June – Picasso makes a gift to Matisse of a portrait of Dora.

20 – In response to Vlaminck's attack, a letter of support for Picasso and cubism is published in *Comoedia*, written by Gaston Diehl and signed by forty-one artists.

29 – Dora tells Cocteau that a bronze cast has been made of Picasso's *Head of a Bull*, fashioned from a bicycle seat and handlebars. Despite all the difficulties posed by the Occupation and shortages of metal, Picasso manages to have numerous major works cast in bronze. He stores them in his annex studio in the rue des Grands-Augustins, and Brassaï eventually makes photographs of them all.

La relève, a scheme to attract workers to Germany, is instituted. For every three volunteers for labor, one French prisoner will be released.

1 – An ordinance is published requiring all Jews aged six and above to wear a yellow star in public, to go into effect on 7 June.

18 – Ninety Communists are arrested. Eluard, who had recently rejoined the Communist Party, has to go underground. He and Hugnet are active in the Resistance.

JULY 1942

15 – Picasso prepares the first studies for the sculpture *Man with a Lamb* (cat. no. 66), based on figures in his print *14 July 1942*.

Sometime after mid-July, Gerhard Heller, a German officer working as a censor in the literary office of the German embassy in Paris, visits Picasso's studio, taken there by Jean Paulhan, a critic and writer who contributed to different Resistance publications as well as wartime newspapers.

18 – Newspaper reports indicate that a painting donated by Picasso is sold in a charity auction by L'Union des artistes for 650,000 francs.

22 – Ernst Jünger, a well-known German writer serving as an army officer in Paris, visits Picasso's studio. Picasso supposedly queries him about his book *Sur les falaises de marbre* and remarks, "Between the two of us, as we sit here, we could negotiate the peace this very afternoon."

16-17 – La Grande Rafle du Vél' d'Hiv takes place, a massive roundup of Jews in Paris by 9,000 French police in which 12,884 persons are arrested. They are transported by bus to the Vélodrome d'Hiver, a sports arena south of the Eiffel Tower, from where they go to the concentration camp at Drancy. Only 400 eventually survive.

AUGUST 1942

6 – The inaugural exhibition opens at the Musée National d'Art Moderne at the Palais de Tokyo. Picasso is not included among the many modern artists shown.

SEPTEMBER 1942

Fritz René Vanderpyl's *L'Art sans patrie, un mensonge: Le pinceau d'Israël* is published (Paris: Mercure de France), a Fascist attack on Jewish art and, by way of association, Picasso and cubism.

The second volume (parts 1 and 2) of *Pablo Picasso*, Zervos's catalogue raisonné of works by Picasso (1906–12 and 1912–17), is printed in Paris for *Cahiers d'Art* (first volume published in 1932).

13 – Picasso dines with Dora, André-Louis Dubois, and Cocteau at the Paris home of the wealthy Argentinean couple Marcello and Hortensia Anchorena, who commissioned a painted door from Picasso that he never delivered.

4 – A labor conscription law for Service du travail obligatoire (STD) is passed, requiring all fit males between 18 and 50 and single women from 20 to 35 to be available for work. Protest strikes and demonstrations follow.

20 – The first issue of the clandestine *Les Lettres françaises* is published by mimeograph.

OCTOBER 1942

Works by Picasso ("maquettes de ballets") are included in an exhibition of recent acquisitions at the Bibliothèque Nationale.

3 – Maurice Toesca, a writer working for the French police, visits Picasso's studio with the publisher Flammarion. Picasso later provides illustrations for a book by Toesca.

NOVEMBER 1942

Two poems by Picasso appear in the literary magazine *Confluence*, published in the Free Zone in Lyon.

30 – Picasso renews his *carte d'identité d'étranger,* for which the Statut des Juifs compels him to sign an affirmation that he is not Jewish. In an effort to avoid the normal official channels, which might arouse the attention of antagonists at the Spanish embassy, Picasso seeks the aid of Toesca, who through his job at the prefecture is able to expedite the renewal.

8 – In Operation Torch, the Allies invade French North Africa.

11 – German forces seize the unoccupied zone in France.

DECEMBER 1942

12-13 – In the sale of the Georges Viau collection by Etienne Ader at the Hôtel Drouot, two paintings by Picasso fetch the extraordinarily high prices of 1,610,000 and 1,300,000 francs.

10 – Hitler orders the arrest and deportation from France of all Jews and other enemies of the Reich.

JANUARY 1943

A painting by Picasso is included in the exhibition *Fleurs et fruits depuis le romantisme* at the Galerie Charpentier.

German authorities require the provision of 250,000 workers as supplement to the STD.

5 – Electricity is rationed in Paris.

11 - 30 – Metro stations are closed.

30 –Joseph Darnard creates the Milice, a paramilitary police force of Frenchmen organized to fight the *maquis.*

31 – After severe losses in the Battle of Stalingrad, Field Marshal Friedrich von Paulus of Germany surrenders his Sixth Army to Russia's Marshal Georgy Zhukov, marking a decisive turning point in the war.

MARCH 1943

Picasso makes his last dated drawings for *Man with a Lamb*. Although Brassaï later quoted Picasso as saying that he modeled the sculpture in February, it must date from March or soon after. Picasso told Brassaï that he completed it in clay in one session with the help of Marcel and Eluard, but the mass of clay was too heavy for the armature, began to collapse and had to be tied to the ceiling beam for support. To preserve it, Picasso later had it cast in plaster in two halves for greater ease of handling.

Freundlich, who had been arrested at St.-Paul-de-Fenouillet and then interned at Drancy before deportation, dies at the camp at Majdanek in Poland.

Picasso in his rue des Grands-Augustins studio with the two sculptures *Head of Dora Maar* and *Man with a Lamb,* September 1944. Photograph by Robert Capa.

APRIL 1943

16 – Nazis reportedly order a painting by Picasso at the Galerie Charpentier removed from exhibition.

28 – While dining at Le Catalan with Picasso and Hugnet, the writer Léon-Paul Fargue suffers a stroke that leaves him partially paralyzed. Picasso notifies Fargue's wife, Chériane, of the attack.

The Vichy government deports to Germany former government and military leaders Léon Blum, Edouard Daladier, Georges Mandel, Paul Reynaud, and General Gustave-Maurice Gamelin.

MAY 1943

Picasso meets Françoise Gilot at Le Catalan, where she is dining with a friend named Geneviève and the actor Alain Cuny. She becomes a regular visitor to his studio.

27 – The first meeting of the Conseil national de la Résistance is held, with Jean Moulin in charge.

27 – According to Rose Valland, a staff member attached to the Musée du Jeu de Paume who secretly kept accounts of confiscated art works, the Occupation authorities organize a massive burning of "degenerate" art in the Tuileries, including works by Picasso, Miró, Max Ernst, André Masson, Klee, and Léger.

JULY 1943

Works by Picasso are added to a long-running exhibition of contemporary painting at the Galerie Art du Printemps, 64, boulevard Haussmann.

Françoise leaves Paris for Fontès, near Montpellier in the Free Zone, and does not see Picasso again until November.

23 – Picasso is visited at his studio by the dealer Martin Fabiani and makes five portrait drawings of him.

10 – Allied forces land in Sicily.

25 – Benito Mussolini is relieved of power in Rome by order of Victor Emmanuel, king of Italy, who has been restored to command of the armed forces by the Fascist Grand Council. Mussolini is put in protective custody but later released by the Germans.

AUGUST 1943

9 – From his secluded home in Champigny-sur-Vende, Chaim Soutine is rushed to Paris by his companion Marie-Berthe Aurenche for an operation. He dies of a perforated ulcer. Picasso and Cocteau attend the funeral.

Having broken off all relations with the Vichy government, the Allies formally recognize the Comité français de libération nationale, presided over by de Gaulle.

Kahnweiler's house at St.-Léonard-de-Noblat is searched by the gestapo, on a tip that he was hiding arms. He and his wife flee to a village in the Lot-et-Garonne.

SEPTEMBER 1943

Brassaï visits Picasso's studio late in September to begin photographing sculptures for a book by Les Editions du Chêne, which was eventually published in 1948 as *Les Sculptures de Picasso* (Paris) with a text by Kahnweiler. He remarks upon the large number of bronzes that had been cast in recent years. Picasso gives him the somewhat suspicious story that friends moved the plasters to the foundry and the bronzes back to the studio by hand carts, at night, "right under the nose of the German patrols."

16 – A letter is sent to Picasso from German authorities (Office de placement allemand) ordering him to report on 20 September for physical and aptitude examinations, in preparation for deportation to Essen as part of the forced labor program. Although it is not known for sure how Picasso is able to evade this summons, he possibly receives aid from the German sculptor Breker.

3 – Italy signs an armistice with the Allies. German troops occupy Northern and Central Italy.

3 – Bombing raids continue on Paris, but now the Left Bank is hit as well as the suburbs.

25 – A special exhibition of Braque's work is included in the Salon d'Automne held at the Palais des Beaux-Arts. Matisse exhibits four works including *Tulips and Oysters on a Black Background,* which he subsequently gives to Picasso. Until 31 October.

OCTOBER 1943

12 – The publisher of Les Editions du Chêne, Maurice Girodias, visits Picasso's studio with Brassaï and insults him by suggesting that a bird assemblage is an "object" rather than a "sculpture."

19 – Zervos discusses with Picasso the possibility of publishing a group of his drawings, eventually resulting in the facsimile publication in 1948 of one of the Royan sketchbooks by *Cahiers d'Art.*

NOVEMBER 1943

Françoise returns to Paris and resumes her visits to Picasso's studio. During one of them, she meets André Malraux as he takes a respite from action with the *maquis.* She continues to live at her grandmother's house in Neuilly.

By 12 November, the rationing inspectors make an unexpected visit to Le Catalan and catch Picasso and others eating chateaubriands on a meatless day. The patrons are forced to pay fines, and the restaurant is closed for a month.

9 – At the annual commemoration of Apollinaire's death at Père-Lachaise Cemetery, Picasso refuses to shake hands with his former friend, André Salmon, because of his pro-Franco stance as a writer for the *Petit Parisien*.

DECEMBER 1943

The book on recent work by Picasso entitled *Picasso: Seize peintures 1939–1943,* with a text by Desnos, is published in Paris by Les Éditions du Chêne.

Portraits of Apollinaire by Picasso are included in the exhibition *Le Temps d'Apollinaire* at the Galerie René Breteau, 70, rue de Bonaparte.

24 – Brassaï makes his last visit until April 1944 to Picasso's studio to photograph the sculptures. As an ex-officer of the Romanian army, he has been mobilized by the Germans and must go into hiding.

FEBRUARY 1944

24 – Max Jacob is arrested at the abbey of St.-Benoît-sur-Loire, where he is a lay brother, and is sent to the concentration camp at Drancy. He dies there of pneumonia on 5 March. There is a question about how and when Picasso first learns of the arrest, but the statement often attributed to him–"Max is an elf. He doesn't need us to fly out of his prison"–may be apocryphal. Cocteau prepares, in league with the collaborationist publisher Georges Prade, a petition to the German embassy on Jacob's behalf, but it is not known who signed it and if it ultimately was sent. Picasso attends the mass for Jacob at St.-Roch on 21 March, after it had been postponed from the 18th. Also in attendance are Braque, Salmon, Derain, Eluard, Pierre Reverdy, and Cocteau, among others.

MARCH 1944

19 – Friends of Picasso present a reading of *Le Désir attrapé par la queue* at the apartment of the Leirises at 53 bis, quai des Grands-Augustins, around the corner from Picasso's studio. Albert Camus directs and roles are acted by Michel and Louise Leiris, Zanie and Jean Aubier, Simone de Beauvoir, Jean-Paul Sartre, Dora, Germaine Hugnet, Raymond Queneau, and Jacques-Laurent Bost. Georges Hugnet prepares the musical accompaniment. Over a hundred people are crowded together in the audience, including Brassaï, Braque and his wife, Valentine Hugo, Jacques Lacan, Sabartés, Reverdy, Jean-Louis Barrault, Georges and Sylvia Bataille, Toesca, Dubois, Henri Michaux, and Lucienne and Armand Salacrou. Picasso displays a portrait of Jacob during the proceedings. After the reading, Picasso escorts a group back to his studio and shows them an original manuscript by Alfred Jarry. Others remain at the Leiris apartment for dinner and extend the party beyond the curfew, through the whole night. Despite criticism of the play by some of Picasso's friends, the event generally is deemed a major success.

22 – Desnos is arrested. He is taken first to Fresnes then interned at Camp Royallieu in Compiègne before deportation to Flossenbürg. He dies of typhus on 8 June 1945 in a hospital at Terezín, Czechoslovakia, just days after liberation by the Russian army.

Participants in the reading of Picasso's play *Le Désir attrapé par le queue* in his studio, March 1944. Standing from the left: Jacques Lacan, Cécile Eluard, Pierre Reverdy, Louise Leiris, Zanie Aubier, Picasso, Valentine Hugo, Simone de Beauvoir. On the floor: Jean-Paul Sartre, Albert Camus, Michel Leiris, Jean Aubier, and Kazbek the dog. Photograph by Brassaï.

APRIL 1944

Brassaï resumes his visits to Picasso's studio. Allied bombing raids on Paris are proceeding day and night, and Brassaï reports that a painting by Picasso entitled *Still Life with Chinese Lantern* is hit by flying glass in the studio of Picasso's printer, Lacourière.

27 – At the request of the actor Jean Marais, Picasso burns a design into a broomstick for him to use as a scepter in his leading role in *Andromaque* at the Théâtre Edouard-VII.

The album *Vaincre* is published by the underground network Front national des arts, with graphics by artists including Fougeron, Goerg, Pignon, and Montagnac, to benefit the Francs-Tireurs and Partisans français, Resistance groups attached to the French Communist Party.

MAY 1944

Picasso is included in an exhibition entitled *L'Oeuvre et la palette de 1830 à nos jours* at the Galerie René Breteau, which includes artists' palettes with their works.

Numerous paintings and drawings of city views from this period show monuments such as bridges, the Vert Galant, and Notre Dame cathedral, near Picasso's studio.

5 – Brassaï begins working at Picasso's studio annex in the rue des Grands-Augustins, photographing sculptures stored there.

JUNE 1944

The exhibition *Picasso*, organized by the Sociedad de arte moderno at the Universidad Iberoamericana in Mexico City, contains fifty-five works.

14 – Picasso concludes an exchange with his paint manufacturer, trading a still life for a country house.

4 – Rome is occupied by the Allies.

6 – The Allies land at Normandy in Operation Overlord.

JULY 1944

Works by Picasso are included in the exhibition *Bains de mer* at the Galerie Paul Prouté, rue de Seine.

15 – Picasso is included in the inaugural exhibition of the Galerie Vendôme, place Vendôme, entitled *Maîtres de l'art indépendant.*

AUGUST 1944

19-25 – With intensifying street fighting between the Resistance (led by the Comité parisian de libération) and Vichy and German forces, Picasso moves to Marie-Thérèse's apartment in the boulevard Henri-IV to be with her and Maya. During these days, he works on two gouaches after Nicolas Poussin's *Triumph of Pan* as a personal celebration of the Liberation. He is back in his studio by 8 August, when he is visited by the first of many American and British journalists and soldiers who seek him out to pay tribute, conferring on him and his work a special heroic status.

25-27 – Picasso is commissioned to design the frontispiece for the commemorative book *Florilège des poètes et peintres de la Résistance,* presented to General de Gaulle upon his entry into Paris.

10-12 – French railroad workers go on strike.

15 – The Paris police go on strike, and the metro stops running.

25 – General Jacques Leclerc, commander of the French Second Armored Division, leads the first armed forces into Paris for its liberation. General Dietrich von Choltitz signs the surrender.

26 – De Gaulle arrives in Paris.

SEPTEMBER 1944

Picasso meets Geneviève Laporte, who visits his studio to research an article for her student newspaper. She attends the Lycée Fénelon in the rue de l'Eperon. His intermittent affair with her lasts for more than a decade.

3 – Picasso presides at a meeting in his studio of the Comité directeur du front national des arts (section peinture, sculpture, gravure), which includes among its members the artists Lhote, Goerg, Desnoyer, Grüber, Pignon, and Fougeron. The committee is authorized to present the Prefect of Police with a demand for the arrest and sentencing of collaborationist artists and critics. It calls for the arrest of Othon Friez, Paul Belmondo, Paul Landowski, Jacques Beltrand, Jean-Marc Campagne, and Camille Mauclair, and it sanctions Derain, Segonzac, Despiau, Legueult, Maillol, Vlaminck, and Oudot with exclusion from the next official salons.

4 – Picasso joins the French Communist Party (PCF) in a private ceremony at the offices of *L'Humanité,* the party newspaper. Marcel Cachin, director of *L'Humanité,* presides together with Jacques Duclos, secretary of the PCF. Aragon, Eluard, Fougeron, and Camus are also in attendance. This event is announced in *L'Humanité* on 5 October with front page coverage and an illustration of a drawing for *Man with a Lamb.*

4 or 5 – Picasso donates a still-life painting to the Musée de Saint-Etienne in recognition of the city's workers.

6 – The Salon d'Automne at the Palais des Beaux-Arts, popularly known as the Liberation Salon, features a special exhibition of seventy-four paintings and five sculptures by Picasso, all dating from recent years. In a reactionary manifestation against Picasso's work and his politics, a number of students precipitate a melee in the galleries, and several paintings are forcibly removed from the walls. Other young people counterreact by standing guard. A letter from Le Front national des étudiants, denouncing the attacks on Picasso, is published in *Marseillaise* on 12 October. A letter from the Comité national des écrivains in support of Picasso, published in *Les Lettres françaises* on 21 October, is signed by Eluard, Hugnet, Bost, Sartre, Queneau, Francis Ponge, Aragon, and Michel Leiris, among others. Until 15 November.

16 – With more than 100,000 participants at the Père-Lachaise Cemetery Picasso takes part in a ceremony to honor French intellectuals killed in the war and the more than 75,000 Nazi victims executed in the region of Paris.

24 – An interview with Picasso by Pol Gaillard, entitled "Why I Joined the Communist Party," is published in *New Masses.* A longer version of the same article appears in *L'Humanité* in the 29–30 October issue. Picasso states: "I have always been in exile, now I no longer am; until the day when Spain can welcome me back, the French Communist Party opened its arms to me, and I have found in it those that I most value. I am once more among my brothers."

Picasso supports various benefit events by donating works to be sold; these include a gala at the Théâtre de la Porte-Saint-Martin on 10 October in support of deported prisoners; a benefit at the Salle Pleyel on 23 October in support of families of Spanish victims of the war for France; and an exhibition opening 27 October on *La Presse clandestine* with a benefit sale at the Maison de l'Université Française.

The Kahnweilers return to Paris and move in with the Leirises.

9-20 — Winston Churchill meets with Josef Stalin in Moscow and agrees to Russian control of Eastern Europe and new boundaries for Poland.

[top]
Installation view of the Picasso exhibition at the Salon d'Automne, Paris, October–November 1944. Photograph by Marc Vaux.

[above]
Picasso and Paul Eluard leading a procession in the ceremony at Père-Lachaise Cemetery to honor Nazi victims in the region of Paris, 16 October 1944.

NOVEMBER 1944

Picasso is named honorary chairman of the Comité des amis de l'Espagne, formed to aid Spanish refugees and anti-Franco political efforts.

Picasso is included in the exhibitions *Maîtres et jeunes de l'art indépendant* at the Galerie de France and *Paris* at the Galerie Charpentier. He donates works for benefit sales at a gala *cinématographique* at the Palais de Chaillot on 10 November to support social services of the Forces françaises de l'intérieur, and at the Hôtel Drouot on 17 November, also to support the FFI.

2 – Picasso and Eluard are part of a delegation formed to honor war victims in the Resistance.

3 – Picasso attends an *Hommage à Max Jacob,* presented by Michel Leiris at the Théâtre des Mathurins.

11 – Armistice Day is celebrated.

DECEMBER 1944

18 – Eluard's book *A Pablo Picasso* is printed for Editions des Trois Collines, Geneva and Paris; it is distributed for sale later in 1945.

13 – Vassily Kandinsky dies in Paris.

JANUARY 1945

Picasso is included in an exhibition of still-life paintings at Galerie Visconti and in drawings exhibitions at the Galerie Granoff and Galerie René Drouin.

27 – Auschwitz is liberated by the Russian army.

FEBRUARY 1945

Zervos photographs Picasso's painting *The Charnel House* (cat. no. 82) in an early state and continues to photograph it as work progresses.

Picasso is included in a show at the Galerie Martin Fabiani to benefit the American cabaret group Stage Door Canteen and in an exhibition at the Galerie Drouin to benefit Soviet prisoners and deportees. His painting *The Cock* sells there for 500,000 francs. He is mentioned in news stories as a candidate for a new government program called "service of artists at war," in which artists would serve the war effort by working on war-related themes.

27 – An exhibition of Picasso's work at the Buchholz Gallery in New York shows paintings and drawings from a private collection. Until 17 March.

4 – 11 – The Big Three meetings between Franklin D. Roosevelt, Churchill, and Stalin take place in Yalta.

MARCH 1945

Picasso is included in an exhibition of modern art at the Galerie Parvillée and *Sculptures d'aujourd'hui* at the Galerie Drouin.

24 – In an interview with Simon Téry in *Les Lettres françaises* ("Picasso n'est pas officier dans l'armée française") in response to the "service of artists at war" initiative, Picasso makes the well-known statement that painting "is an offensive and defensive instrument of war against the enemy."

22 – 23 – Allied armies under General George Patton cross the Rhine.

APRIL 1945

3 – Allied armies cross the Rhine.

12 – Roosevelt dies and Harry S. Truman takes office.

27 – Mussolini is arrested and executed one day later.

29 – American forces enter the concentration camp at Dachau.

30 – Hitler commits suicide.

MAY 1945

Boris Kochno visits Picasso's studio. Ballet director for Jacques Prévert's *Le Rendez-vous*, he chooses a painting of a candlestick and mask to serve as the curtain design.

15 – Malraux visits Picasso at his studio.

Zervos publishes a special edition of *Cahiers d'Art* (nos. 15–19), his first since the beginning of the war, dedicated to art made in France from 1940 to 1944, with special emphasis on the work of Picasso.

25 – Picasso is represented with nine works in *Le Cubisme 1911–1918* at the Galerie de France. Until 30 June.

5 – Denmark is liberated.

7-8 – The German army surrenders at Reims and Berlin.

7 – VE Day is celebrated.

JUNE 1945

At its Tenth Congress, the French Communist Party honors Picasso, but also declares its support of realism in art.

Newspaper announcements list Picasso on the board of directors of the Communist-sponsored book *Encyclopédie de la renaissance française*.

15 – *Le Rendez-vous*, with curtain based on a painting by Picasso, sets by Brassaï, and choreography by Roland Petit, is performed by the Ballets des Champs-Elysées at the Théâtre Sarah Bernhardt. Picasso attends the opening with Brassaï and his wife and Dora. His curtain receives a mixed reaction.

20 – An exhibition of *Peintures récentes* by Picasso takes place at the Galerie Louis Carré, organized in conjunction with the Comité France-Espagne to benefit Spanish relief efforts. It includes twenty-one works and is accompanied by the catalogue *Picasso libres: 21 peintures, 1940–1945*. Until 3 July.

[above]
Victims of the German concentration camp at Buchenwald, 1945. Photograph by Lee Miller.

[below]
Installation view of the Picasso exhibition at the Galerie Louis Carré, June 1945.

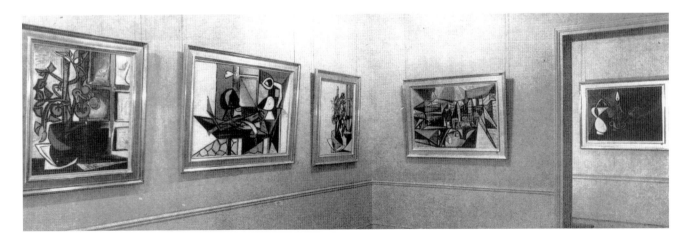

JULY 1945

Picasso leaves for Cap d'Antibes with Dora, where they stay with Marie Cuttoli. Françoise goes to Brittany, although Picasso arranges a room for her at Golfe-Juan at the house of Louis Fort. With Dora, he visits Ménerbes, where he had acquired a house by trading a painting. At some point he gives the house to Dora. He does not see Françoise again until 26 November.

Picasso is represented in *Portraits français* at the Galerie Charpentier and *Le Pathétique dans l'art* at the Galerie Jan-Marc Vidal.

17 – The Potsdam Conference between Stalin, Truman, and Churchill (and later Clement Attlee) results in agreement on the partition of Germany and the German-Polish border. Until 7 August.

AUGUST 1945

Picasso returns to Paris.

6 and **9** – Atomic bombs are dropped on Hiroshima and Nagasaki.

15 – Emperor Hirohito announces the surrender of Japan.

SEPTEMBER 1945

The dealer Martin Fabiani is arrested for doing business with Germans during the Occupation. Picasso reportedly had received a painting from him by Henri Rousseau, which left the Wertheimer collection under suspicious circumstances. Newspaper articles report that he is slated to give testimony.

28 – Two paintings by Picasso are shown in the Salon d'Automne, which features a retrospective exhibition of work by Matisse. Until 29 October.

NOVEMBER 1945

2 – Picasso begins to work in the lithographic workshop of Fernand Mourlot, whom he met through Braque. He returns regularly for four months and produces over 200 lithographs there over the next three and a half years.

26 – Françoise visits Picasso's studio for the first time since July.

13 – After a constitutional referendum, de Gaulle is elected head of the provisional government of France. He forms a coalition government on 21 November.

DECEMBER 1945

Picasso begins work on his large painting *Monument to the Spanish Who Died for France* (Monument aux Espagnols morts pour la France) (cat no. 83). According to certain sources, he shows this work (*hors catalogue*) together with the *Charnel House* in the Communist-sponsored exhibition *Art et résistance* in February and March 1946 at the Musée National d'Art Moderne.

By **14** – An *Exhibition of Paintings by Picasso and Matisse* opens at the Victoria and Albert Museum in London, with twenty-five works by Picasso dating between 1939 and 1945, and a catalogue essay on Picasso by Zervos. It unleashes a storm of public controversy. In an amended form, it travels next to the Palais des Beaux-Arts in Brussels, opening in May 1946.

Sometime during the winter of 1945–46 Picasso travels to Toulouse with Sabartés. There he visits the Varsovie hospital, which was established for Spaniards wounded in the civil war and which Picasso supports financially.

Notes

Picasso, War, and Art
Steven A. Nash

1. The first quotation comes from a statement sent by Picasso to the American Artists' Congress in New York, which was published in the *New York Times,* 18 December 1937; reprinted in Alfred Barr, *Picasso: Fifty Years of His Art* (New York: The Museum of Modern Art, 1946), 264. The second statement is derived from an interview published by Téry in "Picasso n'est pas officier dans l'armée françaises," *Les Lettres françaises* 5, no. 48 (24 March 1945): 6. This interview is often quoted as a manifesto of Picasso's views concerning the sociopolitical purposes of art: "Que croyez-vous que soit un artiste? Un imbécile qui n'a que des yeux s'il est peintre, des oreilles s'il est musicien ou une lyre à tous les étages du coeur s'il est poète. . . . Bien au contraire, il est en même temps un être politique, constamment en éveil devant des déchirants, ardents ou doux événements du monde, se façonnant de toute pièce à leur image. . . . Non, la peinture n'est pas faite pour décorer les appartements. C'est un instrument de guerre offensive et défensive contre l'ennemi."

2. Peter D. Whitney, "Picasso is Safe," *San Francisco Chronicle,* 3 September 1944.

3. Pierre Daix, *La Vie de peintre de Pablo Picasso* (Paris: Editions du Seuil, 1977), 322: "Tu vois, une casserole aussi, ça peut crier . . . Tout peut crier. Une simple bouteille. Et les pommes de Cézanne!"

4. Françoise Gilot and Carlton Lake, *Life with Picasso* (New York: McGraw-Hill, 1964), 46.

5. Michèle Cone, *Artists under Vichy: A Case of Prejudice and Persecution* (Princeton, N. J.: Princeton University Press, 1992), 34; quoted from Edith Thomas.

6. See note 1.

7. Roland Penrose, *Picasso: His Life and Work* (Berkeley and Los Angeles: University of California Press, 1981), 48. Daniel-Henry Kahnweiler later noted: "Picasso was the most apolitical man I have known. . . . He had never thought about politics at all, but the Franco uprising was an event that wrenched him out of this quietude and made him a defender of peace and liberty." *My Galleries and Painters,* trans. Helen Weaver (London: Thames and Hudson, 1971), 108. For an overview of the debate concerning political content in Picasso's earlier art, see Gertje Utley, "Picasso and the 'Parti' de la Renaissance Française: The Artist as a Communist, 1944–1953" (Ph.D. diss., Institute of Fine Arts, New York University, 1997), 38

8. Sidra Stich, in "Picasso's Art and Politics in 1936," *Arts Magazine* 58 (October 1983): 113–18, places Picasso's work from 1936 into the context of political and social events associated with the leftist Front populaire in France and the rise of fascism in Germany, Italy, and Spain.

9. See the drawing of 5 April 1936 in Zervos VIII, 276.

10. Zervos VIII, 285, 286, 287.

11. Zervos VIII, 321, 322, 323.

12. This work is discussed by Ludwig Ullmann in *Picasso und der Krieg* (Bielefeld: Karl Kerber Verlag, 1993), 73–74, and also by Franz Meyer in "Picasso und die Zeitgeschichte," *Picasso im Zweiten Weltkrieg,* exh. cat. (Cologne: Museum Ludwig, 1988), 93–94.

13. See, for example, his *Procession in Valencia* of ca. 1810–12 (Pierre Gassier and Juliet Wilson, *Goya: His Life and Work* [London: Thames and Hudson, 1971], 249 and cat. no. 952), and his *Procession of Flagellants* (ibid., cat. no. 967). Many affinities exist between the *Dream and Lie of Franco* and Goya's two series of etchings the *Disasters of War* and *Los Proverbios.* Compare, for example, Picasso's scene of Franco tightrope walking with a giant phallus and religious banner and Goya's plate entitled *Que se rompe le cuerda* (ibid., cat. no. 1128). The folio edition of the etchings included a sheet of poetry by Picasso.

14. The clearest interpretations of meaning and possible sources remain those by Anthony Blunt in *Picasso's Guernica* (London and New York: Oxford University Press, 1969), 9–13, and Ullmann, *Picasso,* 66–73. On the possible influence of political cartoons, see Phyllis Tuchman, "Guernica and *Guernica,*" *Artforum* 21, no. 8 (April 1983): 44–51. In an interview with Georges Sadoul at his studio in early summer 1937, Picasso said of the *Dream and Lie of Franco:* "C'est . . . un 'acte d'exécration de l'attentat dont est victime le peuple espagnol.' Cet album on me demandé pour le vendre au profit du peuple espagnol et je l'ai fait bien volontiers. Je n'avais l'intention de faire que deux ou trois eaux-fortes. Et puis cela m'est venu je ne sais comment, j'en ai fait beaucoup." In "Une demi-heure dans l'atelier de Picasso," *Regards* (29 July 1937): 8.

15. On Picasso's interest in Jarry, see John Richardson, with Marilyn McCully, *A Life of Picasso,* vol. 1 (New York: Random House, 1991), esp. 359–67.

16. Reproduced in, among other sources, Sidra Stich, *Anxious Visions: Surrealist Art* (Berkeley: University of California Press, 1990), pl. 67. Picasso met Dora Maar late in 1935; they became lovers soon after.

17. The Museum of Modern Art Archives, New York: Alfred H. Barr Jr. Papers; box 16, subgroup 8, series B2; quoted in Barr, *Fifty Years,* 264.

18. See Musée Picasso I, M.P. 1155, 1157, 1162.

19. The most thorough reconstructions of the development of *Guernica* through its many preparatory studies are found in Jean-Louis Ferrier, *De Picasso à Guernica: Généalogie d'un tableau* (Paris: L'Infini, Denoël, 1985), passim; Herschel Chipp, *Picasso's Guernica: History, Transformations, Meanings* (Berkeley, Los Angeles, and London: University of California Press, 1988), 58–135; Judi Freeman, *Picasso and the Weeping Women: The Years of Marie-Thérèse Walter & Dora Maar,* exh. cat. (New York: Los Angeles County Museum of Art, 1994), 32–81; and Ullmann, *Picasso,* 80f. Chipp reproduces the studies of the artist and model in pls. 5.26, 5.33–38, and those including the *Orator* in pls. 5.38 and 5.43.

20. The architect Josep Lluis Sert, designer of the Spanish Pavilion, reported that Picasso said to him early in June, "I don't know when I will finish it [the mural], maybe never. You had better come and take it whenever you need it." The typescript of a statement by Sert at the symposium on *Guernica* held at the Museum of Modern Art on 25 November 1947, including this quote, is found in the Alfred Barr Papers; quoted by Freeman, *Weeping Women,* 60, and Chipp, *Guernica,* 135 and 218 n. 20, who reports that Sert repeated this account in conversations with him in December 1978. Photographs of Picasso inside the Spanish Pavilion at the time of *Guernica*'s installation in mid-June are published by Catherine Blanton Freedberg in *The Spanish Pavilion at the Paris World's Fair* (New York: Garland, 1986).

21. For example, the large *Milliner's Workshop* of January 1926 in the Musée National d'Art Moderne, Paris (reproduced in William Rubin, ed., *Pablo Picasso: A Retrospective,* exh. cat. [New York: The Museum of Modern Art, 1980], 262).

22. The question of the symbolism of the horse and bull is discussed most recently by Brigitte Léal in "'Le taureau est un taureau, le cheval est un cheval': Picasso, peintre d'histoire, de *Guernica* au *Charnier,*" in *Face à l'histoire,* exh. cat. (Paris: Centre Georges Pompidou, 1996), 142–49. Picasso told Jerome Seckler that "the *Guernica* mural is symbolic . . . allegoric. That's the reason I used the horse, the bull, and used symbolism." He further elaborated: "Yes, the bull there represents brutality, the horse the people. . . . the bull is not fascism, but it is brutality and darkness." Quoted in "Picasso Explains," *New Masses* 54, no. 11 (13 March 1945): 4–7. In a letter to Alfred Barr written in May 1947, however, Kahnweiler quotes Picasso as saying, "But this bull is a bull and this horse is a horse. . . . It's up to the public to see what it wants to see." (MoMA Archives: AHB Papers; letter read at the symposium on *Guernica* held at the Museum of Modern Art on 25 November 1947; quoted by Dore Ashton, *Picasso on Art: A Selection of Views* [New York and Harmondsworth: Penguin Books, 1977], 155.)

23. Between January and November of 1937, Picasso made nearly sixty individual works on the theme of the Weeping Woman. For the most inclusive study of this theme, see Freeman, *Weeping Women,* passim.

24. See André Malraux, *Picasso's Mask* (New York: Holt, Rinehart and Winston, 1976), 138, and Gilot and Lake, *Life with Picasso,* 122: "I couldn't make a portrait of [Dora Maar] laughing. For me she's the weeping woman. For years I've painted her in tortured forms, not through sadism, and not with pleasure, either; just obeying a vision that forced itself on me."

25. Brigitte Baer, *Picasso: Gravures 1900–1942,* exh. cat. (Paris: Musée Picasso,

1996), 48. Roland Penrose describes a visit with Picasso's mother, during which she reported the incident of a burning convent near her apartment, in *Scrap Book, 1900–1981* (New York: Rizzoli, 1981), 85.

26. A photograph of this sculpture is reproduced by Rosamond Bernier, *Matisse, Picasso, Miro as I Knew Them* (New York: Knopf, 1991), 147, who also quotes Picasso on the origin of the work as a flea market bust of Venus that Picasso's father reworked with plaster and then painted.

27. Baer, *Gravures,* 52, and her essay in this volume.

28. On Picasso's connections with the Republican government, and his support of different relief efforts, see Chipp, *Guernica,* 7 f.; Cone, *Artists Under Vichy,* 151–52; Utley, "Picasso and the 'Parti,'" 53–54, 57–59. Alfred Barr quotes Mary Callery, purchaser of the important painting *Woman with a Cock,* as saying that Picasso did not wish to sell the work but agreed to do so only because he wanted to raise money for Spanish aid. (*Fifty Years,* 265.) In fall 1938, Picasso sent *Guernica* for exhibition in England under the auspices of the National Joint Committee for Spanish Relief.

29. Penrose, *Life,* 324, reported that he went to Picasso's apartment and saw the recently finished *Night Fishing at Antibes* on the night after Hitler's invasion of Poland. He must have been mistaken in his dates, however, since Jaime Sabartés recorded Picasso's departure from Antibes on 26 August (*Picasso: An Intimate Portrait* [New York: Prentice Hall, 1948], 182–83).

30. For reviews of the considerable literature on this painting, see William Rubin, *Picasso in the Collection of the Museum of Modern Art* (New York: The Museum of Modern Art, 1972), 232–33, and Timothy Anglin Burgard, "Picasso's *Night Fishing at Antibes:* Autobiography, Apocalypse, and the Spanish Civil War," *Art Bulletin* 68, no. 4 (December 1986); esp. 656 n. 1.

31. Harriet and Sidney Janis, *Picasso: The Recent Years 1939–1946* (Garden City, N.Y.: Doubleday, 1946), text to pl. 5.

32. These towers are generally described in literature on the painting as both belonging to the château Grimaldi, but this is not the case.

33. A suggestion first made by George Levitine; the painting is reproduced in Rubin, *Museum of Modern Art,* 233.

34. On the painting and engravings after it, see *Anniversary Exhibition,* exh. cat. (London: Trafalgar Galleries, 1996), cat. no. 3.

35. Christian Zervos, *L'Art de la catalogne de la seconde moitié du neuvième siècle à la fin du quinzième siècle* (Paris: Editions Cahiers d'Art, 1937), pl. 80, no. 133. A major exhibition on medieval Catalonian art entitled *L'Art catalan du Xe au XVe siècle* was presented at the Musée du Jeu de Paume in Paris in March and April of 1937, and Picasso served on the organizing committee.

36. Ibid., pl. 5. On the influence of Catalonian art on Picasso, see also Chipp, *Guernica,* 87–89, and Pierre Cabanne, *Pablo Picasso: His Life and Times* (New York: William Morrow, 1977), 77–78.

37. Lydia Gasman throws much new light on the question of Picasso's fear of aerial bombardment, and its reflection in his work, in her essay in this book. Sabartés brief comments on the painting are also illuminating vis-à-vis its underlying emotive message: "[Picasso] could not have refrained from expressing the heavy emotions and the increasingly tragic presentiments which hovered over us in those days." (Sabartés, *Intimate Portrait,* 181.)

38. See, for example, *Cheveaux et personnage* from 11 September 1939 in *Picasso: Die Sammlung Ludwig* (Munich: Prestel Verlag, 1993), cat. no. 39.

39. Léal, cat. no. 42, folios 3–9.

40. These sources are thoroughly analyzed in Jean Boggs, ed., *Picasso & Things,* exh. cat. (Cleveland: Cleveland Museum of Art, 1992), 263–64.

41. See Zervos X, 549–51.

42. Kahnweiler, *Galleries and Painters,* 118.

43. Bouguereau's famous *Birth of Venus* is illustrated, for example, in *William Bouguereau,* exh. cat. (Montreal: Montreal Museum of Fine Arts, 1984), cat. no. 89.

44. Sketchbook from 10 January to 26 May 1940, published in Léal, cat. no. 45; see folios 20–48; the motif continues into the sketchbook from March 1940 (ibid., cat. no. 44). The drawing dated 14 March 1940 is reproduced in Léal, cat. no. 44, folio 69V.

45. Ibid., cat. no. 43, folios 28–40.

46. Ibid., cat. no. 46, folio 11R. It is theorized that work on the canvas progressed in two phases, with a first, considerably different composition painted in March and a second added over the top in June. See Rubin, *Museum of Modern Art,* 234 n. 3.

47. Ibid., 158.

48. Published in Léal, cat. no. 42.

49. Rumors that Picasso had taken part in the Resistance movement began to circulate internationally at the time of the Liberation. Some of these rumors were put into writing, for example, by Alfred Barr in "Picasso 1940–1944: A Digest with Notes," *Museum of Modern Art Bulletin* 12, no. 3 (January 1945), where he notes that "[Picasso's] position in the Resistance Movement is of unique importance" (2), and that "[Picasso's] very existence in Paris encouraged the Resistance artists, poets and intellectuals who gathered in his studio or about his café table" (2). Other writers sympathetic to Picasso's postwar politics also have sought to fortify any possible linkage with the Resistance and paint an activist role for his art. Emile Szittya, for example, claims that "the works of Picasso, particularly those that he created during the Occupation, all demonstrate a barely concealed action against fascism" (in "Notes sur Picasso," *Courrier des arts et des lettres* [Paris, 1947], 24). Pierre Daix writes, "Il suffit dire que Picasso a été considéré par tous les résistants actifs–Eluard, Yvonne et Christian Zervos, . . . Louise et Michel Leiris qui hébergèrent le dirigeant communiste Laurent Casanova, Laurent Casanova lui-même–comme un des leurs par les idées et le courage" (*La Vie de peintre,* 296). For some of the false accusations of collaborationist activities, see Seckler, "Picasso Explains," 4. Utley lists more sources on this subject, "Picasso and the 'Parti,'" 60 and 111 n. 226.

50. It became a common ploy for Picasso's detractors during the war years to label him as Jewish or group him among artists negatively influenced by "Jewish" elements in modern art. For example, Fernand Demeure wrote, "Picasso, c'est le délire juif. Il a le don inné du pastiche et cette soif native de détruire, comme à tout fils ou demi-fils d'Israël" (in "Explications de quelques maîtres modernes," *Le Reveil du Peuple* [Paris, 29 March 1944]). The most famous denouncements of Picasso as a Jewish artist came in Fritz René Vanderpyl, *L'Art sans patrie, un mensonge: Le pinceau d'Israël* (Paris: Mercure de France, 1942); John Hemming Fry, *Art décadent sous le règne de la démocratie et du communisme* (Paris: Henri Colas, 1940); and Maurice de Vlaminck, "Opinions libres . . . sur la peinture," *Comoedia* 2, no. 50 (6 June 1942): 1, 6 (reprised in his *Portraits avant décès* [Paris: Flammarion, 1943], 181–89).

51. The letter from the Office de placement allemand dated 16 September 1943 instructing Picasso to appear for his preliminary examination and to sign a work contract was discovered in the archives of the Musée Picasso by Gertje Utley (see Utley, "Picasso and the 'Parti,'" 61). The letter reads in part: "you have been selected to leave as part of the program of voluntary workers to Germany. . . . We expect that you will understand your duty towards Europe and that . . . you will answer our appeal willingly. You are forewarned that any attempt at sabotage or any failing will be mercilessly punished." In 1941, Picasso had transformed press photographs propagandizing the work program in Germany into blistering parodies by drawing over them in pencil, changing the faces of happy workers into monstrosities. See Anne Baldassari, *Picasso and Photography: The Dark Mirror,* exh. cat. (Paris: Flammarion; Houston: Museum of Fine Arts, 1997), figs. 246–47.

52. André-Louis Dubois, *A travers trois républiques: Sous le signe de l'amitié* (Paris: Plon, 1972), 144: "Des bruits circulaient que répercutait Maurice Toesca [another friend of Picasso's]. Nous voulions que Picasso reste invisible pour que personne ne pense à lui, qu'il soit oublié."

53. For specific auctions, exhibitions, and dates, consult the Chronology in this book.

54. Jean Cocteau is one source for the report that a Picasso painting was ordered off of view. See *Journal 1942–1945* (Paris: Editions Gallimard, 1989), 298–99. Picasso repeated many times to friends and interviewers that he had been prohibited from exhibiting during the Occupation specifically due to a request by the Spanish Embassy to German authorities.

55. Sabartés, *Intimate Portrait,* passim, and Brassaï, *Picasso and Company,* trans. Francis Price (Garden City, N.Y.: Doubleday, 1966), passim.

56. See the accompanying Chronology for a list of participants. Several sources on Picasso's life during the war give listings of the participants and members of the audience, sometimes with slightly contradictory information. See, for example, Brassaï, *Picasso and Company,* 144–45;

Dubois, *A travers trois républiques,* 136; and Simone de Beauvoir, *La Force de l'âge* (Paris: Editions Gallimard, 1960), 583–85.

57. Different pieces of legislation passed after the beginning of the Occupation allowed for the confiscation of public sculptures, to be melted down for their bronze content. Even though it was highly illegal and risky, Picasso managed to have numerous works cast during the Occupation. Brassaï relates the rather suspicious story that Picasso's friends transported the new casts in handcarts from a clandestine foundry to Picasso's studio, at night and right under the noses of the Nazis (Brassaï, *Picasso and Company,* 49–51). In letters written in July and August of 1940, when Picasso was still living in Royan, Christian Zervos says he is looking after Picasso's sculptures and is waiting for the "uncle of Valsuany [*sic*]" to come to Paris so that other bronzes and plasters could be transported to Picasso's studio (letters of 24 July and 8 August 1940, Picasso Archives, Musée Picasso, Paris). This implies a relationship still active in 1940 with the Valsuani foundry, and may provide a clue about the casting of sculptures over the next few years. In his diaries, Cocteau reported that the famous *Head of a Bull* fashioned from a bicycle seat and handlebars had been newly cast as of 29 June 1942 (see *Journal,* 142, 171).

58. Gilot and Lake, *Life with Picasso,* 44–45.

59. Zervos informed Picasso of this development in a letter dated 24 July 1940, (Picasso Archives, Musée Picasso, Paris). He writes: "Sur la porte de vôtre appartment 23 rue La Boétie et sur celle de l'atelier Grds Augustins, l'ambassade d'Espagne a apposé des feuilles mettant ces deux locaux sous sa protection."

60. Soutine died on 4 August 1943 and Jacob on 24 February 1944. Hélène Seckel and André Cariou have laid to rest the old suspicions that Picasso willfully ignored the plight of his friend Jacob, when he was arrested by the Nazis. For an account of attempts led by Cocteau to intervene on Jacob's behalf, see *Max Jacob et Picasso,* exh. cat. (Paris: Musées des Beaux-Arts, and Paris: Musée Picasso, 1994).

61. Dubois, *A travers trois républiques,* 145; Gilot and Lake, *Life with Picasso,* 43–44.

62. Whitney, "Picasso is Safe," 3.

63. See note 50.

64. See note 50 for full reference. Vlaminck writes, in his attack on cubism: "Quelle duperie, n'est-ce pas, de vouloir pénétrer le sens divin du monde à l'aide de l'absurdité métaphysique d'une Kabale ou d'un Talmud? . . . Le Cubisme! Perversité de l'esprit, insuffisance, amoralisme, aussi éloigné de la peinture que la pédérastie de l'amour."

65. Maurice Toesca, *Cinq ans de patience (1939–1945)* (Paris: Editions Emile-Paul, 1975), 178–79.

66. Arno Breker, *Paris, Hitler et moi* (Paris: Presses de la Cité, 1970), 234–36. "C'est ainsi qu'on me signala que Picasso était sur le point d'être arrêté . . . Il aurait été un communiste actif et aurait tenté de faire passer en fraude des devises en Russie par le Danemark, et en Espagne." Breker also took credit for saving Maillol's Jewish model Dina Vierny. Cocteau confirmed that Breker had been of help to both him and Picasso: "C'est grâce à Breker que Picasso et moi avons étés sauvés du pire. Je ne l'oublierai jamais." From *Le Passé défini I, 1951–1952, Journal* (Paris: Editions Gallimard, 1983), 352.

67. Ernst Jünger, *Journal de guerre et d'occupation, 1939–1948* (Paris: René Julliard, 1965), 149–51, and Gerhard Heller, *Un Allemand à Paris: 1940–1944* (Paris: Editions du Seuil, 1981), 117–19. Heller tells of a German corporal named Hans Kuhn who visited Picasso at his studio and took many photographs (123). One German soldier is known to have bought from Picasso, through the dealer Jeanne Bucher, a drawing of a reclining nude. See "Ein Stuttgarter Sammler: Als Soldat bei Picasso in Paris," *Pablo Picasso in der Staatsgalerie Stuttgart,* exh. cat. (Stuttgart: Staatsgalerie Stuttgart, 1981), 36f. Picasso supposedly had an incriminating discussion with this soldier in which he is said to have expressed pleasure with the German-enforced curfew in Paris since it gave him more uninterrupted time for work, but this discussion, if it took place, is reported without any of the irony or sarcasm that it must have contained.

68. Picasso apparently told the story about Abetz to a number of different people. To a correspondent for *Newsweek,* however, he reported that the incident actually involved an unnamed German army officer ("Picasso and the Gestapo," *Newsweek* 24, no. 13 [25 September 1944]: 98, 100).

And with other interviewers, the story changed to Picasso handing out postcards of *Guernica* to German visitors as "souvenirs."

69. Gertje Utley disputes this possibility, underscoring the genuineness of Picasso's commitment to the Communist Party ("Picasso and the 'Parti,'" 64).

70. Brassaï, *Picasso and Company,* 65.

71. "Hommage à Pablo Picasso, qui vécut toujours de la vie de la France," *Les Lettres françaises* 4, no. 20 (9 September 1944) 8.

72. MoMA Archives: AHB Papers; 8, unit 3, letter of 28 March 1945; reprinted and translated in Cone, *Artists under Vichy,* 233–34.

73. Picasso's painting has been reproduced many times, starting with Janis and Janis, *Recent Years,* pl. 99, although the present whereabouts of the work are now unknown.

74. John Groth, "Letter from Paris," *Art Digest* 19 (1 December 1944): 9; Lee Miller, "In Paris . . . Picasso Still at Work," *Vogue* (15 October 1944): 98–99, 149–50, 155; John Pudney, "Picasso: A Glimpse in Sunlight," *The New Statesman and Nation* 28, no. 708 (16 September 1944): 182–83; Peter Whitney, "Picasso is Safe."

75. Utley, "Picasso and the 'Parti,'" 73.

76. By far the most thoroughly researched source on Picasso's involvement with the Communist Party, and the reflection of these commitments in his art, is Utley, ibid., passim. Fougeron claimed that the initial idea for honoring Picasso at the Salon d'Automne had no ulterior motives, and that even he was surprised to learn that Picasso was planning to join the Party (73).

77. Naturally, support for Picasso came most rapidly and most strongly from left-wing writers through the Communist-affiliated *Les Lettres françaises.* See, for example, André Lhote, "Le Salon d'Automne? Un rassemblement de la libre peinture," on 23 September, and Louis Parrot, "Picasso au Salon," on 7 October 1944; but also Georges Limbour, "Picasso au Salon d'Automne," *Le Spectateur des Arts,* no. 1 (December 1944): 4–8, and Regine Raufast, "Picasso au Salon d'Automne," *Formes et Couleurs* 6 (1944): 185–87.

78. For Picasso's various contributions to charities and involvement with different boards and committees, see the accompanying Chronology and also Utley, "Picasso and the 'Parti,'" 176–77, 209 no. 180–82. On the *épuration* proceedings against artists, see ibid., 123, 180 n. 9.

79. For Picasso's statement of why he joined the Communist Party, see Pol Gaillard's interview of Picasso published as "Why I Became a Communist," in *New Masses* 53, no. 4 (24 October 1944): 11, and in an expanded version in *L'Humanité* 41, no. 64 (29–30 October 1944): 1–2; reprinted in Barr, *Fifty Years,* 267–68. Picasso stated: "Mon adhésion au Parti communiste est la suite logique de toute ma vie, de toute mon oeuvre. . . . Je suis de nouveau parmi mes frères!"

80. On issues of nationalistic reaction in post-Liberation criticism, and perceptions of Picasso as an outsider, see Utley, "Picasso and the 'Parti,'" 118 n. 279, 231 f., and 278 n. 85.

81. "Picasso: The Painter Who Defied the Germans Finds Himself the Hero of a Revolutionary Mood," *New York Times Magazine* (29 October 1944), 18, 39.

82. "Picasso and Matisse," *Spectator,* no. 6129 (14 December 1945): 567.

83. For example, N. Bercovici, "Picasso and Mr. Ayrton," *Spectator,* no. 6130 (21 December 1945): 595, and H. Nicolson, "Afterthoughts Regarding the Picasso Controversy," *Spectator,* no. 6132 (4 January 1946): 10.

84. Zervos, "Pablo Picasso," *Exhibition of Paintings by Picasso and Matisse,* exh. cat. (London: British Council and Victoria and Albert Museum, 1945), 1–4.

85. Zervos XI, 92.

86. Heller, *Allemand,* 118: "Devant la *Nature morte au crâne de boeuf* il nous disait: 'J'ai peint cela la nuit, car je préfère en ce moment l'éclairage nocturne à l'éclairage naturel . . . Il faudrait que vous reveniez de nuit pour le voir!'"

87. See the interpretations given by Boggs in *Picasso & Things,* 268, and Brigitte Baer in her essay in the present catalogue. Zervos did not give the painting a precise date in his catalogue raisonné, but it is listed as "10 May 1941" in Janis and Janis, *Recent Years,* pl. 60. Any inscription it may have had on its reverse has been covered by a relining.

88. For some of the more simplistic still lifes of the period, see Zervos XXIII, 129–32, 223–28, 274–89. On the series of tomato plants, see the catalogue entry on one of these paintings in Boggs, *Picasso & Things,* 286.

89. Gilot and Lake, *Life with Picasso,* 120.

90. Malraux, *Picasso's Mask,* 138.

91. James Lord, *Picasso and Dora: A Personal Memoir* (New York: Farrar Straus Giroux, 1993), 121–22; Brassaï, *Picasso and Company,* 224. The painting is currently in the collection of Mr. Stephen Wynn, Las Vegas.

92. Georges Wildenstein, *Ingres* (London: Phaidon, 1954), cat. nos. 27 and 280.

93. Baer, *Gravures,* 59, and her essay in this volume.

94. Cowling in Elizabeth Cowling and John Golding, *Picasso: Sculptor/Painter,* exh. cat. (London: Tate Gallery, 1994), cat. no. 105, dates the sculpture to February or March 1943, based in part on Brassaï's assertion (Brassaï, *Picasso and Company,* 51). Picasso told Brassaï that he was aided in his work on the sculpture by Paul Eluard and his chauffeur Marcel. He modeled the form in clay in a single session. Because the armature was not strong enough to support the weight of the clay, however, the sculpture began to collapse and had to be held up with ropes tied to the ceiling. To stabilize it, Picasso had the work cast into plaster and it was this plaster, made in two sections for greater ease of handling, that stood in Picasso's studio for the remainder of the war and is now part of the collection of the Centro de Arte Reina Sofia in Madrid (ibid., 161). The animal in the sculpture is referred to in early sources, and by Picasso himself, as both "mouton" and "agneau." We have chosen to use the title *Man with a Lamb* because it better fulfills the sacrificial implications of the sculpture.

95. Quoted in Musée Picasso I, 145.

96. See Cowling and Golding, *Sculptor/Painter,* cat. no. 105, and Albert Elsen, "Picasso's Man with a Sheep: Beyond Good and Evil," *Art International* 21, no. 2 (March–April 1977): 8–15, 29–31. Recently, Phyllis Tuchman has proposed that the man in the sculpture is a portrait of Max Jacob. See "Picasso's Sentinel," *Art in America* 86, no. 2 (February 1998): 86–95.

97. See Zervos XIII, 59–64, 296–300; XIV, 101–108.

98. Pudney, "Picasso: A Glimpse," 182–83: "[Picasso] believes that outside events caused him to seek a greater objectivity. He said that the tendency in the creative artist is to stabilize mankind on the verge of chaos. 'A more disciplined art, less constrained freedom, in a time like this is the artist's defense and guard,' Picasso said. 'Very likely for the poet it is a time to write sonnets. Most certainly it is not a time for the creative man to fail, to shrink, to stop working.'" Gertje Utley discusses the painting in the context of the neonationalistic thinking that arose in France after the Liberation as a reassertion of traditional French values, a movement that included some factions highly critical of Picasso. "Picasso and the French Post-war 'Renaissance': A Questioning of National Identity," in *Picasso and the Spanish Tradition* (New Haven and London: Yale University Press, 1996), 107–108. For more on Picasso's bacchanal, see Susan Grace Galassi, in *Picasso's Variations on the Masters: Confronting the Past* (New York: Harry N. Abrams, 1996), 90–94.

99. Although the *Monument to the Spanish* does not appear in the exhibition catalogue, various writers who saw the show record its presence there. For example, see Daix, *La Vie de peintre,* 328, and Kahnweiler, *Galleries and Painters,* 120. On the iconography of the painting, see Utley, "Picasso and the 'Parti,'" 172–75 (who questions its inclusion in *Art et résistance*), and Cowling and Golding, *Sculptor/Painter,* cat. no. 114. Picasso owned a bugle very similar to the one in the painting, which he loved to blow. It is shown, complete with its tassels, in a photograph by Cecil Beaton of Picasso in his studio (Picasso Archives, Musée Picasso, Paris).

100. See Robert Rosenblum, "The Spanishness of Picasso's Still Lifes," in Jonathon Brown, ed., *Picasso and the Spanish Tradition* (New Haven and London: Yale University Press, 1996), 92–93.

101. Lord, *Picasso and Dora,* 325.

102. Discussion of the possible influence of news about the concentration camps is found in Utley, "Picasso and the 'Parti,'" 127 f., and Baldassari, *Photography,* 214, figs. 244 and 245. William Rubin, among others, wrote that Picasso had painted *Charnel House* in response to revelations of the camps (Rubin, *Museum of Modern Art,* 166). However, the fact that photographs of the camps and their victims taken during the Allied liberations did not appear until April 1945 after the painting was begun, has cast doubt on this assertion. Utley and Baldassari show, nevertheless, that Picasso was certainly aware of the camps and had even seen photographs of them well before starting work on *Charnel House.*

Picasso sought out Daix at one point, who was a survivor of a German concentration camp, to ask him how closely *Charnel House* matched the reality of the camps and exterminations (Daix, *La Vie de peintre,* 322).

103. See Rubin, *Museum of Modern Art,* 238–41, and Gertje Utley's essay in this volume for photographs of different stages of the painting's development and discussion of the dates involved. The most detailed account of this development is found in Utley, "Picasso and the 'Parti,'" 127 f.

104. Picasso exhibited the painting in *Art et résistance* in Paris in February and March of 1946. He agreed to donate it to the Communist veterans association to be sold to raise money but apparently desired to work on it further. He kept it for several more years before selling it in 1954. Although it is signed and dated 1945, he definitely worked on it later but seems to have made the last changes by April 1946.

105. Rubin (*Museum of Modern Art,* 169) discusses the expressive qualities of this lack of finish.

106. See Brassaï, *Picasso and Company,* 224, 257; and Pierre Daix, *Picasso Créateur: La Vie intime et l'oeuvre* (Paris: Editions du Seuil, 1987), 294–95.

107. Rubin, *Museum of Modern Art,* 166.

108. Gilot and Lake, *Life with Picasso,* 74.

109. "Picasso's *Guernica,*" *London Bulletin,* no. 6 (October 1938): 6.

Picasso's Disasters of War: The Art of Blasphemy
Robert Rosenblum

Some of the material in this essay was first given as a lecture at the Museo Nacional del Prado on 14 January 1996, and then published, in a Spanish translation, as "El *Guernica* de Picasso: El conjunto y las partes," in *El Museo del Prado: Fragmentos y detalles* (Madrid: Fundación Amigos del Prado, 1997), 175–90.

1. On Picasso's intentions for the eventual display of *Guernica* in Madrid, see the statement by his lawyer, Roland Dumas, in Ellen C. Oppler, ed., *Picasso's Guernica* (New York and London: Norton, 1988), 153–55.

2. The relationship between *Guernica* and Goya's *Third of May, 1808* and *Disasters of War* was already noted in 1937 by José Bergamín in "Le Mystère tremble: Picasso furioso," *Cahiers d'Art* 7, nos. 4–5 (1937): 137–39. Since then, the comparison of *Guernica* to Goya's war imagery has been made countless times in both general and specific ways. See, for example, Herschel B. Chipp, *Picasso's Guernica: History, Transformations, Meanings* (Berkeley, Los Angeles, and London: University of California Press, 1988), passim.

3. This plausible suggestion was made in Hugh Thomas, *Goya: The Third of May 1808* (New York: Viking Press, 1973), 94. The actual buildings depicted by Goya seem to elude precise identification.

4. "La lanterne, c'est la Mort." See André Malraux, *La Tête d'obsidienne* (Paris: Editions Gallimard, 1974), 42. Picasso also commented on the strange overall lighting of the painting, which resembled, but was different from, moonlight. For a fascinating study of Goya's lantern in the context of scientific invention and the symbolism of the Enlightenment, see Albert Boime, "La luz mortífera de Goya y la Ilustración," in *El Museo del Prado: Fragmentes y detalles,* 291-323. Boime also refers here to the parallel symbolism of the lightbulb in *Guernica.*

5. For some provocative comments on the newness of Goya's religious paintings, see Fred Licht, *Goya and the Origins of the Modern Temper in Art* (New York: Universe Books, 1979), ch. 3.

6. *Goya: Exposition de l'oeuvre gravé, de peintures, de tapisseries et de cent-dix dessins* (Paris: Editions des Bibliothèques Nationales, 1935).

7. On this drawing, see Josep Palau i Fabre, *Picasso: The Early Years, 1881–1907* (New York: Rizzoli, 1981), 92–93.

8. On this joke and its sources, see Temma Kaplan, *Red City, Blue Period: Social Movements in Picasso's Barcelona* (Berkeley: University of California Press, 1992), 55–56.

9. See the discussion in John Richardson, "Picasso's Apocalyptic Whorehouse," *New York Review of Books* 36, no. 7 (23 April 1987): 40–47.

10. The theme is fully studied in Suzanne L. Stratton, *The Immaculate Conception in Spanish Art* (Cambridge: Cambridge University Press, 1994)

11. I have already proposed this irreverent reference to El Greco's *Assumption* in "The Spanishness of Picasso's Still Lifes," in Jonathan Brown, ed., *Picasso and the Spanish Tradition* (New Haven and London: Yale University Press, 1996), 75–77. It should be added that the mixture of sacred and profane and the appearance of whores in heaven have ample precedence in Picasso's art, especially in the *Burial of Casagemas* (1901). On these matters, see especially Theodore Reff, "Themes of Love and Death in Picasso's Early Work," in *Picasso, 1881–1973,* eds. Roland Penrose and John Golding (London: Paul Elek, 1973), 11–47.

12. A less subtle fusion of virgin and whore in one Spanish image may be found in Ramón Casas' poster, *Sífilis,* an advertisement for a sanitarium offering cures for syphilis. The woman depicted holds the white lily of the Virgin Annunciate in her left (sinister) hand, while revealing behind the mantilla on her back that she holds in her right hand the snake from the Garden of Eden, the ultimate symbol of sexual temptation. It is illustrated in Marilyn McCully, *Els Quatre Gats: Art in Barcelona around 1900* (Princeton: Princeton University Press, 1978), 73.

13. For a telling comparison with T. S. Eliot's mixture of the imagery of aerial bombings with Catholic iconography, as well as for comments on related readings of the symbolism of *Guernica,* see James Leggio, "Alfred H. Barr Jr. as a Writer of Allegory: Art History in a Literary Context," in *The Museum of Modern Art at Mid-Century: Continuity and Change; Studies in Modern Art, no. 5* (New York: The Museum of Modern Art, 1995), 120-31.

14. The visual analogies between one particular page of the Beatus manuscripts, *The Deluge* in the *Apocalypse of Saint Sever,* and *Guernica* are often cited, probably first in Juan Larrea, *Guernica: Pablo Picasso* (New York: Curt Valentin, 1947), fig. 12. Larrea, in fact, offers in his text (written in 1945) many elaborately speculative readings of *Guernica* in the context of apocalyptic imagery, in particular, and Christian imagery, in general. Subsequently, Picasso's awareness and use of these Romanesque manuscripts, from the late 1920s on, became a frequent theme in the literature. For a compilation of useful references, see Timothy Anglin Burgard, "Picasso's *Night Fishing at Antibes:* Autobiography, Apocalypse, and the Spanish Civil War," *Art Bulletin* 68, no. 4 (December 1986): 656–72, especially notes 29–35.

15. Oppler, *Picasso's Guernica,* 100–1, points out a related cartoon by René Dubosc, published on the front page of *L'Humanité* (28 April 1937), which shows a dove of peace lying decapitated on a mock-Roman sacrificial altar serving fascist dictators.

16. Picasso's father's pigeons turn up often in the first three chapters of John Richardson, *A Life of Picasso, 1881–1906,* vol. 1 (New York: Random House, 1991), including a reference (52) to the 1912 cubist still life.

17. This painting is discussed in fascinating detail and, for the first time, in reference to its subliminal Christian readings in Jean Sutherland Boggs, *Picasso & Things,* exh. cat. (Cleveland: The Cleveland Museum of Art, 1992), no. 32.

18. On these still lifes and their reading as humanoid "disasters of war," see José López-Rey, "Goya's Still Lifes," *Art Quarterly* 11 (1948): 251–60; and William B. Jordan and Peter Cherry, *Spanish Still Life from Velázquez to Goya* (London: National Gallery Publications, 1995), 175–85.

19. On this painting, *Dog and Cock,* see the full discussion in Boggs, *Picasso & Things,* no. 78.

20. The richest and most sharp-eyed account of this extraordinary series is found in Judi Freeman, *Picasso and the Weeping Women: The Years of Marie-Thérèse Walter & Dora Maar,* exh. cat. (Los Angeles: Los Angeles County Museum of Art, 1994), where a passing reference is made to the Spanish tradition of the *mater dolorosa* (29).

21. On this drawing, see also ibid., 54.

22. See Roland Penrose, *Picasso: His Life and Work,* 2nd ed. (New York: Shocken Books, 1962), 275.

23. The story is told, and the work reproduced, in Rosamond Bernier, *Matisse, Picasso, Miró as I Knew Them* (New York: Alfred A. Knopf, 1991), 146–47.

24. The most extreme example of this kind of interpretation is found in the indefatigable multiple readings of every image in the painting by Melvin E. Belcraft in his *Picasso's Guernica: Images within Images* (Rohnert Park, California: Melvin E. Belcraft Publisher, 1981), with later revised editions and many epistolary postscripts.

25. For the fullest account of Grünewald's impact on Picasso, see Susan Grace Galassi, *Picasso's Variations on the Masters: Confronting the Past* (New York: Harry N. Abrams, 1996), ch. 3.

26. On Dix's triptych, see Fritz Löffler, *Otto Dix, Leben und Werk* (Dresden: Verlag der Kunst, 1960), 93–96.

27. On this and other newspaper accounts of the bombing in the French press, see especially Herbert R. Southworth, *Guernica! Guernica!: A Study of Journalism, Diplomacy, Propaganda, and History* (Berkeley: University of California Press, 1977) 407–8. For later accounts of the impact of newspaper accounts and illustrations on *Guernica,* see Phyllis Tuchman, "Guernica and *Guernica*," *Artforum* 21, no. 8 (April 1983): 44–51; and Chipp, *Picasso's Guernica,* ch. 4.

28. The often-repeated comparison with Poussin's and Reni's *Massacre of the Innocents* was probably first made in Anthony Blunt, *Picasso's "Guernica"* (London: Oxford University Press, 1969), 45, 47.

29. The works of Gutiérrez-Solana, with their recurrent Spanish themes and images of war and apocalyptic disaster, often offer foreshadowings of *Guernica* (as well as of the *Girl before a Mirror*). For the fullest account of his art, see José Luis Barrio-Garay, *José Gutiérrez Solana: Paintings and Writings* (Lewisburg, Pennsylvania: Bucknell University Press, 1978).

30. This source was first suggested by Dustin Rice, according to Joseph Masheck, "*Guernica* as Art History," *Art News* 66, no. 8 (December 1967): 66. Masheck, who includes many other art-historical sources for the painting (Poussin, Reni, Rubens, Ingres, etc.), then goes on to suggest that Saint Paul's conversion (Paul = Pablo) may allude to Picasso's "conversion" to the Communist Party. Picasso, incidentally, was quite aware of Caravaggio's *Conversion of Saint Paul* while painting *Guernica.* Dalí, who visited him then, recounts that Picasso said that he wanted the horse to be as realistic as in Caravaggio, so that you could smell the sweat, and joked that his younger compatriot, a master of hyperrealism, should paint the horse for him. See Carlton Lake, *In Quest of Dali* (New York: G. P. Putnam's Sons, 1969), 46. A related image, Saint George and the Dragon (in a painting by Vitale de Bologna), has also been proposed as a source for the horse in *Guernica.* See Manuela Mena Marqués, "Un precedente italiano en el *Guernica* de Picasso," *Actes de las I Jornadas de Arte organizadas por el Instituto "Diego Velázquez"* (Madrid: Consejo Superior de Investigaciones Científicas, 1982), 165–72.

31. Pointed out in Chipp, *Picasso's Guernica,* 127–28.

32. This remark, which may be apocryphal, is cited in Tomás Harris, *Goya: Engravings and Lithographs,* vol. 1 (Oxford: B. Cassirer, 1969), vii.

33. The comparison between this kneeling figure and Ingres's *Jupiter and Thetis* seems to go back to the late 1960s. See my *Jean-Auguste-Dominique Ingres* (New York: Harry N. Abrams, 1967), 23–24; and Blunt, *Picasso's "Guernica,"* 47.

34. As evidenced, for example, in the woman who looks up at the miracle-working Saint Anthony of Padua in the frescoes at San Antonio de la Florida, Madrid.

35. See above, note 14.

36. A Christian reading of the painting, involving references to the Crucifixion and animal sacrifice, has also been proposed in Mark Rosenthal, "Picasso's *Night Fishing at Antibes:* A Meditation on Death," *Art Bulletin* 65, no. 4 (December 1983): 649–58.

37. Illustrated in Burgard, "Night Fishing," 666.

38. Alfred H. Barr, Jr., ed., *Masters of Modern Art* (New York: The Museum of Modern Art, 1954), 94.

39. See Burgard, "Night Fishing," 669–70.

40. For further remarks on this painting, see *Picasso: The Love and the Anguish – The Road to Guernica,* exh. cat. (Kyoto: The National Museum of Modern Art, 1995), no. 109.

41. Boggs, *Picasso & Things,* nos. 103–5.

42. For the most recent interpretation of the proper identity of the animal and the sacrificial character of this sculpture, see Phyllis Tuchman, "Picasso's Sentinel," *Art in America* 86, no. 2 (February 1998): 86–94.

43. For the fullest discussion of Zurbarán's painting, of which there are several versions, see Jeannine Baticle, *Zurbarán* (New York: The Metropolitan Museum of Art, 1987), no. 52.

44. For a wide-ranging, erudite, and enjoyable account of Picasso's treatment of sheep, birds, and many other animals, see Neil Cox and Deborah Povey, *A Picasso Bestiary* (London: Academy Editions, 1995).

45. See Boggs, *Picasso & Things,* no. 104. I have also discussed the relevance of Goya's painting in "The Spanishness of Picasso's Still Life," 87-90.

46. For the earliest detailed description and analysis of the *Charnel House,* see William Rubin, *Picasso in the Collection of the Museum of Modern Art* (New York: The Museum of Modern Art, 1972), 166–69, where the date of the painting's inception is given as late 1944 rather than February 1945.

47. See Elizabeth Cowling and John Golding, *Picasso: Sculptor/Painter,* exh. cat. (London: The Tate Gallery, 1994), no. 44.

48. I have already suggested the relevance of Goya's *Ravages of War* in Rubin, *Picasso in the Collection,* 238 n. 7, fig. 161.

49. See Anne Baldassari, *Picasso and Photography: The Dark Mirror,* exh. cat. (Paris: Flammarion; Houston: The Museum of Fine Arts, 1997), 214, fig. 244.

50. Rubin, *Picasso in the Collection,* 166.

Death falling From The Sky: Picasso's Wartime Texts
Lydia Csató Gasman

In memory of my Icarus, Horel-Zwi.

1. Picasso, cited in Simone Gauthier, "Picasso, The Ninth Decade: A rare interview with the 86-year old master and his 40-years-younger wife," *Look* 20 (November 1967): 87–88.

2. Brassaï, *Picasso and Company,* trans. Francis Price (Garden City, N.Y., 1966), 40.

3. For relevant discussions of air power see: Eugene M. Emme, *The Impact of Air Power: National Security and World Politics* (Princeton: Van Nostrand, 1959); Jesús Salas Larrazábal, *Air War over Spain,* trans. Margaret A. Kelly (London: Allan, 1974); and R. J. Overy, *The Air War 1939–1945* (New York: Stein and Day, 1981).

4. Fresco attributed to Francesco Traini, before 1345, Camposanto in Pisa; see Millard Meiss, *Francesco Traini,* ed. Hayden B. J. Maginnis (Washington, D.C.: Decatur House Press, 1983), 40–43.

5. *Minotaure* 10 (winter 1937): 19.

6. Picasso, 1 May and 2 April 1938, cited in *Picasso: Collected Writings,* ed. Marie-Laure Bernadac and Christine Piot (New York: Abbeville Press, 1989), 195, 193. Unless otherwise specified, the English translations from Picasso's original Spanish and French texts cited in *Picasso: Collected Writings* are my own.

7. Inspired by "l'argot des poilus," bees were used to mean "bombs" and "airplanes" in Apollinaire's poems of World War I (J. G. Clark, "De fil en aiguille, complément à une étude," in *La Revue des lettres modernes*: *Guillaume Apollinaire* 15, 53*;* and Guillaume Apollinaire, *Calligrammes: Poems of Peace and War (1913–1916),* trans. Anne Hyde Greet (Berkeley: University of California Press, 1980), 249, 265.

8. For the "cognitive appraisal" of the danger represented by air raids, see Ronald A. Kleinknecht, *The Anxious Self: Diagnosis and Treatment of Fears and Phobias* (New York: Human Sciences Press, 1986), 20, 25; Kleinknecht's emphasis.

9. Marc Bloch, *Strange Defeat: A Statement of Evidence Written in 1940,* trans. Gerard Hopkins (New York: Oxford University Press, 1968), 57; Bloch's emphasis.

10. Ibid., 54.

11. Ibid., 56. Note that the English translation leaves out the adjective "hostile" that was attached to the sky in the original French text: "ciel hostile." Marc Bloch, *L'Etrange défaite: Témoignage écrit en 1940* (Paris: A. Michel, 1957), 84. See also Jean-Pierre Azéma, *1940, l'année terrible* (Paris: Seuil, 1990), 365; and Carole Fink, *Marc Bloch: A Life in History* (Cambridge: Cambridge University Press, 1989). Parallelling Bloch's phenomenological insights into aerial terror, Picasso's wartime poetry presents the "bombs going into a dive" (172), the "wailings of sirens" (214), the "cement of the sky" (205), its "liquid bricks" (239) "fall[ing] from the high furnaces of the blue" (234), heaven and its "mantle of cruelty" (236). And, almost exactly like the "pictures of torn flesh" conjured up by the "dropping of bombs from the sky" in Bloch (ibid.), the "skin is ripped off" the autobiographical "house" (210) in Picasso's Christmas

1939 text. On the wooden, small house, in Spanish, *caseta,* see n. 91.

12. Bloch, *Strange Defeat,* 57.

13. Herman Parret, "'Ma Vie' comme effet de discours," *La Licorne* 14 (1988): 163; see also 17, 169, 172–75. Although a model for many semiological formalists, in *Circumfessions* Jacques Derrida refutes the reductive theory that autobiographical texts (and events) are, in fact, linguistic-cultural constructs. See Geoffrey Bennington and Jacques Derrida, *Jacques Derrida,* trans. Geoffrey Bennington (Chicago: University of Chicago Press, 1993), 205–9. Robert Smith notes that Derrida's *Circumfessions* is his "most thickly autobiographical text." Robert Smith, *Derrida and Autobiography* (Cambridge: Cambridge University Press, 1995), 45.

14. As in note 1, supra.

15. Allan Young, *The Harmony of Illusions: Inventing Post-Traumatic Stress Disorder* (Princeton: Princeton University Press, 1995), 289. Recent studies on the psychological effects of war include the anthology *Psychological Dimensions of War,* ed. Betty Glad (Newbury Park, California: Sage Publications, 1990).

16. Curtis Cate, *André Malraux, A Biography* (London: Hutchinson, 1995), 229.

17. On strategic terror bombing see *The Laws of War: Constraints on Warfare in the Western World,* ed. Michael Howard, George J. Andreopuolos, and Mark R. Shulman (New Haven: Yale University Press, 1994); and Lee Kennett, *A History of Strategic Bombing* (New York: Scribner, 1982).

18. Giulio Douhet, *The Command of the Air (1921–1929),* trans. Dino Ferrari (New York: Coward-McCann, 1942).

19. André Malraux, *Man's Hope,* trans. Stuart Gilbert and Alistair MacDonald (New York: Modern Library, 1983), 347, 369. Malraux also notes that Franco's "rebel army" was instructed to "adhere strictly" to the Douhet-based rule that "it is essential to inspire a certain salutary dread in the [enemy] population" because it entails a "lowering effect on the morale of his troops." Ibid., 377. Picasso "considered illustrating" *Man's Hope.* André Malraux, *Picasso's Mask* (New York: Holt, Rinehart, Winston, 1976), 45.

20. Malraux, *Man's Hope,* 367.

21. Picasso was prescient. As early as 14 December 1935, in an untitled poem appended to his (handwritten) collage-text (61, 65) made up of clippings from *Le Journal* (8 December 1935, 2–3) that mentioned the Third Reich and the "Italo-Ethiopian conflict" (ibid.) – when the Duce's air force bombed hospitals and civilians – the "threat of the wing" (65) hovers over a couple in love and their sobbing infant. Picasso's menacing wing elicits, specifically, the "Italian squadrons" that, as the headlines in *Le Journal* broadcast (ibid., 1, 5), heavily bombed Dese, the capital of central Ethiopia, while the French and the British were discussing the possibility of a "règlement amiable du conflit italo-étiopien" and Mussolini was declaiming an "ardent discours contre les sanctions" against Italy imposed by the League of Nations. Read in relation to these headlines dominated by the air war in Ethiopia, such purposefully selected citations in Picasso's collage-text inevitably suggest the connection he established between death coming down from the sky, life on earth, and his personal existence: "les enfants martyrisés" (61) (*Le Journal,* 8 December, 2); "l'appel des morts de la guerre" (61) (*Le Journal,* ibid.); "oiseaux qui . . . partirent, laissant derrière eux des figures de nouveau ravagées" (65) (*Le Journal,* ibid.); "expirante . . . sous une armoire" (65) (*Le Journal,* ibid.); "la mort mystérieuse d'une infirmière" (65) (*Le Journal,* ibid., 3); "l'arbre de Noël des petits Italiens" (65) (*Le Journal,* ibid., 2). Even "donneuses de lait" (65)(*Le Journal,* ibid.) becomes an allusion to Marie-Thérèse nursing Maya under the "threat of the wing," a scene that one day later Picasso conjured in his elegiac drawing, *Marie-Térèse nourissant Maya* (15 November 1935; Robert Rosenblum, "Picasso's Blond Muse: The Reign of Marie-Thérèse," in *Picasso and Portraiture,* exh. cat. (New York: The Museum of Modern Art, 1996), 366. On 14 December, for the first time in his writings, Picasso replaced the traditional benevolent wing, which not long ago touched the "harmonium with its caress" (17 August 1935, 23), with a hostile apparition, the "threat of the wing" (65). And a few months later, just three days after a brutal skirmish between the Republican Left and the Falange, "which suggested that civil war had almost begun," Picasso contemplates the "first rendezvous of the wings" in the "blue [sky] setting on fire [the] black of the space" (19 April 1936, 122). The news concerning the savage bombings in Spain reached

Picasso through numerous channels, including Paul Eluard and Roland Penrose. The latter visited Picasso's mother, sister, and nephews in Barcelona, probably in the summer-fall of 1936. Picasso's mother told him about the fire, smoke, and stench at a convent next to her apartment. Roland Penrose, *Scrap Book* (New York: Rizzoli, 1981), 85. In *Picasso: His Life and Work* (Berkeley: University of California Press, 1981), 296, Penrose does not mention his visit with Picasso's mother, and is vague about the way in which Picasso learned the troubling news concerning the convent in Barcelona. At the end of 1936, David Gascoyne, who just returned to Paris after having visited Picasso's family in Barcelona with Penrose, noted Picasso's eagerness to learn "news" from those whom he loved, as well as his "depressed and anxious" state of mind caused by the civil war. See Gascoyne, "Journal 1936–1937," in *Spanish Front: Writers on the Civil War,* ed. Valentine Cunningham (New York: Oxford University Press, 1986), 271–2. From letters sent by Kahnweiler to Max Jacob at the beginning of July 1936 and on 20 November 1936, we also learn that Picasso was oppressed by the situation in Spain: "Picasso est sombre, sombre, deprimé. Les événments d'Espagne le préoccupent." See Hélène Seckel, *Max Jacob et Picasso,* exh. cat. (Paris: Musée des Beaux-Arts, 1994), 239.

22. To André Malraux and José Bergamín; see Malraux, *Picasso's Mask,* 10–11.

23. Penrose, *Picasso: His Life and Work,* 307.

24. Picasso, cited in Pierre Cabanne, *Le Siècle de Picasso,* 4 vols. (Paris: Editions Denoël, 1975), 2:33.

25. Irving Pflaum, "Death from the Skies," in *Nothing but Danger,* ed. Frank C. Hanighorn (New York: National Travel Club, 1939), 222.

26. Hugh Thomas, *The Spanish Civil War,* rev. and enlrg. (New York: Harper and Row, 1977), 807.

27. Picasso remarked to Laporte that his symbol for peace was a "pigeon" that contradicted the commonplace notion of the "gentle dove"; as far as he was concerned there was "no crueller animal" than the dove. His own doves "pecked a poor little pigeon to death because they didn't like it. They pecked its eyes out, then pulled it to pieces. It was horrible. How's that for a symbol of Peace?" See Geneviève Laporte, *Sunshine at Midnight: Memoirs of Picasso and Cocteau,* trans. D. Cooper (London: Weidenfeld and Nicolson, 1975), 7–8.

28. Malraux, *Man's Hope,* 339.

29. Marie-Thérèse Walter, conversation with author, January 1972. Marie-Thérèse also told me that Picasso was relieved when, on 25 June 1940, the Franco-German armistice came into force. Picasso told Marie-Thérèse: "c'est mieux comme ça." The war had been too much for him. He was not alone, the "great majority of the French felt relieved" for obvious reasons. See Azéma, *1940: l'année terrible,* 194.

30. Gertrude Stein had already observed that Picasso had the capacity to imagine things as if they were hallucinatorily real, to "see" graphically what he thinks; see Edward Burns, ed., *Gertrude Stein on Picasso,* (New York: Liveright, 1970), 24.

31. Thomas, *Spanish Civil War,* 714.

32. *The Guardian Book of the Spanish Civil War,* ed. R. H. Haigh, D. S. Morris, and A. R. Peters (Aldershot: Wildwood House, 1987), 206.

33. See the discussion of Picasso's "Samson complex" in Gasman, "Mystery, Magic and Love: Picasso and the Surrealist Writers, 1925–38," (Ph.D. diss. Columbia University, 1981), 696–98.

34. Françoise Gilot with Carlton Lake, *Life with Picasso* (New York: McGraw-Hill, 1964), 23.

35. Jaime Sabartés, *Picasso: An Intimate Portrait,* trans. from the Spanish by Angel Flores (New York: Prentice Hall, 1948), 107.

36. On 3 and 4 September, *L'Excelsior* reported that the Luftwaffe bombed the city of "CZESTOHOVA, LIEU SAINT DE POLOGNE . . ."; and its 16th century cloister housing the effigy of the miraculous "black Virgin" (3 September, 2, 3; 4 September, front page); the analogy with the bombing of Guernica in 1937 would not have escaped Picasso.

37. From the mid-1930s, *Le Figaro,* though adhering to the traditional "positions of the right" was against the pro-Fascist extreme right and consistently denounced the dangers of Nazism. See *Histoire générale de la presse française,* 5 vols, eds. Claude Bellanger, Jacques Godehot, Pierre Guiral, and Fernand Terrou (Paris: Presses Universitaire de France, 1972), 3: 544.

38. *Le Figaro,* 3 August 1939, 3; see also 7 August 1939, 3.

39. *Le Figaro,* July 1939.

40. *Le Figaro*, August 1939.

41. *Le Figaro,* 29 August 1939, C5; aspects of "La France devant la crise," its "agonie vers la guerre" were encapsulated in photographs showing the procedure for blocking the windows of cellars (to be used as shelters against bombs) in Parisian buildings (*Le Figaro,* 26 August 1939, 1; 28 August 1939, 5; 30 August 1939, 5).

42. Georges Bataille, *Oeuvres Complètes,* vol. 6 (Paris: Editions Gallimard, 1973), 142, 144, 174, 174–175.

43. Simone de Beauvoir, *Journal de guerre: Septembre 1939 – Janvier 1941,* Sylvie Le Bon de Beauvoir (Paris: Editions Gallimard, 1990); and *La Force de l'age* (Paris: Editions Gallimard, 1960).

44. See André Breton, "Interview de Charles-Henri Ford" (1941) in André Breton, *Entretiens* (Paris: Editions Gallimard, 1973), 225–26, and "Prolegomena to a Third Surrealist Manifesto or Not" (1942), in André Breton, *Manifestoes of Surrealism,* trans. R. Seaver and H. R. Lane (Ann Arbor: University of Michigan Press, 1972), 293; see also Henri Béhar, *André Breton: Le Grand Indésirable* (Paris: Cahmann-Levy, 1990), 324–29.

45. See Max Jacob, *Méditations,* ed. René Plantier (Paris: Editions Gallimard, 1972), 144, 145–46, 194.

46. Eugene Jolas, *Vertical: A Yearbook For Romantic-Mystic Ascensions* (New York: Eugene Jolas, 1941), 17–18, 75, 77, 79, 84.

47. Thomas Mann, *Journal: 1918–1921, 1933–1939,* ed. Peter de Mendelssohn, trans. Robert Simon (Paris: Editions Gallimard, 1985), 578–81.

48. Antony Penrose, *Les Vies de Lee Miller,* trans. from English by Christophe Claro (Paris: Arléa/Seuil, 1994), 110–113.

49. Denis De Rougemont, *The Devil's Share,* trans. H. Chevalier (New York: Meridian Books, 1956). See St. John Perse, "Rougemont l'occidental," in André Reszler and Henri Schwamm, *Denis De Rougemont: l'Écrivain, l'Européen* (Neuchatel: Editions de la Baconniere, 1976).

50. See Lionel Richard, "André Suarès face au nazisme," in *Suarès et l'Allemagne,* ed. Yves-Alain Favre (Paris: Lettres Modernes, 1976), 169; and "Un inédit de Suarès: *Tiers Faust,"* in *L'Univers mythique de Suarès,* ed. Yves-Alain Favre (Paris: Minard, 1983), 211.

51. Simone Weil, *The Iliad or The Poem of Force* (Wallingford, Pennsylvania: Pendle Hill, 1976), 26 (written in the fall of 1940); see also, *Simone Weil: Philosophe, Historienne et Mystique,* ed. Gilbert Kahn (Paris: Aubier Monteigne, 1978).

52. See "Une Forme nouvelle des conflits internationaux. La Paix," no author given, *La Revue des deux mondes* 52 (15 August 1939), 766–89. The following thesis is defended in this article: "La Paix-Guerre repose sur l'idée de profiter de la crainte de la guerre catastrophe pour excercer des pressions plus importantes qu'autrefois, tout en évitant de créer une tension suffisante pour amener l'ennemi á recourir á la guerre totale." Ibid., 769.

53. Jean-Paul Sartre, *The War Diaries: November 1939/March 1940,* trans. Quintin Hoare (New York: Pantheon Books, 1984), 100, 97.

54. Ibid., 52.

55. Ibid., 59; Sartre's emphasis.

56. Blaise Cendrars, *Sky Memoirs (Le Lotissement du ciel,* 1949), trans. Nina Rootes (New York: Paragon House, 1992), 63, 181–82; see Jacqueline Chadourne, *Blaise Cendrars poète du cosmos* (Paris: Seghers, 1973), 110–18.

57. See Charles F. Wallraff, *Karl Jaspers: An Introduction to His Philosophy* (Princeton, New Jersey: Princeton University Press, 1970), 137, 208.

58. Thomas, *Spanish Civil War,* 587; Thomas points out that the "attempted defense of this tragic exodus from the air was the last fight in which André Malraux's air squadron took part." Jean Lacouture, who refers to "more than 100,000 refugees from Málaga hunted down and machine gunned" by the Italian navy and pursuit planes, also discusses Malraux's involvement in the Málaga campaign and its record in *Man's Hope.* Jean Lacouture, *Malraux: Une vie dans le siècle, 1901–1976* (Paris: Editions du Seuil, 1976), 235–39; by the end of February, Malraux was back in Paris, where he might have talked with Picasso about the fall of Málaga (ibid., 239–40).

59. Analogous to what Gertrude Stein thought about Picasso's experience of objects, it may be said that Picasso did not imagine bombs raining from heaven, he saw them. Burns, *Gertrude Stein on Picasso,* 24.

60. Picasso, *The Four Little Girls (1947–1948),* trans. Roland Penrose (London: Calder and Boyars, 1970), 24.

61. Louis Aragon, *Anicet ou le panorama* (1921) (Paris: Editions Gallimard, 1969), 86.

62. André Breton, *L'Amour fou* (1937) in *Oeuvres completes, vol. 2* (Paris: Editions Gallimard, 1992), 779; Breton's emphasis.

63. Sabartés, in *Picasso: An Intimate Portrait*, trans. from the Spanish by Angel Flores (New York: Prentice Hall, 1948), states that Picasso left Paris "towards midnight" (188) on "September 3," 1939 (187), and arrived in Royan on "September 4," 1939 (189). But the French translation of the original Spanish text by Sabartés, *Picasso: Portraits et souvenirs*, trans. Paule-Marie Grand and Andre Chastel (Paris: Louis Carré and Maximilien Vox, 1946), states that Picasso left Paris "vers minuit" (198) on "29 aout" 1939 (196) and arrived in Royan on "2 Septembre" 1939 (199). Though these same dates are later given in Sabartés's *Picasso:Recuerdos y retratos*, published in 1953 (208–10), the four days ascribed to Picasso's trip from Paris to Royan do not make sense. Given that there are some 500 kilometers between Paris and Royan and since, as we read in *Picasso: Portraits et souvenirs* itself, Picasso and Sabartés traveled "à plus de cent à l'heure. . .le plus vite possible" (198) "toute la nuit" (199) – making the trip in one single night – it could not have possibly lasted four days, from 29 August to 2 September.

    Picasso: An Intimate Portrait offers the more consistent account. Similarly, the chronology in the Rubin 1980 catalogue for the Picasso retrospective at the Museum of Modern Art establishes that Picasso left Paris on 3 September 1939 (350). However, the chronology in Musée Picasso I states that Picasso left for Royan on 1 September 1939 (291). The inconsistent, confusing dates given in *Picasso: Portraits et souvenirs* also seem to account for the contradictory and apparently erroneous dates given for Picasso's departure from Paris, and for his arrival in Royan, by, for example, Brassaï, *Picasso and Company,* 40; Cabanne, *Le Siècle de Picasso,* 2:49; Daix, *Picasso créateur: La Vie intime et l'oeuvre* (Paris: Editions du Seuil, 1987), 273; and Patrick O'Brian, *Picasso: Pablo Ruiz Picasso, A Biography* (New York: Putnam, 1976), 344. Penrose seems to have given up the task of specifying the dates of Picasso's departure from Paris and arrival in Royan (*Picasso: His Life and Work*, 324-25).

64. Sabartés, *Picasso: An Intimate Portrait,* 188.

65. Ibid., 189.

66. *Le Clairon de Saintonge* (Royan), 20 August 1939, 1.

67. Christian Genet and Louis Moreau, *Les Deux Charentes sous l'Occupation et la Résistance* (Gémozac: La Caillerie, 1983), 11, 23, 20.

68. Guillaume Apollinaire, "Couleurs du Temps," in *Oeuvres poètiques* (Paris: Editions Gallimard, 1965), 948–49: "Voyez ces gros nuages qui montent . . . D'autres nuages . . . Je les vois arriver ce sont les dieux . . . tous les dieux de notre humanité/Qui s'ensemblent ici . . . pour parler au soleil."

69. The "charettes" in Picasso's phrase "nuages charettes" (trans. from his Spanish original "nubes carretas") (11 August 1940, 234) can be read as "avion[s]." See Jean-Marie Cassagne, *Le Dictionnaire de l'argot militaire* (Paris: Zelie, 1994), 55.

70. See Ovid *Metamorphoses,* trans. Rolfe Humphries (Bloomington: Indiana University Press, 1955), 8.230–260. Guillaume Apollinaire in "To Italy" (1915) wrote about the "flight of partridges of the 75s," in Apollinaire, *Calligrammes,* 265, "75" was the name of a cannon used for harassing "enemy lines"; note that Picasso dated his 7 February 1914 letter to Apollinaire: "7 Fevrier 1915/Journée du 75." See *Picasso/Apollinaire Correspondence,* ed. Pierre Caizergue and Hélène Seckel (Paris: Editions Gallimard, 1992), 129. The landing of Wilbur Wright's flying machine on 8 August 1908 was compared to a "partridge returning to its nest." See Robert Wohl, *A Passion for Wings: Aviation and the Western Imagination, 1908–1918* (New Haven: Yale University Press, 1994) 5, 7. The "eyes of the partridge" stand for the eyes of the bull in Joseph Peyré, *Sang et Lumière* (Paris: B. Grasset, 1935), 259, a novel about turbulent Spain in the mid-1930s. A "low-flying partridge" introduces *Men under Stress* by Roy R. Grinker and John P. Spiegel (Philadelphia: Blakiston, 1945), 3–4. The traditional symbolic meanings of the partridge are discussed *in extenso* by Beryl Rowland in *Birds with Human Souls: A Guide to Bird Symbolism* (Knoxville, Tennessee: University of Tennessee Press, 1974), 123–27. See also Hugh of Foilloy, *The Medieval Book of Birds: Hugh of Foilloy's Aviarium,* trans. Willene B. Clarck (Binghamton, New York: Medieval and Renaissance Texts and Studies, 1992), 235–37; Rev. Charles Swainson, *The Folk Lore and Provincial Names of British Birds* (London: Publishers for the Folk-lore Society, 1986), 172–73.

71. In 1957, commenting (in a conversation with Jean-Marie Magnan) on nonsensical passages in a Spanish translation of a French article, Picasso seemed to allude to the almost systematic recurrence of euphemism in his oeuvre: "we the Spanish place everything upside down. When a little girl is pretty we say 'que mona,' in other words, 'what a monkey.' With inversion everything becomes more forceful, more distinct." Cited in *Picasso: Toros y toreros,* exh. cat. (Paris: Museé Picasso, 1993), 72.

72. Hervé Coutau-Bégarie and Claude Huan, *Mers El-Kébir (1940): La rupture franco-britannique* (Paris: Economica, 1994), 180; and Azéma, *1940, l'année terrible,* 204.

73. Picasso cited in Malraux, *Picasso's Mask,* 11.

74. The aerial war on the Channel seems to have been in the back of Picasso's mind because on 17 July, for example, he spontaneously associated the "mechanism among the most complicated" with the "cheese manchego" ("Fromage de la région de la Manche") (222).

75. Winston Churchill's speech is reprinted in Eugene Emme, *Impact of Air Power,* 78–79. Daix notes: Picasso "is evidently on the side of the English who fight alone" in 1940. Daix, *Picasso créateur,* 276. I thank John Richardson for having informed me in a 1996 telephone conversation that Dora Maar, whom he had just visited in Paris, confirmed *en passant* that Picasso naturally allied himself with the English in the Battle of Britain.

76. See Derek Wood and Derek Dempster, *The Battle of Britain and the Rise of Air Power 1930–1940* (New York, Toronto, London: McGraw-Hill, 1961), 235–259.

77. Pseudo-Dionysius, *The Celestial Hierarcy,* in *Pseudo-Dionysius: The Complete Works,* trans. Colm Luibheid (New York: Paulist Press, 1987), 143–91. Pseudo-Dionysius was active "between the third and the fifth centuries." Ibid., 45.

78. Martin Gilbert, *The Second World War: A Complete History* (New York: Henry Holt, 1989), 116.

79. The "winged scarab" is an Egyptian hieroglyphic representation of sun and king associated with the rearing cobra, the "uraeus" – which had crowned Fernande Olivier in the drypoint by Picasso and Max Jacob, *Planche de Dessins de Max Jacob et Picasso* (end 1904–1905); see Hélène Seckel, *Max Jacob et Picasso,* cat. 48, 40; the "winged scarab" appears directly below Horus's "winged eye" in the famous *Pendant with Symbols of the Sun and the Moon,* from Tutankhamun's tomb; see, for example, *Masterpieces of Tutankhamun,* introduction and commentary by David P. Silverman (New York: Abbeville Press, 1978), 112–13; and Richard H. Wilkinson, *Reading Egyptian Art: A Hieroglyphic Guide to Ancient Egyptian Painting and Sculpture* (London: Thames and Hudson, 1992), 113, 109.

80. Werner Spies, *Pablo Picasso on the Path to Sculpture: The Paris and Dinar Sketchbooks of 1928* (Munich: Prestel Verlag, 1995), pls. 13–20.

81. Many thanks to John Richardson who, generous as always, provided me with a photocopy of this formerly unpublished page.

82. See Genet and Moreau, *Les Deux Charentes,* 16–19.

83. See Zervos XI, 21–26, 31–34, 51.

84. This is also the case of his compulsive linear scribbles intended, Picasso suggests in his writings, to trap the entrapping spaces of the air filled with a "network of threads" (213), "entangled threads" (212), "veins entangled with the electric lines" (223), and the "play of parabolas and the amusement of hyperbolas" (159).

85. For a detailed chronology of Picasso's stay in Royan, including his round trips to Paris, see Sabartés, *Picasso: An Intimate Portrait,* 190–205.

86. Genet and Moreau, *Les Deux Charentes,* 193; J. R. Colle, *Royan, son passée, ses environs* (La Rochelle: Quartier Latin, 1965), 67.

87. See "Studio at Royan" in Sabartés, *Picasso: An Intimate Portrait,* 190–205.

88. Ibid., 203–204.

89. Details on Botton Square are given in Yves Delmas, *Royan* (Royan: Yves Delmas, 1991), 83, 85, 89.

90. Sabartés, *Picasso: An Intimate Portrait,* 194–95.

91. The Spanish noun *caseta* means "bathing cabin" as well as "small house" (a diminutive noun formed from *casa* = house). See Gasman: "Mystery, Magic and Love," 7–49; and "Picasso's *Caseta,* His Memories, and His Poems," *Poetry East* (1984): 83–114.

92. The information regarding the wooden cabanas on the Grande Conche, as well as the photographs, was generously provided to the author in

November 1987 by Robert Colle, who was close to Picasso during his stay in Royan. Colle, a member of Academie Saintonge and curator of the Musée Royan, published such basic books on the history and folk-lore of Royan and the neighboring regions as *Royan, son passé, ses environs* (see note 86 supra), and *Sorciers, sourciers et guerisseurs en Aunis et Saintonge* (La Rochelle: Rupella, 1979).

93. This is my reading of Picasso's cabanas (see note 91, supra); it is gener-ally accepted in the literature on the artist, and was most recently endorsed by Kirk Varnedoe in *Picasso: Masterworks from The Museum of Modern Art*, exh. cat. (New York: The Museum of Modern Art; Atlanta: The High Museum of Art, 1998), 96.

94. The holy wanderers of Galicia became famous through the *modernista* writings of Valle-Inclan, who dedicated his poetic novel, *Saintly Flower* (1904), to a mendicant on his "way to Santiago de Compostella" – some sixty-four kilometers from La Coruña – believed by a young Galician girl to be "Jesus traveling through the land to see where charity is to be found." See Verity Smith, *Ramon del Valle-Inclan* (New York: Twayne, 1973), 17, 119, 120. At La Coruña, in 1895, the year of Conchita's illness and death, Picasso had already celebrated the beggars peregrinating through the mystical land of Galicia. His incisive portraits of mendicant pilgrims in, for example, *Old Pilgrim, Bearded Man with His Hands Resting on His Stick,* and the often-reproduced *Beggar in a Cap* (see Josè Palau i Fabre, *Picasso: Life and Work of the Early Years: 1881–1907* (Oxford: Phaidon Press, 1981), 61, nos.: 65, 52, 63), capture the wisdom and spiritual strength of socially alienated creatures and, at the same time, disclose some of their Christian aura. The "pilgrim," as Palau i Fabre remarks, is the "*man whose body has become his own house*." Ibid., 61; italics mine.

95. Prime Minister Daladier's radio address was published under the title "Le martyre des innocents crie vengeance du fond de cette nuit" in *Le Figaro,* 25 December 1939, 3.

96. "Casas derruidas de la carne" = "maisons détruites de la chair" (227), 30 July 1940.

97. Sabartés, *Picasso: An Intimate Portrait,* 190–205.

98. André Breton, *L'Amour fou,* 44; Breton's emphasis. Breton, who served as a "medical officer at the aviation training field in Poitiers," visited Picasso in January–July 1940 in Royan. Mark Polizzotti, *Revolution of the Mind: The Life of André Breton* (New York: Farrar Straus and Giroux, 1995), 439, 480; see also *André Breton: La beauté convulsive,* exh. cat. (Paris: Editions du Centre Pompidou, 1991), 346. Picasso's assemblage of bicycle saddle and handlebars, *Head of a Bull* (1943; Musée Picasso), was first tested by Picasso, while he was looking for eloquent garbage in the reliquaries of Royan. Robert Colle (letter from Royan to this writer, 11 September 1987) witnessed the occasion on which Picasso experimented with the *Head of a Bull* in his studio at Les Voiliers. Colle recalled how the artist "placed automatically a bull's head upon the handlebars of a bicycle" and then "had a good time drawing them." While Picasso, "amused," was ready to "tear that drawing up," his "customer" cried out: "What a masterpiece! The alliance of modern technology and primitive brutality!" (ibid.). A 1940 photograph of a "bicycle saddle of exactly the same type" as that in *Head of a Bull,* hanging on the "wall above a group of Picasso's recent paintings" in his studio at Les Voiliers, that has recently come to light appears to confirm Colle's memory. See Elizabeth Cowling, "Objects in Sculpture," in *Picasso: Sculptor/Painter,* exh. cat. (London: Tate Gallery, 1994), 235. The photograph is held in the Picasso Archives, Musée Picasso, Paris. (See chronology, page 213.) The bull was a prominent deity in the mythology of the Royan region, the "archeolog-ical museum" in Saintes, for example, exhibiting "heads of bulls deco-rated with garlands and ready for immolation," and the "chair of the horned god Cernunos," supported by "two bull heads." Colle, *Sorciers,* 239.

99. Like his attraction to the past, Picasso's temptation to rehearse in Royan the transgressive sexuality he had appreciated for a long time was an attempt to journey back into a warless era. He made love to both Marie-Thérèse and Dora Maar to access liberating pleasure and through it the solace of reunion with an alien cosmos. Yet he could not love the "sky void of caresses and kisses" (210). Marie-Thérèse and Dora are the "two shutters" mimicking the blackout shutters on the windows of Royan, who

"abandon to its fate the house [emptying] its tripes on the sky" (212).

100. "Un marin allemand est lachement assassiné," *La Dépêche de Royan,* 18 August 1940, 1. Robert Colle writes: "On a apprit plus tard que le soldat [the sentinel at the Kommandatur] s'était suicidé" (*Royan,* 62).

101. Andrée Rolland, *Picasso et Royan aux jours de la guerre et de l'occupation* (Royan: Impr. Nouvelle, 1967), n.p.

102. *Journal de Marennes,* 11 August 1940.

103. Rolland, *Picasso et Royan,* n.p.

104. Bypassing the principle of identity, Picasso created a similar image in a text written on 6 July 1940: "angular, twisted circumference [surround-ing] . . . the globe of the [foul] smell" (217).

105. Colle, *Royan,* 62. The memory of a "Royan emptied" on 15 August, the day when Picasso painted "Le café des Bains" – and the Germans celebrated with "great pomp" the "funeral" of the sentinel from the Kommandatur – is recalled in Guy Binot, *Histoire de Royan et de la presqu'ile d'Avert* (Paris: Le Croît Vif, 1994), 321.

106. Sabartés, *Picasso: An Intimate Portrait,* 213–14.

I wish to thank Johanna Bauman for assisting me in finalizing my summaries of the texts I wrote on "Picasso's Great Fear of Air Raids," and Amy Lemley for striving to instill an everyday tone in the language of those texts.

From *Guernica* to *The Charnel House:* the Political Radicalization of the Artist
Gertje R. Utley

Part of this essay is derived from research related to my doctoral thesis, "Picasso and the 'Parti de la Renaissance Française': The Artist as a Commu-nist, 1944–1953" (Ph.D. diss., Institute of Fine Arts, New York University, 1997; Yale University Press, forthcoming). I welcome the opportunity to reiterate my deep gratitude to my professors Kirk Varnedoe, Robert Rosenblum, William Rubin, and Tony Judt for their continued support, and I thank Suzanne Stratton for her helpful editorial comments. I am also deeply indebted to Brigitte Léal for her untiring counsel in all matters pertaining to Picasso, and to the entire staff of the Musée Picasso, Paris, without whose dedicated help none of my work would be possible.

1. Picasso, in an interview with Pol Gaillard, which appeared in condensed form in Pablo Picasso, "Why I Became a Communist," *New Masses* 53, no. 4 (24 October 1944): 11; reprinted in full version in Pablo Picasso, "Pourquoi j'ai adhéré au Parti Communiste: Une interview de Picasso à la revue américaine New Masses," *L'Humanité* 41, no. 64 (29–30 October 1944): 1–2. See reprint in French in Alfred H. Barr Jr., *Picasso: Fifty Years of His Art* (New York: The Museum of Modern Art, 1946; London: Secker & Warburg, 1975), 267.

2. See Daniel-Henry Kahnweiler, "Pablo Picasso et son temps," "Picasso" special edition, *La Nouvelle Critique* (1961): 33; André Fermigier, "La Gloire de Picasso," *Revue de l'art* 1, no. 2 (1968): 114–22; Roger Garaudy, "Guernica, l'Espagne, la politique," in Jean Cassou, *Pablo Picasso* (Paris: Somogy, 1975), 197; Marilyn McCully, *Els Quatre Gats: Art in Barcelona around 1900* (Princeton, N.J.: Princeton University Press, 1978); Patricia Leighten, *Re-Ordering the Universe: Picasso and Anarchism, 1897–1914* (Princeton: Princeton University Press, 1989); Robert Lubar, book review for Patricia Leighten, *Re-Ordering the Universe,* in *Art Bulletin* 72, no. 3 (September 1990): 505–10; Temma Kaplan, *Red City, Blue Period: Social Movements in Picasso's Barcelona* (Berkeley, Los Angeles, and London: University of California Press, 1992).

3. Picasso told Pierre Daix that the clipping with the article on Jean Jaurès in the 1912 collage *La Bouteille de Suze* was consciously chosen for its political content. Daix, in conversation with the author, 16 October 1992, and in his "Eluard et Picasso," *Paul Eluard et ses amis peintres 1895–1952* (Paris: Centre Georges Pompidou, 1982), 26. Robert Rosenblum was the first to look into the newspaper texts of the collages; see Robert Rosenblum, "Picasso and the Typography of Cubism," in Roland

Penrose and John Golding, eds., *Picasso in Retrospect* (New York: Harper and Row, 1973), 33–48. Leighten, *Re-Ordering the Universe,* gives the most extensive account of this.

4. J. Granié, "Les Cubistes," *Revue d'Europe et d'Amérique;* G. Kahn, "Le Salon d'Automne: Peinture et sculpture," *Mercure de France* (16 October 1911): 868–70; cited in Lubar's review of Leighten, *Re-Ordering the Universe,* 509.

5. For a primary testimony of surrealist politics, see André Breton, *Position politique du surréalisme* (Paris: Edition du Sagitaire, 1935; Société Nouvelle des Editions Pauvert, 1962, 1971). On Breton's subsequent views of Picasso's politics, see André Breton, "80 carats . . . mais une ombre," *Combats-Arts* (2 November 1961), trans. Simon Watson Taylor, reprint, in Marilyn McCully, ed., *A Picasso Anthology: Documents, Criticism, Reminiscences* (London: The Arts Council of Great Britain with Thames and Hudson, 1981), 243–45. See also André Thirion, *Revolutionaries without Revolution* (New York: MacMillan, 1975), 301; trans. Joachim Neugroschel, *Révolutionnaires sans révolution* (Paris: Robert Laffont, 1972); Pierre Daix, *Aragon, une vie à changer* (Paris: Editions du Seuil, 1975), 240–88; Helena Lewis, *The Politics of Surrealism* (New York: Paragon House, 1988); Sidra Stich, *Anxious Visions: Surrealist Art* (Berkeley: University Art Museum; New York: Abbeville Press, 1990).

6. On Eluard's politics and his relations with Picasso, see the excellent studies by Jean-Charles Gateau, *Paul Eluard ou le frère voyant 1895–1952* (Paris: Editions Robert Laffont, 1988), in particular 215–30; and *Eluard, Picasso et la peinture (1936–1952)* (Geneva: Librairie Droz, 1983), 265–67.

7. With Georges Bataille, whose mistress she had been in the early thirties, Dora Maar had been a member of Boris Souvarine's radical group Le Cercle, and was in the mid-1930s close to Bataille's militant organization, Contre-Attaque, which positioned itself to the left of the Popular Front. On Dora Maar see Judi Freeman, " . . . the gift of metamorphosis," in her *Picasso and the Weeping Women: The Years of Marie-Thérèse Walter & Dora Maar,* exh. cat. (Los Angeles: Los Angeles County Museum of Art, 1994), 174.

8. Thirion, *Revolutionaries,* 301. See also Michel Fauré, *Histoire du surréalisme sous l'Occupation: Les Réverbères – La Main à plume* (Paris: La Table Ronde, 1982).

9. "The Political Picasso," BBC Picasso Season, BBC 2, televised program, 20 February 1994.

10. Sidra Stich, "Picasso's Art and Politics in 1936," *Arts Magazine* 58 (October 1983): 113–18, interprets the gouache as an allegory of the Popular Front's resistance to the spread of fascism.

11. It was assumed that the gouache was selected among Picasso's works to serve as model for the stage curtain for Romain Rolland's play, *Le 14 juillet,* commissioned for that year's 14 July celebrations. I have found evidence, however, that Picasso actually produced the drawing expressly for the event.

12. A.B., "Les spectacles des fêtes du 14 juillet," *Le Jour,* 10 June 1936; *Le Nouveau Cri,* 27 June 1936. See also *Le Front Populaire et l'Art Moderne, 1936–1939: Hommage à Jean Zay,* exh. cat. (Orleans: Musée des Beaux Arts, 1995), 175; financing for the project had received governmental approval on 5 June 1936.

13. The two plays are published together in one volume. Romain Rolland, *La Théâtre de la révolution: Le 14 juillet–Danton–Les Loups* (Paris: Albin Michel, 1926); *Two Plays of the French Revolution,* trans. Barret H. Clark (New York: Henry Holt, 1918), 128, 236.

14. Pencil drawing, 68 × 67 cm, 13 June 1936, Musée Picasso, Paris, M.P. 1167.

15. Stefan Priacel, "Théâtre pour le peuple et par le peuple," *Regards,* 16 July 1936. The musical contributions were by Darius Milhaud, Arthur Honegger, and Georges Auric, among others.

16. Annie de Méredieu, "A l'Alhambra, c'est devant une salle enthousiaste que c'est déroulé la représentation populaire de '14 juillet'," *Paris-Soir,* 16 July 1936; Pierre Audiat, "A l'Alhambra, 'le 14 juillet' de Romain Rolland," *Paris-Soir,* 20 July 1936; "14 juillet l'Alhambra," *Vu,* 15 July 1936.

17. A notice in *Europe,* 15 August 1936, reads that the Maison de la culture sent a telegram of support to President Campanys of the Spanish Republic. Among the signatories was Picasso.

18. In a letter from Valencia dated 17 December 1936, the undersecretary of Public Education and Art confirmed the nomination and invited Picasso to come and assure himself of the work that had been done to safeguard the national collections. See the Picasso Archives, Musée Picasso, Paris. The author of the article "Prudence mère de sûreté," *La Liberté,* 27 February 1937, claims that the Republic had even put a plane at Picasso's disposal – in vain.

19. Georges Sadoul, "Une demi-heure dans l'Atelier de Picasso," *Regards,* 29 July 1937, 8; Roberto Otero, *Forever Picasso: An Intimate Look at His Last Years* (New York: Harry N. Abrams, 1975), 116. Brassaï, *Conversations avec Picasso* (Paris: Editions Gallimard, 1964), 199; Brassaï, *Picasso and Company,* trans. Francis Price (Garden City, N.Y.: Doubleday, 1966).

20. See in particular Zervos VIII, 323; Zervos VIII, 336; Zervos IX, 97. Ludwig Ullmann, *Picasso und der Krieg* (Bielefeld: Karl Kerber Verlag, 1993), 73–80.

21. Gateau, *Eluard, Picasso,* 237.

22. Ibid., 56–57. This belief also informed the attitudes of the intellectual Resistance in France, in particular of writers such as Sartre and Camus.

23. The last three scenes were drawn in June only and relate more directly to *Guernica.*

24. In an interview with Georges Sadoul, Picasso called the etchings "un acte d'exécration de l'attentat dont est victime le peuple espagnol" (*Regards,* 29 July 1937, 8). In December 1937 the work was part of the exhibition *L'Art cruel* at the Galerie Billiet-Worms in Paris.

25. Eluard, who was present, recalled how distressed Bergamín's report had left them. Gateau, *Eluard, Picasso,* 52. Bergamín was also responsible for safeguarding the artistic treasures of the Prado. The political opinions of Bergamín, who was a Catholic leftist, were to remain very influential for Picasso, as Roberto Otero, the photographer and nephew of Raphael Alberti, told me in our conversation.

26. In 1932 Picasso had declared: "I will never make art with the preconceived idea of serving the interest of the political, religious, or military art of a country." He pointed out, however, what side he meant in this by adding: "I will never fit in with the followers of the prophets of Nietzsche's superman." Cited in Gert Schiff, ed. *Picasso in Perspective* (Englewood Cliffs, N. J.: Prentice Hall, 1976), 15; Dore Ashton, ed. *Picasso on Art: A Selection of Views* (New York: Viking Press, 1972), 148.

27. The most comprehensive text on the Spanish Civil War is Hugh Thomas, *The Spanish Civil War* (London: Penguin Books, 1961; New York: Simon and Schuster, 1986).

28. Letter, Javier Vilato to the author, 20 January 1998. Although the foreign press continued to promote the myth of a united Popular Front, Picasso had ample opportunity to be informed of the dissentions. Vilato and his brother Fin had taken up arms against Franco by joining the militias in Barcelona. Christian Zervos was in Barcelona at the end of November 1936, where he visited Picasso's family, and a close friend of Kahnweiler had enlisted in the left-wing militia under the legendary Buenaventura Durruti. On the events in Spain, see Thomas, *Spanish Civil War,* in particular, the chapter "Rising and Revolution," 199 ff.; François Furet, *Le Passé d'une illusion: Essai sur l'idée communiste au XXe siècle* (Paris: Robert Laffont/Calmann-Lévy, 1995), "Communisme et antifascisme," in particular, 289–310. For the most detailed and fascinating firsthand account read George Orwell, *Homage to Catalonia* (New York: Harcourt Brace, 1952).

29. We know of Picasso's sympathies for the radical left militias as, according to the surrealist poet Noël Arnaud, Picasso's financial support after the war would mainly help former militants of the militia organizations FAI (Federación anarquista ibérica) and POUM (Partido obrero de unificación marxista). Arnaud is cited in Michèle Cone, *Artists under Vichy: A Case of Prejudice and Persecution* (Princeton, N.J.: Princeton University Press, 1992), 152. The POUM was the group with which Orwell fought. Revolutionary in vocation and hostile to Stalinism, its members became the main target of Communist persecution; many were incarcerated and killed. On the Communists' hold on the Republican government in Valencia, see Furet, *Le Passé,* 254–59; Thomas, *Spanish Civil War,* 341, 452.

30. Only the inclusion, in a sketch of 19 April 1937, of several raised fists holding Picasso's version of the Communist hammer and sickle, betrays a modicum of militant disposition. For publication of those drawings see Ludwig Ullmann, "Zur Vorgeschichte von Picasso's Guernica," *Kritische Berichte* 14, no. 1 (1986): 4–26.

31. Gertrude Stein asserted that it was not really the events themselves as much as their happening in Spain that shook Picasso; in her *Picasso*

(London: Batsford, 1938), 46–47; (New York: Dover Publications, 1984), 47–48.

32. Juan Larrea, *Guernica: Pablo Picasso* (New York: Curt Valentin, 1947), 72.

33. Werner Spies, *Picasso: Die Zeit nach Guernica, 1937–1973*, exh. cat. (Stuttgart: Verlag Gerd Hatje, 1993), 20.

34. Madrid, Museo Nacional del Prado, *Guernica–Legado Picasso* (Madrid: Ministerio de Cultura 1981), 153–55. The offer by an American collector to buy *Guernica* and its related works was not accepted. See the correspondence Christian Zervos (5 October 1939, 6 October 1939) to Pablo Picasso in the Musée Picasso Archives.

35. The prints were reproduced and sold, together with Picasso's accompanying text, in a limited edition of 1,000 copies to benefit the Spanish Refugee Relief Campaign. Gateau, *Eluard, Picasso*, 53.

36. Gertje R. Utley, "Picasso and the 'Parti' de la Renaissance Française: The Artist as a Communist, 1944–1953" (Ph. D. diss., Institute of Fine Arts, New York University, 1997; New Haven: Yale University Press, forthcoming), 175–78. For Picasso's support of the Spanish Republicans see also Juan Larrea, letter to Alfred Barr, The Museum of Modern Art Archives, New York: Alfred H. Barr Jr. Papers; Record Group 12 Picasso.VIII.B.3.

37. Larrea, letter to Barr (MoMA Archives: AHB Papers; 12.VIII.B.3); *L'Humanité*, 18 February 1939; Javier Vilato in conversation with the author. On Picasso's help to Republican refugees, see, in particular, Mercedes Guillén, *Picasso* (Madrid: Alfaguara, 1973).

38. Utley, "Picasso and the 'Parti'," 175. On the French government's policies with respect to the Civil War in Spain, see David Wingeate Pike, *Les Français et la guerre d'Espagne* (Paris: Presses Universitaires de France, 1975) and Jean-Baptiste Duroselle, *La Décadence 1932–1939* (Paris: Imprimerie Nationale, 1985), in particular ch. 10.

39. Picasso's generosity to friends and strangers was described by Josep Palau i Fabre in conversation with the author, 2 November 1992; and in his *Picasso i els seus Amics Catalans* (Barcelona: Editorial Aedos, 1971), 186–87; Guillén, *Picasso*, passim. See also the numerous references and letters of acknowledgment in the Picasso Archives, Musée Picasso, Paris.

40. According to Roberto Otero, in conversation with the author, Jacqueline Roche, Picasso's last companion, told him how she was spending nights counting money for huge cash donations for Spanish Communists in need, because Picasso did not want to handle such matters by check.

41. According to one report, Picasso was accused of trafficking in foreign currencies via Denmark to Spain and the Soviet Union. Only the intervention of Arno Breker rescued him from this dangerous situation. Jacques Dubois, "Etre une vedette sous l'occupation: La face cachée d'un astre turbulent," "Picasso," special edition, *Amateur d'art*, no. 724 (1986): 31. See also David Pryce-Jones, *Paris in the Third Reich: A History of the German Occupation: 1940–1944* (London: Collins, 1981), 220. Mary-Margaret Goggin, "Picasso and His Art during the German Occupation: 1940–1944" (Ph.D. diss., Stanford University, 1985), 233.

42. *New York Times,* 19 December 1937, cited in Herschel B. Chipp, *Picasso's Guernica: History, Transformations, Meanings* (Berkeley, Los Angeles, and London: University of California Press, 1988), 160. As the civil war in Spain started as a right-wing military uprising engineered by Franco against the elected Popular Front government, the allusion to the military caste is clear.

43. Otero, *Forever Picasso*, 117.

44. For future generations *Guernica* became an inspiration for political activism in art and in posters. See, for example, the group Crónica in Georg Eichinger, "Picasso's *Guernica* als Zitat: Zur Funktion des Kunst-Zitats in drei Bildern der Gruppe Crœnica," *Guernica: Kunst und Politik am Beispiel Guernica – Picasso und der Spanische Bürgerkrieg* (Berlin: Neue Gesellschaft für Bildende Kunst, 1975), 77–80.

45. Picasso, "Why I Became a Communist," 11.

46. Eluard: "Il a été un des rares peintre à se conduire comme il faut, et il continue"; quoted in Cabanne, *Le Siècle de Picasso*, vol. 3, *Guernica – La Guerre (1937–1955)* (Paris: Editions Denoël, 1975), 142; Cabanne, *Pablo Picasso: His Life and Times,* trans. Harold J. Salemson (New York: Morrow, 1977), 363. Antonina Vallentin, for example, recalled, "one knew about his refusal of all concession and compromise with the enemy." *Pablo Picasso* (Paris: Albin Michel, 1957), 365. Among the intellectuals who vouched for Picasso's uncompromising behavior were

Jacques Prévert, Brassaï, Louis Parrot, Christian Zervos, and Jean Cocteau. Although his reputation as a collaborationist has been somewhat cleansed by the recent publication of his wartime diaries, Cocteau's credibility is still questionable in this respect.

47. None of the accusations is ever accompanied by a substantiating footnote. See, for example, Dubois, "Etre une vedette," 31; Brigitte Baer, "Eine Leseart von Picasso's Werk in den Kriegsjahren: Eine traumatische Trauer," in Siegfried Gohr, ed., *Picasso im Zweiten Weltkrieg: 1939 bis 1945,* exh. cat. (Cologne: Museum Ludwig, 1988), 51; Cabanne, *Le Siècle,* 141; as well as "Picasso et . . . la politique," *Le Crapouillot,* no. 25 (May/June 1973).

48. See Philippe Burrin, *France under the Germans: Collaboration and Compromise,* trans. Janet Lloyd (New York: The New Press, 1996); Pryce-Jones, *Third Reich;* Gilles Ragache and Jean-Robert Ragache, *La Vie quotidienne des écrivains et des artistes sous l'Occupation, 1940–1944* (Paris: Hachette, 1988); Herbert R. Lottman, *The Left Bank: Writers, Artists, and Politics from the Popular Front to the Cold War* (Boston: Houghton Mifflin, 1982); Fauré, *Histoire,* as well as more personal accounts by Brassaï, *Conversations;* Jean Cocteau, *Journal 1942–1945* (Paris: Editions Gallimard, 1989); Michel Leiris, *Journal 1922–1989* (Paris: Editions Gallimard, 1992).

49. Sabartés writes that he would admit the occasional German soldier who claimed to be an artist and admirer of Picasso's work. Jaime Sabartés, *Gespräche und Erinnerungen,* trans. Oswalt von Nostitz (Zurich: Arche Verlag, 1956; Frankfurt: Luchterhand, 1990), 237. See also Gerhard Heller, *Un Allemand à Paris 1940–1944* (Paris: Editions du Seuil, 1981), 118; Ernst Jünger, *Premier Journal parisien* (Paris: Christian Bourgois, 1980), 158; Collector from Stuttgart, "Als Soldat bei Picasso in Paris," in Gohr, *Picasso im Zweiten Weltkrieg,* 281–82. Hans Kuhn was a corporal in the Komman-dantur and an abstract, surrealist painter.

50. Burrin, *France under the Germans,* 193. See also Jean-Paul Sartre, "Paris sous l'Occupation," *Situations, III: Lendemains de guerre* (London: La France Libre, 1945; Paris: Editions Gallimard, 1949).

51. Jean Paulhan embodies the complexity of the situation under the Occupation. He was the director of *La Nouvelle Revue française* from 1925–40, at which time the Germans took control of the paper and fired him. During the Occupation he continued to work for the collaborationist paper, all the while using his office for his Resistance activities. A leading figure in the intellectual Resistance, he was instrumental in publishing the underground *Les Lettres françaises.* See Pierre Herbey, *La Nouvelle Revue française des années sombres, 1940–1941* (Paris: Editions Gallimard, 1992). Sartre, in his 1945 essay, "Paris sous l'Occupation," comments on the complexities of life with the enemy. On the peculiar "color blindness" in relations between resistants and collaborators, see for example Cocteau, *Journal 1942–1945,* 110 n.1; on 5 May 1942, only days before his "Salut à Breker," he dined in the company of Paul Eluard and other resistants at the home of Lise Desharmes, herself "a queen of the resistance."

52. Ragache and Ragache, *La Vie quotidienne,* 150–51; Laurence Bertrand Dorléac, *L'Art de la défaite, 1940–1944* (Paris: Editions du Seuil, 1993), 194–97, 318 n23. The rumored visits by Rudolf Hess or Otto Abetz, on the other hand, have never been corroborated.

53. Among Picasso's frequent companions who served in the Resistance were Michel Leiris, Jean Cassou, Paul Eluard, Louis Aragon, Georges Hugnet, and Robert Desnos, who, caught in early 1944, would perish in the camp in Theresienstadt (Terezín) on 8 June 1945.

54. Fougeron, in conversation with the author.

55. Françoise Gilot and Carlton Lake, *Life with Picasso* (New York: McGraw-Hill, 1964), 41–42.

56. Ibid., 62, 63.

57. The rumor that Picasso had participated in the Resistance emerged after the Liberation and was published by Alfred H. Barr Jr., "Picasso 1940–1944: A Digest with Notes," *The Museum of Modern Art Bulletin* 12, no. 3 (January 1945): 1–9. It drew a sharp reply from Christian Zervos in a letter dated 28 March 1945. (MoMA Archives: AHB Papers; 12.VIII.B.3.

58. Fritz René Vanderpyl, *L'Art sans patrie un mensonge: Le Pinceau d'Israel* (Paris: Mercure de France, 1942), quoted in Goggin, *Art and Picasso,* 232.

59. On the auction in Lucerne, see Stephanie Barron, *"Degenerate Art": The Fate of the Avant-Garde in Nazi Germany* (New York: Harry N. Abrams, 1991), 99, 136, 144, 168. On the fate of the "entartete kunst" looted from

Jewish collections in France and stored at the Musée du Jeu de Paume, see Hector Feliciano, *The Lost Museum: The Nazi Conspiracy to Steal the World's Greatest Works of Art* (New York: HarperCollins, 1997), 107–108.

60. In his review of the exhibition of contemporary Spanish art in the Galerie Charpentier in September 1942, the notorious Lucien Rebatet of the collaborationist *Je suis partout* made no secret of that fact. Lucien Rebatet, "L'Art espagnol contemporain," *Je suis partout*, 9 September 1942. See also Y. B.,"Une exposition d'artistes espagnols contemporains," *Le Figaro*, 18 August 1942; Jean-Marc Campagne, " L'Art espagnol contemporain à la Galerie Charpentier," *Les Nouveaux Temps*, 30 September 1942. As Steven Nash writes in his essay in this volume, the ban on exhibiting works by Picasso was not always respected. André Warnod, "Une exposition d'art espagnol," *Le Figaro*, 6 October 1942. On the Galerie Charpentier and its questionable dealings with the Germans during the Occupation, see Felicano, *Lost Museum*, 150–52.

61. The exhibition was held at the Galerie Berri-Raspail. Picasso's participation in this exhibition inspired at least one journalist to call Picasso a Jew who was aping Negro art. See Henri Labroue, "La Peinture juive," *Le Pilori*, 27 May 1943: "ce juif livournais n'est qu'un singe de l'art nègre."

62. R. T., "Une curieuse exposition rue Bonaparte," *Aujourd'hui*, 16 May 1944. The exhibition was called *L'Oeuvre et la palette, 1830 à nos jours.*

63. Brassaï, *Conversations*, 69.

64. Republished by Olivier Dussiau, "Requins et faisans de l'édition," *Union Française* (Lyon), 6 October 1943, with the following commentary: "N'y-a-t-il pas là un des signes les plus éclatants de décadence litéraire, spirituelle et morale."

65. Pétain believed that France's defeat was caused less by military conquest than by moral disintegration.

66. The title was derived from a phrase by Rimbaud: "La main à plume vaut la main à charrue" (the hand at the quill is as valuable as the hand at the plough). The most exhaustive account of the *Main à plume* is in Fauré, *l'Histoire.*

67. Gilot and Lake, *Life with Picasso,* 46.

68. See André-Louis Dubois, *A travers trois républiques: Sous le signe de l'amitié* (Paris: Plon, 1972). On his help to Picasso, see Gilot and Lake, *Life with Picasso,* 44. On his friendship with Cocteau, see Cocteau, *Journal 1942–1945,* passim. Dubois worked at the prefecture as director for the reconstruction of bombed areas. It was through the connections of his previous employment, as police chief of the Ministry of the Interior before Vichy fired him from that post, that he was able to help. Maurice Toesca, *Cinq Ans de patience (1939–1945)* (Paris: Editions Emile-Paul, 1975). Toesca, whose work for Vichy was only a cover for his Resistance activities, was able to renew Picasso's identity papers in 1942 and can probably also be recognized as saving Picasso from being sent to Germany for work service. On Toesca, see also Cocteau, *Journal, 1942–1945,* 196, passim; Pryce-Jones, *Third Reich,* 46–47. More famously, it was through Arno Breker's powerful connections and his friendship with Cocteau that Picasso and Cocteau "were spared the worst." See Cocteau, recollections in his *Le Passé défini* (Paris: Editions Gallimard, 1983), 352. Cocteau had met Breker when the German sculptor lived in Paris as the student of Maillol. For more on their friendship, see Cocteau, *Journal 1942–1945,* 112, 125–28, 132, 133. Apparently Breker also protected Dina Vierny, the Jewish mistress of his old teacher Maillol; Pryce-Jones, *Third Reich,* 250. It is more than probable that Breker was also Picasso's mysterious source of bronze for the casting of his sculptures.

69. Hélène Seckel and André Cariou, *Max Jacob et Picasso,* exh. cat. (Paris: Réunion des Musées Nationaux, 1994), 272–79.

70. Emile Szittya, "Notes sur Picasso," *Courrier des arts et des lettres* (1947): 24; cited in Cone, *Artists under Vichy,* 145. On the idea that during the Occupation subversive painting was seen as a form of Resistance, see Laurence Bertrand Dorléac, *L'Histoire de l'art: Paris 1940–1944. Ordre national, traditions et modernité* (Paris: Presses de la Sorbonne, 1986).

71. Brassaï, *Conversations,* 314, 315.

72. On French art at the time of the Popular Front government in France, see *Le Front Populaire et l'Art Moderne 1936–1939: Hommage à Jean Zay,* exh. cat. (Orleans: Musée des Beaux Arts, 1995). On French art during the Occupation, see Fauré, *Histoire;* Bertrand Dorléac, *L'Art de la défaite;* Cone, *Artists under Vichy,* and Pontus Hulten, *Paris 1937–Paris 1957: Créations en*

France, exh. cat. (Paris: Centre Georges Pompidou, 1981), 82–125.

73. Others were Lurçat's tapestry, which incorporated Eluard's poem "Liberté," and Francis Grüber's *Hommage à Callot* (1942). On Fougeron, see Raymond Perrot, *Esthétique de Fougeron* (Paris: E. C. Editions, 1996); Jean-Jacques Dutko, *Fougeron* (Paris: Editions Person, 1987).

74. Fougeron had installed a printing press in his studio, where he created the clandestine journal *L'Art français* and cooperated in the publication of such other underground papers as *Les Lettres françaises.* Bertrand Dorléac, *L'Art de la défaite,* 279–85, 578. See also David Cascaro, *Edouard Pignon et la politique* (Paris: Université Panthéon-Assas Paris, 1996), 92–93; Cone, *Artists under Vichy,* 169–70.

75. "Est-ce que si peu d'artistes étaient insurrectionnaires par rapport aux écrivains et poètes, à cause de l'impossibilité de la tâche?" cited in Hélène Parmelin, *Picasso sur la place* (Paris: Julliard, 1959); trans. Humphrey Hare, *Picasso Plain* (London: Secker and Warburg, 1963), 190, and in Ashton, *Picasso on Art,* 151.

76. Bertrand Dorléac, *L'Art de la défaite,* 282; Cone, *Artists under Vichy,* 172.

77. "La peinture d'avant-garde, c'était comme une voix de la Résistance," is cited in Cascaro, *Edouard Pignon,* 92. Yves Sjöberg, "Vingt jeunes peintres de tradition française," *Construire,* no. 5 (May 1941), in his review of their exhibition in the Galerie Braun in May 1941, recognized in their work the desire "de surmonter le chaos actuel, de créer envers et contre tout, d'échapper au servage intellectuel et de maintenir intact les traditions d'indépendance de l'école de Paris." See also Cone, "'Abstract' Art as a Veil: Tricolor Painting in Vichy France, 1940–44," *Art Bulletin* 74, no. 2 (June 1992): 191–204; Hulten, *Paris 1937,* 106.

78. For the liberal attitude of the Germans in cultural matters, see Burrin, *France under the Germans,* 324. Ragache and Ragache, *La Vie quotidienne,* passim.

79. Brassaï, *Conversations,* 209: "le symbole de la liberté retrouvée"; Antonina Vallentin, *Picasso* (Garden City, N.Y.: Doubleday, 1963), 226; "le porte-drapeau de la France résistante." Among those who vouched for Picasso's honorable conduct during the Occupation, see also Louis Parrot, "Hommage à Pablo Picasso, qui vécut toujours de la vie de la France," *Les Lettres françaises* 4, no. 20 (9 September 1944): 8, and Christian Zervos's letter to Alfred H. Barr Jr., 29 March 1945 (MoMA Archives: AHB Papers; 12.VIII.B.3).

80. See the photos of Picasso surrounded by members of Le Front nationale des intellectuels, in the Père-Lachaise cemetery in *Le Patriote,* 15 October 1944, and again heading a procession with Paul Eluard on 2 November. And he appeared with Le Front national universitaire at a memorial for the victims of fascism in October 1944 (photo courtesy Roger-Viollet in *L'Histoire,* October 1988, 75).

81. "Le plus grand peintre aujourd'hui vivant, Picasso, à apporté son adhésion au Parti de la Renaissance Française," *L'Humanité,* 5 October 1944, 1.

82. See for example Fontanel, "Picasso . . . J'ai quelques réactions," *Gavroche,* 20 October 1944; "N'avait il pas une importance capitale, ce premier Salon de la Libération? Un salon qui devait être spécifiquement français – un salon enfin libre – un salon qui devait exprimer la véritable pensée, la véritable culture française." Janet Flanner, *Men and Monuments* (New York: Harper, 1957) 195.

83. For the details on the scandal surrounding Picasso's presence at the Salon, see: "Un essai de sabotage absurde au Salon d'automne," *Le Parisien Libéré,* 10 October 1944; "Scandale au Salon," *Libération,* 10 October 1944; "A 'Tokio' Picasso provoque une insurrection," *Aurore,* 10 October 1944; J. B., "Au Salon d'automne on avait volé trois Picasso," *Ce Soir,* 10 October 1944; Sherry Mangan, "L'Affaire Picasso," *Time,* 30 October 1944, 78; G. H. Archambault, "Picasso: The Painter Who Defied the Germans Finds Himself the Hero of a Revolutionary Mood," *New York Times Magazine,* 29 October 1944, 18–19, 39; Barr Jr., "Picasso 1940–1944," 6; Gwen Harrison, "L'Affaire Picasso," *Maelström* 1, no. 2 (summer 1945): 13–15; Gilot and Lake, *Life with Picasso,* 61; André Fermigier, "La Gloire de Picasso," *Revue de l'art* 1, no. 2 (1968): 114–22; Harriet and Sidney Janis, *Picasso: The Recent Years, 1939–1946* (New York: Doubleday, 1946), 13–15.

84. In "Picasso et le C.N.E.," *Les Lettres françaises,* 21 October 1944, 7, the writer equates the action of the anti-Picasso protesters with the "procédés de la brutalité physique et d'intimidation qui sont ceux des hitlériens" and he adds "de telles manifestations ne peuvent être que le vestige de

l'occupation allemande." "Nous tenons à dire que directement ou indirectement nous les considerons comme le fait de l'ennemi."

85. Picasso, "Why I Became a Communist," 11. For an extensive account of Picasso's relationship with the French Communist Party, see Utley, "Picasso and the 'Parti.'" For an autobiographical recounting of the reasons leading young French Communists to join the party during and shortly after the war, see in particular Annie Kriegel, *Ce que j'ai cru comprendre* (Paris: Robert Laffont, 1991) and Edgar Morin, *Autocritique* (Paris: Editions du Seuil, 1970). For a historical and critical view of the fascination of communism for the intellectuals, see Tony Judt, *Past Imperfect: French Intellectuals 1944–1956* (Berkeley, Los Angeles, and London: University of California Press, 1992), as well as his earlier *Marxism and the French Left* (Oxford: Clarendon Press, 1986). See also Furet, *Le Passé.*

86. For Péri's last words, see Kriegel, *Ce que j'ai cru,* 462 n. 1.; for Picasso's reaction to the letter see Guillén, *Picasso,* 91. To Guillén, who judged the letter a bit theatrical, Picasso replied vehemently that he thought the letter was magnificent and that whatever one wrote before being executed is authentic.

87. Geneviève Laporte, who, as a member of Le Front national des étudiants, interviewed Picasso for her school paper, was shocked to hear that he had not even read Marx before joining the Communist Party. Geneviève Laporte, *Un amour secret de Picasso: Si tard le soir . . .* (Monaco: Editions du Rocher, 1989), 18, and in conversation with the author.

88. Malraux is quoted by David Caute, *Communism and the French Intellectuals, 1914–1960: Western Europe* (New York: Macmillan, 1964), 13. Jeannine Verdès-Leroux, *Au service du Parti: Le parti communiste, les intellectuels et la culture (1944–1956)* (Paris: Fayard/Editions de Minuit, 1983), 85.

89. A recent publication on the subject is Furet, *Le Passé.*

90. Judt, *Past Imperfect,* 5; Pascal Ory and Jean-François Sirinelli, *Les Intellectuels en France, de l'Affaire Dreyfus à nos jours* (Paris: Armand Colin, 1986), 151; Verdès-Leroux, *Au service du Parti,* 18. In the twelve months after the Liberation the Grand Parti de la Résistance, the Parti aux 75, 000 fusillés, as they liked to be known, won 500,000 new members. The Communists' exaltation of their role in the Resistance was in opposition to de Gaulle's policy. In his efforts to reunite the French, de Gaulle propagated the myth that the Resistance was the domain of all the French. See Henry Rousso, *Le Syndrome de Vichy de 1944 à nos jours* (Paris: Editions du Seuil, 1987, 1990), 34.

91. On the role and organization of the French Communists in the Resistance, see Germaine Willard, "Le P.C.F. et la Deuxième Guerre mondiale," in Roger Bourderon et al., *Le P.C.F. Etapes et problèmes 1920–1972* (Paris: Editions Sociales, 1981), 199–226. On the French Resistance under Vichy, see Roderick Kedward and Roger Austin, eds., *Vichy France and the Resistance* (Totowa, N.J.: Barnes and Noble, 1985); James D. Wilkinson, *The Intellectual Resistance in Europe* (Cambridge, Mass.: Harvard University Press, 1981).

92. Morin, *Autocritique,* 36, 47, 52. See also Ory and Sirinelli, *Les Intellectuels,* 151; see also Ariane Chebel d'Appollonia, *Histoire politique des intellectuels en France (1944–1954),* vol. 2 (Paris: Editions Complexe, 1991), 12. Jean-Pierre Rioux, *La France de la Quatrième République,* vol. 1, *L'Ardeur et la nécessité 1944–1952* (Paris: Editions du Seuil, 1980), 86. For further evidence of this point, read also *L'Humanité* of late 1944 and early 1945.

93. Morin, *Autocritique,* 77. The postwar image of the Soviet Union as chief victim of and victor over the Fascist invaders had for a time obscured the memory of the Moscow trials of the 1930s.

94. Albert Camus affirmed in 1944 that "anti-communism is the beginning of dictatorship," *Combat,* 7 October 1944.

95. See Utley, "Picasso and the 'Parti,'" passim.

96. Louis Aragon emphasized Picasso's importance for the party. In one of his articles following the famous scandal surrounding Picasso's portrait of Stalin, Aragon insisted: "nous avons avec nous un homme que l'ennemi nous envie furieusement," *Les Lettres françaises,* 9 April 1953.

97. André Warnod, "En peinture tout n'est que signe, nous dit Picasso," *Arts,* no. 22 (29 June 1945): 1, 4; Gilot and Lake, *Life with Picasso,* 74, 221.

98. Claude Morgan in his front-page editorial in *Les Lettres françaises,* 16 September 1944, deploring the inefficiency of the proceedings to purge collaborators, wrote, "Pour sauver l'Homme, la haine – aujourd'hui – est encore nécessaire."

99. For Picasso's role in the *épuration* (the purges of intellectuals after the Liberation), see the correspondence of Othon Friesz and of André Fougeron in the Picasso Archives, Musée Picasso, Paris. See also "Le Front national des Arts réclame des arrestations," *France libre,* 5 October 1944; André Fougeron, "A propos du Salon," *La Marseillaise,* 5 October 1944; "Epuration dans les Arts," *Franc-Tireur,* 6 October 1944; Jacques Vingtras, "L'Epuration et les artistes," *Le Populaire,* 24 October 1944. See also Gilot and Lake, *Life with Picasso,* 138. On the subject of the purges, read Pierre Assouline, *L'Epuration des intellectuels, 1944–1945* (Brussels: Editions Complexe, 1985); Herbert Lottman, *The Purge* (New York: Morrow, 1986). On the purges and their relevance for the Communists, see *Les Lettres françaises* and *L'Humanité,* late 1944, 1945, for examples of the vociferous debate on the topic of *épuration* in the Communist press. For the purges in the artistic community, see Sarah Wilson, "Art and the Politics of the Left in France ca. 1935-1955" (Ph.D. diss. Courtauld Institute of Art, 1993), 262.

100. Simone Téry, "Picasso n'est pas officier dans l'Armée française," *Les Lettres françaises* 5, no. 48 (24 March 1945): 6; also in catalogue of the exhibition *Picasso libre* at the Galerie Louis Carré in Paris; trans. Alfred H. Barr Jr., *Picasso: Fifty Years,* 357–58.

Where Do They Come From–Those Superb Paintings and Horrid Women of "Picasso's War"?
Brigitte Baer

1. Picasso had, in fact, seen that aspect, putting in the 1938 *Crucifixion* this square with rays, which is not a veil of Veronica but the cubical lantern from Goya's *Third of May, 1808.* At least that is how it looks to me.

2. *The Shadow of Death.* One of the three replicas is in the Manchester City Museum and Art Gallery.

3. Musée Picasso I, M.P. 122; Zervos VII, 287.

4. Musée Picasso II, M.P. 1071–1082. See Zervos VIII, 49, 55, 53, 56, 50, 51, 52; and Musée Picasso II, M.P. 1210, Zervos IX, 193.

5. Jean Clair, "Cette chose admirable, le péché," in *Corps crucifiés,* exh. cat. (Paris: Musée Picasso, 1993).

6. His mother, Olga, Marie-Thérèse, Dora Maar, and perhaps even little Nusch whom Eluard, according to his practice, had brought in as a third participant in their friendship, which must have amused Picasso, but also perturbed the child within him; in any case on 15 August 1937 (the day of the Assumption of the Virgin) he depicted Nusch as a wicked beast of prey, with the devouring smile of Little Red Riding Hood's wolf-grandmother; Zervos, VIII, 369.

7. Musée Picasso II, M.P. 1083; not in Zervos.

8. Léal, cat. no. 46, folios 17 recto and 18 recto, 11 and 19 July 1940, Royan; Zervos XI, 18 and 19.

9. When I was a very little girl, I, too, was in Royan at that time: I saw, I drank, and was put to bed.

10. The unconscious is buried so deeply in the psyche that it is impossible even to be approached by the person, although it does compel acts and lifelong positions. It has nothing to do with the so-called unconscious of the surrealists, which is no more than reverie that is, in theory, not controlled; a reverie that is so superficial that it resembles seaweed floating near the surface of the water, and the surrealists' absence of control is subject to caution, a nice parlor-game.

11. Carl Einstein (1885–1940) – German Jew who was an art historian, philosopher, and friend of Daniel-Henry Kahnweiler, and of the cubists – committed suicide on the way to Spain, trying to escape the Germans.

12. *Face à l'histoire, 1933–1996,* exh. cat. (Paris: Centre Georges Pompidou, 1996), 19 December 1996-7 April 1997, and *Années 30 en Europe, Le temps menaçant, 1929-1939,* Musée d'Art Moderne de la Ville de Paris, 20 February–25 May 1997.

13. Jean Cocteau, *Journal 1942–1945* (Paris: Editions Gallimard, 1989), 554.

14. Zervos III, 76.

15. Christian Zervos, "Conversation avec Picasso," in *Cahiers d'Art, Picasso 1930–1935,* 10, nos. 7–10 (1935): 40. This issue was in fact published in 1936, although dated 1935.

16. Jaime Sabartés, *Picasso, Portraits et souvenirs* (Paris: Louis Carré and

Maximilien Vox, 1946; Paris: L'Ecole des lettres, 1996). Also, *Picasso: An Intimate Portrait,* trans. Angel Flores (New York: Prentice Hall, 1948) and *Picasso, Retratos y recuerdos* (Madrid: A. Aguado, 1953). This apparently simplistic little book has a lot to tell us about Picasso, neither indulgently nor hatefully.

17. Zervos, "Conversations avec Picasso," 40.

18. Guillaume Apollinaire, "L'adieu du cavalier," in *Ombre de Mon Amour,* poem 68, written on 20 September 1915: "Ah God! how pretty war is." (Geneva: Pierre Cailler, 1948).

19. Picasso's situation in France could have become difficult if Franco, in Hendaye in October 1940, had allowed Hitler to move his troops across Spain to fight in North Africa, for Hitler might have given him some "lollipops" in exchange, such as Spanish Republicans who had taken refuge in France; but Franco had the sense to refuse.

20. One must not lend credence to the "testimony" of Gerhard Heller, an intellectual snob and a minor underling who tended to claim, with much sentimentality and often nauseating "sensitivity," to have protected a lot of people, when in fact he was a simple bystander. See Gerhard Heller, *Un Allemand à Paris: 1940–1944* (Paris: Editions du Seuil, 1981).

21. See Laurence Bertrand Dorléac, *L'Art de la défaite, 1940–1944* (Paris: Editions du Seuil, 1993).

22. I have often wondered just how this bronze was used in an "all-steel" war, but the Germans were master-salvagers. Maybe it was used to cast Arno Breker's supermen and superwomen?

23. Clearly, the English had been so nasty to little Joan of Arc! The libretto was by Paul Claudel, the music by Arthur Honegger.

24. But who knows? Picasso detested pain and suffering, and he had a tendency to burst into a kind of anger toward those who inflicted it on him.

25. See Freud, passim, about *gleichschwebende Aufmerksamkeit.*

26. Little Raymonde, a child adopted for a while by Fernande Olivier during the *Demoiselles d'Avignon* gestation, was around twelve years old, coming right out of a convent, and the studio was small. She must have hampered the lovemaking of the couple by being, which is normal at that age, "all attention." Picasso drew her in his *Demoiselles* sketchbooks. Her curiosity brought back to him his peeping-tom nature as a small boy, and gave the original bordello the shape and impact we know: for curiosity is the sin in that painting.

27. See W. Spies and C. Piot, *Picasso: Das plastische Werk* (Stuttgart: Gerd Hatje Verlag, 1983), nos. 409, 350, 463, respectively.

28. See Marcel Proust, *Le Temps retrouvé,* vol. 1 (Paris: NRF/Editions Gallimard, 1927), 33; he writes that when he thought he was looking at people, he was in fact X-raying them, whereas the Goncourt brothers were simply seeing their outside envelope and, so, could write "descriptions."

29. Zervos XIII, 37.

30. Zervos XIII, 67. It is just possible, however, that these two heads were inspired by the terrible photographs (the first ones) of the death camps, published in *Défense de la France,* 30 September 1943. This was a clandestine paper. The snapshots might have been shown to Picasso by someone like Desnos; they are of Greek children and Russian prisoners.

31. Zervos XIII, 36, 21 May.

32. Zervos XIII, 95, 24 August.

33. In *Hôtel du Nord,* a film by Marcel Carné, 1938.

34. Having, some ten years ago, been skimming through Mary Mathews Gedo, *Picasso: Art as Autobiography* (Chicago and London: University of Chicago Press, 1980), I noticed, after having written this obvious remark, that the author had written about the link between *Guernica* and the Málaga earthquake, but in another context. See page 181.

35. See this photograph in John Richardson with Marilyn McCully, *A Life of Picasso,* vol. 1 (New York: Random House, 1991), 32. On top, age four; on the bottom, age seven.

36. *Les Demoiselles d'Avignon,* exh. cat. (Paris: Musée Picasso, 1988), sketchbook 4, folios 14 and 15.

37. And it was perhaps from these quarrels that the artist's fear of syphilis arose, although the fear of this disease was widespread at the time.

38. See notes 27 and 40.

39. See Proust, *Du Côté de chez Swann,* (1928).

40. D. W. Winnicot (died 1971) was a world-renowned psychoanalyst, primarily of children. His books have been widely translated. They are at the same time accurate, enlightening, and deeply original; wonderful, too, and tender, they are all written in simple words. The concepts of a "good-enough mother" and that of the capacity, for a baby, and then for the adult "to be alone in the presence of someone" are his. A good-enough mother is one who can adapt herself to the changing needs of a growing infant and child without intruding. Thus, an adult who never had the possibility, as a baby, of playing restfully under the evenly suspended attention of his mother will always be unhappy and will make other people unhappy, among other things. Moreover, the adult never had the "peace" necessary to be creative. His most famous book is *Playing and Reality* (London: Tavistock, 1971; see index for "mother" and "alone."

41. The notion of the "intermediate space of Mothers" in Goethe has been much pondered and discussed for centuries, because it is somewhat nebulous. But artists seem to grasp it, in their own way. See, for example, Giovanni Segantini (1858–1899), *Le cattive madri,* 1894 (Osterreichische Galerie, Vienna), and *Il castigo delle lussuriose,* 1891 (Kunsthaus Zürich); there are also, in Segantini's mountains around Maloja, some round and deep holes that are called "the wells of the Mothers." Hermann Broch made the notion somewhat clearer in his beautiful book, *The Death of Virgil* (trans. Jeanne Starr Untermayer [New York: Pantheon, 1945]). This was much later, as the book was written mostly at Princeton, at the end of his life. It seems that this notion is coming back "en force" in intellectual circles, perhaps because it can only be grasped obscurely, by poets and painters. Picasso, of course, did not know about it but he still had to endure the "intermediate space of the Mothers."

42. Baer, cat no. 623.

43. André Malraux, *La Tête d'obsidienne* (Paris: Editions Gallimard, 1974), 118.

44. See Pierre Cabanne, *Le Siècle de Picasso,* vol. 2 (Paris: Editions Denoël, 1975). The author says that Roland Penrose told him the story.

45. Baer, cat nos. 625 and 626.

46. Baer, cat no. 646.

47. Baer, cat. nos. 649 and 672.

48. It is this "collage" and this lack of balance that twelve years ago plunged me into a study drowned in clouds of tobacco smoke, à la Sherlock Holmes. I had Degas in my head, and ended up finding the precise source.

49. Paul-André Lemoisne, *Degas et son oeuvre* (Paris: Paul Brame et C. M. de Hauck with Arts et Métiers Graphiques, 1946–1949), cat. no. 717. Picasso could have seen the work in Vollard's book, *Degas,* published by Crès in 1924, in Paris. He probably saw it again at the exhibition *Degas,* at the Orangerie, Paris, 1937, where it was lent by Durand-Ruel (no. 120).

50. It was purely by chance that I discovered, while researching Degas, how Picasso's mother died, from a book borrowed from Maya Picasso and annotated by her: her father had sent her to spend a few months at his sister Lola's house in Barcelona, a house that had been the family home. Lola told Maya Picasso exactly what happened.

51. See note 47.

52. Léal, cat. no. 42: Royan, 30 September–29 October 1939; M.P. 1990–111.

53. See Aeschylus, *Oresteia: The Choephori* and *The Eumenides;* i.e, the death of Clytemnestra and after.

54. Léal cat. no. 42, folio 96, recto; Zervos X, 109.

55. Tomás Harris, *Goya: Engravings and Lithographs* (Oxford: Bruno Cassirer, 1964; San Francisco: Alan Wofsy Fine Arts, 1983), cat. no. 119.

56. Léal, cat. no. 42, folio 42, recto; Zervos X, 53.

57. Zervos X, 302.

58. Léal, cat. no. 42, folios 49–53, rectos; Zervos X, 54, 73, 69, 70, 71.

59. Proust, *Du Coté de chez Swann,* vol. 1.

60. See Zervos IX, 352.

61. See note 53.

62. We must never forget that although Picasso's family did not regularly attend church, and that he himself, at least when he was young, "ate clerics alive," as a radical-socialist primary schoolteacher would do during the first half of our century, nevertheless he had been brought up in nineteenth-century Spain. He was imbued with biblical history and the lives of the saints, things that were taught to children in school; hence, he was full of religiosity.

63. Zervos X, 194–196.

64. Baer, cat. no. 682.

65. Brassaï, *Conversations avec Picasso* (Paris: Editions Gallimard, 1964) 137.

66. See note 53.

67. This photograph, reproduced here through the kindness of the Vilato family and especially Xavier Vilato, Picasso's grandnephew, I found only by accident; but, as Picasso *didn't* say, one only finds what, in some corner of one's brain, one is looking for.

68. 23 April 1942; Zervos XII, 43.

69. 26 June 1941; Zervos XI, 199.

70. Zervos XI, 153.

71. Zervos XI, 151.

72. Zervos XI, 272.

73. Zervos IX, 362.

74. Zervos XI, 221 and 222.

75. Bernhard Geiser, rev. and supp. by Brigitte Baer, *Picasso, peintre graveur,* vol. 2 (Berne: Editions Kornfeld, 1992), cat. no. 287.

76. Zervos XI, 112.

77. Little children "believe" that the seeds of babies are swallowed by the mother or else brought in either through the navel or the anus, and that they come out again by one of those orifices, the only ones they know about. The "belief" very often remains in the unconscious, although the adult knows perfectly well how it works, and how to make it work.

78. Spies and Piot, *Picasso,* cat. no. 335.

79. Ibid., cat. no. 238.

80. Rudyard Kipling, "A Friend of the Family," in *Debits and Credits* (London: Penguin, 1993), 232.

Circumventing Picasso:
Jean Paulhan and His Artists
Michèle C. Cone

1. See Tony Judt, *Past Imperfect: French Intellectuals 1944–1956* (Berkeley: University of California Press, 1992), 26; Frédéric Badré's new biography of Paulhan, *Paulhan le juste* (Paris: Grasset, 1997); see also John Culbert, "Slow Progress: Jean Paulhan and Madagascar," *October* 83 (winter 1998).

2. The *Bleu Blanc Rouge* painters included Jean Bazaine, Maurice Estève, Charles Lapicque, Edouard Pignon, André Fougeron, and others who shared a vivid palette, occasionally using the colors of the French flag. Romantic realists included Roland Oudot, Maurice Brianchon, and Raymond Legueult, whose middle-of-the-road approach to painting was neither thoroughly academic nor thoroughly vanguard. Lucien Rebatet, the notorious critic of *Je suis partout,* coined the expression "Between-the-Jew-and-the-Pompier" to signify middle-of-the-roadism. Pompier art was the vulgar way of referring to the academic milieu, while Jewish art stood for extreme vanguardism foreign to the French sensibility.

3. Jean Paulhan, *Choix de lettres II 1937–1945: Traité des jours sombres* (Paris: Editions Gallimard, 1992), 331. In a 1937 letter in the same vein, Paulhan had called *Guernica* "fairly uninteresting," 37. All translations are by the author.

4. For a history of representations of death in the western world, see Philippe Aries, *Essais sur l'histoire de la mort en Occident du Moyen Age à nos jours* (Paris: Editions du Seuil, 1975).

5. See Michèle C. Cone, "Picasso's War in Occupied Paris," *Artists under Vichy: A Case of Prejudice and Persecution* (Princeton, N. J.: Princeton University Press, 1992), 133-34.

6. Ibid., 55.

7. [Pierre] Drieu la Rochelle, "La peinture et les siens," *Comoedia,* 23 April 1941.

8. Paulhan, *Choix,* 224.

9. Jean Paulhan, *Braque le patron* (Paris: Mourlot, 1945; Geneva and Paris: Trois Collines, 1946).

10. *Jean Paulhan/Jean Grenier: Correspondance 1925–1968* (Quimper: Calligrammes, 1984), 145.

11. Fernand Mourlot, *Gravés dans ma mémoire* (Paris: Laffont, 1979), 117.

12. Ibid., 120.

13. All three works are referenced in André Berne-Joffroy, *Jean Paulhan à travers ses peintres* (Paris: Musées Nationaux, 1974), nos. 471, 463, and 467.

14. Paulhan, *Choix,* 264.

15. John Golding, Sophie Bowness, Isabelle Monod-Fontaine, *Braque: The Late Works* (New Haven and London: Yale University Press, 1997), 9.

16. Ibid.

17. Ibid., 3.

18. Ibid., 40.

19. Ibid., 25.

20. Paulhan, *Choix,* 96–97.

21. Lucien Rebatet, "Révolutionnaires d'arriére garde," *Je suis partout,* 29 October 1943.

22. See Bouvier on Braque's sculpture, *Comoedia,* 29 August 1942, and Bazaine on Braque in *Comoedia,* 5 June 1943.

23. Mourlot, *Gravés,* 127. In fact, the Nazi intellectual Gerhard Heller liked Braque's paintings, and one of them had been on view in an exhibition of modern French art held in Nazi Berlin in 1937. See Michèle C. Cone, "French Art of the Present in Nazi Berlin," forthcoming in the *Art Bulletin,* September 1998.

24. René Drouin and Leo Castelli had started the gallery in 1939 and, after Castelli's departure for the United States, Drouin reopened it alone. His first director, a collaborationist, was Georges Maratier; his second director, an active resister, was Gildo Caputo. Paulhan was the *éminence grise* of the gallery.

25. Paulhan, *Choix,* 337.

26. Gerhard Heller, *Un Allemand à Paris* (Paris: Editions du Seuil, 1981), 116.

27. Jean Paulhan, *Fautrier l'enragé* (Paris: Blaizot, 1949).

28. The first to identify this postwar sensibility was the French critic Michel Tapié de Ceyleran. Against formalism and against any kind of Franco / French particularism, he placed Dubuffet as well as Fautrier in the company of American (de Kooning), English (Paolozzi), Dutch (Appel), and Canadian (Rioppelle) artists who, he felt, had rejected tradition and worked from a neo-Dadaist position of artistic tabula rasa.

29. The catalogue of the 1943 Drouin exhibition provides only a list of the exhibited works, and one illustration with no caption, in addition to the Paulhan text.

30. See Marcel-André Stalter, "Fautrier, du permanent au fugace" in Suzanne Pagé, ed., *Jean Fautrier* (Paris: Paris-Musées, 1989), 42–43.

31. Berne-Joffroy, *Jean Paulhan à travers ses peintres,* 218.

32. For details see Jean-Paul Ledeur, "Fautrier, la chair de l'émotion," in Pagé, *Jean Fautrier,* 42–43.

33. Ibid., 95–96.

34. Paulhan, *Choix,* 322.

35. Ibid., 323.

36. Lucien Rebatet, "Les arts et les lettres," *Je suis partout,* 25 November 1943.

37. Jean-Marc Campagne, interview with the author, 16 June 1984. He brings up *"la spiritualité juive," "le paysage mental juif," "les particularismes juifs."*

38. This link is rarely acknowledged by Soutine scholars, as Romy Golan observes in "Blind Alley: The Reception of Soutine in France after World War II," in *Soutine,* exh. cat. (New York: The Jewish Museum, 1998). My thanks to Romy Golan for her valuable advice and for making her text available.

39. Jean Paulhan, *Fautrier l'enragé* (Paris: Editions Gallimard, 1962), 48.

40. The portrait is reproduced in André Verdet, *Jean Fautrier* (Freiburg: Limmer Gallery, 1981).

41. Jacqueline Cousin, Dossier Fautrier, *Cahiers bleus,* 1975. Reprint 1989, 83. Gift of Arno Breker to the author.

42. The name Garde ("keep" but also "nurse" in French) was given to Gerda Groth by Soutine. The artist decided to "keep" Groth after spending an evening with her, and let her become his "nurse."

43. Mlle Garde, "Mes années avec Soutine," *L'Oeil,* January 1956, 27.

44. Elie Faure quoted in *Soutine* (Paris: Orangerie des Tuileries, 1973), 14.

45. Paulhan, *Choix,* 343.

46. Ibid., 317. Masson was the French surrealist painter.

47. Ibid., 329. Roland Oudot and Maurice Brianchon were romantic realists whose best work was designing sets for the Paris Opera productions. See note 2.

48. Paulhan, *Choix,* 311.

49. Maurice Tuchman in Maurice Tuchman, Esti Dunow, and Klaus Perls, *Chaim Soutine (1893–1943),* catalogue raisonné, vol. 1 (Cologne: Benedikt Taschen Verlag, 1993), 16. Tuchman speaks of a transcendental

motif in the invisible presence of wind in the late landscapes, whereas I read a memory of windblown steppes in the late landscapes peopled with children.

50. Mlle Garde, "Mes années," 29.

51. See Michael Marrus and Robert Paxton, *Vichy France and the Jews* (New York: Basic Books, 1981), 250–55.

52. Ibid., 236.

53. The collector Pierre Lévy tells in his memoirs that Max Kaganovitch, a refugee dealer in Lyons, continued to sell his work. See Pierre Lévy, *Des artistes et un collectionneur* (Paris: Flammarion, 1976), 185.

54. Mlle Garde, "Mes années," 31.

55. Paulhan, *Choix,* 311. An article entitled "Contre les peintres d'aujour-d'hui," signed Maurice Sachs, praising Soutine, had appeared in the July 1934 NRF.

56. Ibid., 353. Georges Limbour had been a friend of Dubuffet since the 1920s, when both circulated among the surrealists.

57. Jean Dubuffet, *Bâtons rompus* (Paris: Minuit, 1986), 7.

58. Ibid., 8.

59. Ibid. It was not a funeral but a mass held at Eglise St.-Roch.

60. Berne-Joffroy, "Elements biographiques," *Jean Paulhan à travers ses peintres,* xi.

61. Jean Paulhan, *Les Fleurs de Tarbes ou la terreur dans les lettres* (Paris: Editions Gallimard, 1941), 35.

62. Ibid. Such deconstruction of language evokes Artaud's ideas in the Theatre of Cruelty – the elimination of dialogue from the theatre, and the recourse to gestures, howls, and incantations instead.

63. Paulhan, *Braque le patron,* 22.

64. Culbert, "Slow Progress: Jean Paulhan and Madagascar," 89.

65. Paulhan, *Choix,* 342.

66. Berne-Joffroy, "Elements," xx.

67. Quoted in Frances Morris, *Paris Post War: Art and Existentialism* (London: The Tate Gallery, 1993), 144.

68. Rebatet, "Révolutionnaires d'arrière garde."

Reports from the Home Fronts:
Some Skirmishes over Picasso's Reputation
Michael FitzGerald

I have not cited publications that appear in other texts in this catalogue and are not essential sources for this text. I am especially grateful to Gertje Utley for sharing with me her research into the Picasso Archives, Musée Picasso, Paris. In order to prepare for the birth of a son, I have sometimes abbreviated arguments in this essay. May we all live to fight another day.

1. *San Francisco Chronicle,* 3 September 1944.

2. Brassaï, *Conversations avec Picasso* (Paris: Editions Gallimard, 1964), 182–83.

3. In January to April 1938, the painting toured Denmark and Scandinavia in a nonpolitical exhibition of works by Matisse, Braque, Laurens, and Picasso.

4. Henry McBride, "Picasso's *Guernica* Here," *New York Sun,* 6 May 1939.

5. *Springfield Republican,* 18 July 1937. Although McCausland wrote primarily for a regional newspaper, her criticism was widely followed in the art world.

6. "Art's Acrobat," *Time,* 13 February 1939, 44.

7. *Springfield Republican,* 19 November 1939.

8. Jerome Mellquist, "Picasso: Painter of the Year," *Nation,* 9 December 1939, 658.

9. Press release, August 1943, The Museum of Modern Art Archives, New York: Alfred H. Barr, Jr., Papers; Box 16. Subgroup VIII.B.2. Misidentified as issued in conjunction with *Picasso: Forty Years of His Art.*

10. *Museum of Modern Art Bulletin,* October–November 1942, 19.

11. "The Last Time I Saw Picasso," *Art News,* 1–14 March 1942, 36.

12. For Picasso's relations with dealers before World War II, see Michael FitzGerald, *Making Modernism: Picasso and the Creation of the Market for Twentieth-Century Art* (New York: Farrar Straus and Giroux, 1995).

13. Vlaminck's denunciation first appeared in the Paris newspaper *Comoedia* (6 June 1942) and was reprinted in *Portraits avant décès* (Paris: Flammarion, 1943). Picasso kept a clipping of this article and referred to it when discussing the experience of the Occupation. In the 13 June issue of *Comoedia,* André Lhote offered a somewhat lukewarm defense of Picasso, and others supported him in the 20 June issue. My thanks to Steven Nash for bringing this episode to my attention.

14. Harriet and Sidney Janis, *Picasso: The Recent Years 1939–1946* (New York: Doubleday, 1946), pl. 55. It is not clear whether these paintings were purchased during the war or in the months immediately following the Liberation.

15. Martin Fabiani, *Quand j'étais marchand de tableaux* (Paris: Julliard, 1976), 127.

16. Hector Feliciano reports the aftermath of one transaction. During the war, Fabiani sold or traded a painting by the Douanier Rousseau to Picasso, after Picasso required a certificate from Fabiani stating that the picture was not illegally obtained. After the war, Picasso learned that the painting had been confiscated by the Nazis from Pierre Wertheimer and passed to Fabiani. *The Lost Museum* (New York: Basic Books, 1997), 121.

17. The papers of Louis Carré's gallery are preserved in the French Archives Nationales.

18. Gerhard Heller reported seeing some Picassos at Carré's gallery, but there is no evidence the dealer had a substantial stock during the war. *Un Allemand à Paris: 1940–1944* (Paris: Editions du Seuil, 1981), 115.

19. Auction records indicate the inflated prices in French francs paid for paintings during the war. For example, one of Picasso's paintings brought 610,000 francs at Drouot in early June 1942, and the sale of the Viau collection at Drouot on 12–13 December 1942 included a Picasso that sold for 1,610,000 and another for 1,300,000 francs. These prices are many times those reached at the peak of the pre-Depression market. As one example, in 1929 Viscount de Noailles bought a small Dinard painting for 43,000 francs. Besides sales on the open market, extensive dealings were common in modern paintings confiscated by the Nazis from French citizens, primarily Jews such as Paul Rosenberg. In general, Nazi officials, such as Hermann Göring or Otto Abetz, requisitioned paintings by Picasso or his contemporaries without intending to keep them. They were to be sold on the international market (generally in Switzerland), or swapped with dealers or collectors for old-master pictures. These practices were thoroughly documented at the end of the war by James Plaut and Theodore Rousseau of the OSS Art Looting Unit. See my review of recent publications on this subject: "Nazi Esthetes," *Art in America,* February 1998, 33–35.

20. For some of these exhibitions, see Steven Nash's chronology in this volume and Michèle Cone, *Artists under Vichy: A Case of Prejudice and Persecution* (Princeton, N. J.: Princeton University Press, 1992).

21. The auction is discussed in *Résolution nationale* (18 July 1942). It was held by "L'Union des artistes," and Picasso's painting brought 650,000 francs.

22. Roland Penrose was another deeply interested party. Although there are several notes from Penrose to Picasso during 1938–39 preserved in the Picasso Archives, there are none from late 1939 to mid-1944. They resume with one dated 27 August 1944, in which Penrose wrote, "Il me semble presque incroyable encore de pouvoir vous écrire." My thanks to Steven Nash for bringing this correspondence to my attention.

23. "Excerpts from Gladys Delmas, 'French Art during the Occupation,'" MoMA Archives: AHB Papers. Presumably "occult" is a mistranscription of "cult."

24. G. H. Archambault, "Picasso," *New York Times Magazine,* 29 October 1944.

25. Letter of 28 March 1945. Translation courtesy of Cone, *Artists under Vichy,* 233–34.

26. Correspondence between Plaut and Barr in MoMA Archives: AHB Papers; 16.VIII.B.2.

27. Alfred H. Barr Jr., *Picasso: Fifty Years of His Art* (New York: The Museum of Modern Art, 1946), 245.

28. Ibid., 250.

29. Ibid., 250.

30. Carré held the first exhibition from 20 June through 18 July 1945 and the second from 14 June through 14 July 1946.

Compare with In New York, Rosenberg held exhibitions of Picasso's work in February–March 1942, April and December 1943, February–March 1947, and March–April 1948. Pierre Matisse held an exhibition in December 1943.

31. "The 1940–45 Picasso in His Latest Paris Show," *Art News,* 1–30 September 1945, 11.

32. "Picasso: Late, Later, Latest," *Art News,* February 1947, 20.

33. Françoise Gilot and Charlton Lake, *Life with Picasso* (New York: McGraw-Hill, 1964), 286.

34. Kootz's first exhibition of Picasso's work, which he billed as "the first post-war showing in America of recent paintings by Picasso," occurred from 27 January through 15 February 1947.

35. See Michael FitzGerald, "A Triangle of Ambitions: Art, Politics, and Family during the Postwar Years with Françoise Gilot," in William Rubin, ed., *Picasso and Portraiture: Representation and Transformation* (New York: The Museum of Modern Art, 1996), 444 n. 36.

36. Janis and Janis, *Picasso: The Recent Years,* pl. 55. For the Ganzes' collecting, see Michael FitzGerald, ed., *A Life of Collecting: Sally and Victor Ganz* (New York and London: Christie's, 1997). On 2 May 1949, Kootz wrote to Picasso, "As you know, I have many of your paintings in stock now, as *business has been quite bad.*" Picasso Archives, Musée Picasso, Paris. My thanks to Gertje Utley for bringing this letter to my attention.

37. Elizabeth McCausland, *Picasso* (New York: ACA Gallery, 1944), 12. Jerome Seckler, "Picasso Explains," *New Masses,* 13 March 1945.

38. Charles Wertenbaker, "Pablo Picasso: Portrait of the Artist," *Life,* 13 October 1947.

39. Joseph A. Barry, "Picasso's Dove Takes Off: The New Bird, Like the Old One, Is a Fine Target for the French Humorists," *New York Times,* 22 October 1950. The text concluded:

   Something has frightened [Picasso's dove] badly. And it all happened in Korea. Uncle Joe sent tanks and planes and guns to the North Koreans and pointed them toward the south. It was not enough, so Uncle Joe sent for Picasso and said: "Corporal Picasso, to the rescue! The North Koreans are collapsing! Quick, a dove."

   Picasso's dove is just coming back, and it is coming back as fast as its one wing can take it. The left wing, as anyone can plainly see, has been hit. People who start a war and cry "Peace" are not fit companions for man, beast, nor dove, even if they use the coo coo language, so the new dove is getting away fast.

   As Gertje Utley has carefully documented, a wide range of responses to Picasso's art existed among French critics after the war. Although Picasso probably took very few of them seriously, conservative critics, who had never shown much sympathy for his work, went so far as to accuse him of corrupting "pure" French cultural traditions. "Picasso and the French Post-War 'Renaissance': A Questioning of National Identity," in Jonathan Brown, ed., *Picasso and the Spanish Tradition* (New Haven and London: Yale University Press, 1996), 95–117. This situation is far too complex to allow extensive treatment here.

40. Writing to Roland Penrose regarding Picasso's signing an open letter to *L'Humanité* protesting the Soviet suppression of dissent in Hungary in 1956, Barr stated, "Of course I am pleased that he signed the open letter to *L'Humanité,* but I can't help feeling a certain sense of disgust that it should have taken him so long to declare what has been so painfully obvious to the rest of the world. . . . " Letter, 16 January 1957, MoMA Archives: AHB Papers; Box 2. Subgroup II. Series C.

41. See Michael FitzGerald, "Triangle of Ambitions," 436–41.

Selected Bibliography
Picasso and the War Years: 1937–1945

Note:

The literature on Picasso in general, the Spanish Civil War, and France during World War II is immense. This bibliography is reduced to a highly selective list of the most useful sources on Picasso's life and work during the period 1937–1945. For information and bibliography on the Spanish Civil War, see Hugh Thomas, *The Spanish Civil War,* rev. ed. (New York: Harper and Row, 1977). Among the most authoritative texts on the history of France during World War II are Robert O. Paxton, *Vichy France: Old Guard and New Order, 1940–1944* (New York: Columbia University Press, 1982); Jean-Baptiste Duronselle, *L'Abîme: 1939–1945* (Paris: Imprimerie Nationale, 1982); Henri Amouroux, *La Grande Histoire des Français sous l'occupation* (Paris: Editions Robert Laffont, 1976), and Philippe Burrin, *France under the Germans: Collaboration and Compromise,* trans. from French by Janet Lloyd (New York: New Press, 1996).

Abbreviated References Cited in Notes to the Essays

Baer

Baer, Brigitte. *Catalogue raisonné de l'oeuvre grave et des monotypes, 1935–1945.* Vol. 3 (1986) of Bernhard Geiser and Brigitte Baer. *Picasso: Peintre-graveur.* 7 vols. and addendum. Bern: Editions Kornfeld, 1986–96.

Léal

Léal, Brigitte. *Musée Picasso: Carnets. Catalogue des dessins.* 2 vols. Paris: Editions de la Réunion des Musées Nationaux, 1996.

Musée Picasso I

Musée Picasso: Catalogue sommaire des collections. Peintures, papiers collés, tableaux-reliefs, sculptures, céramiques. Paris: Editions de la Réunion des Musées Nationaux, 1985.

Musée Picasso II

Richet, Michèle. *Musée Picasso: Catalogue sommaire des collections. Dessins, aquarelles, gouaches, pastels.* Paris: Editions de la Réunion des Musées Nationaux, 1987.

Zervos

Zervos, Christian. *Pablo Picasso.* 33 vols. Paris: Editions Cahiers d'Art, 1932–78.

Archives

Hoover Institution Archives, Hoover Institution on War, Revolution and Peace, Stanford University.

Musée Picasso, Paris, Picasso Archives.

The Museum of Modern Art Archives, New York: Alfred H. Barr Jr. Papers.

Picasso Literature

Ades, Dawn, comp. *Art and Power: Europe under the Dictators 1930–45.* Exh. cat. London: Hayward Gallery, 1995.

Archambault, G.H. "Picasso. The Painter Who Defied the Germans Finds Himself the Hero of a Revolutionary Mood." *The New York Times Magazine,* 29 October 1944, 18–19, 39.

Arnheim, Rudolf. *Picasso's Guernica: The Genesis of a Painting.* Berkeley: University of California Press, 1961.

Ashton, Dore, ed. *Picasso on Art: A Selection of Views.* New York: Viking Press, 1972.

Baer, Brigitte. "Eine Leseart von Picasso's Werk im der Kriegsjahren: Eine traumatische Trauer." In Siegried Gohr, ed. *Picasso im Zweiten Weltkrieg: 1939 bis 1945.* Exh. cat. Cologne: Museum Ludwig, 1988.

Baer, Brigitte, and Bernhard Geiser. *Picasso, peintre graveur.* 7 vols. and addendum. Bern: Editions Kornfeld, 1986–96.

Baldassari, Anne. *Picasso and Photography: The Dark Mirror.* Exh. cat. Paris: Flammarion; Houston: Museum of Fine Arts, 1997.

Barr, Alfred H. Jr. *Picasso: Forty Years of His Art.* Exh. cat. New York: The Museum of Modern Art, 1939.

——. "Picasso 1940–1944: A Digest with Notes." *The Museum of Modern Art Bulletin* 12, no. 3 (January 1945): 1–9.

——. *Picasso: Fifty Years of His Art.* New York: The Museum of Modern Art, 1946.

Beauvoir, Simone de. *La Force de l'âge.* Paris: Editions Gallimard, 1960.

Berlin, Neue Gesellschaft für Bildende Kunst. *Kunst und Politik am Beispiel Guernica - Picasso und der Spanische Bürgerkreig.* Berlin: NGBK, 1975.

Bernadac, Marie-Laure, and Christine Piot. *Picasso écrits.* Paris: Réunion des Musées Nationaux and Editions Gallimard, 1989.

Berne-Joffroy, André. *Jean Paulhan à travers ses peintres.* Exh. cat. Paris: Editions des Musées Nationaux, 1974.

Bertrand Dorléac, Laurence. *L'Histoire de l'art; Paris 1940–1944: Ordre national, traditions et modernité .* Paris: Presses de la Sorbonne, 1986.

——. *L'Art de la défaite, 1940–1944.* Paris: Editions du Seuil, 1993.

Bloch, George. *Picasso: Catalogue de l'oeuvre gravé et lithographié.* 4 vols. Bern: Kornfeld and Klipstein, 1968–79.

Blunt, Anthony. *Picasso's Guernica.* London and New York: Oxford University Press, 1969.

Boggs, Jean Sutherland, ed. *Picasso & Things: The Still Lifes of Picasso.* Exh. cat. Cleveland: The Cleveland Museum of Art, 1992.

Brassaï [Gyula Halasz]. *Picasso and Company.* Trans. Francis Price. Garden City, N.Y.: Doubleday, 1966. Originally published as *Conversations avec Picasso* (Paris: Editions Gallimard, 1964).

Brassaï [Gyula Halasz] and Daniel-Henry Kahnweiler. *Les Sculptures de Picasso.* Paris: Editions du Chêne, 1948.

Breker, Arno. *Paris, Hitler, et moi.* Paris: Presses de la Cité, 1970.

Burgard, Timothy Anglin. "Picasso's *Night Fishing at Antibes:* Autobiography, Apocalypse, and the Spanish Civil War." *Art Bulletin* 68, no. 4 (December 1986): 656–72.

Cabanne, Pierre. *Pablo Picasso: His Life and Times.* Trans. Harold J. Salemson. New York: William Morrow, 1977. Originally published as *Le Siécle de Picasso.* 4 vols. (Paris: Editions Denöel, 1975).

Carré, Louis, ed. *Picasso libre: 21 peintures, 1940–1945.* Exh. cat. Paris: Galerie Louis Carré, 1945.

Cassou, Jean. *Picasso.* Trans. Mary Chamot. New York: Harry N. Abrams, 1959. Originally published as *Picasso* (Paris: Hypérion, 1940).

Charbois, Nicole. "Eluard et Picasso." Special Picasso edition, *Europe* 51, no. 525 (January 1973): 188–207.

Chipp, Herschel B. *Picasso's Guernica: History, Transformations, Meanings.* Berkeley, Los Angeles, and London: University of California Press, 1988.

Clark, Vernon. "The Guernica Mural: Picasso and Social Protest." In Gert Schiff, ed. *Picasso in Perspective.* Englewood Cliffs, N.J.: Prentice Hall, 1976. Originally published in *Science and Society* 5, no. 1 (December 1941): 72–78.

Cocteau, Jean. *Le Passé défini I, 1951–1952, Journal.* Paris: Editions Gallimard, 1983.

———. *Journal 1942–1945.* Paris: Editions Gallimard, 1989.

Cone, Michèle. *Artists under Vichy: A Case of Prejudice and Persecution.* Princeton, N.J.: Princeton University Press, 1992.

Council of Europe, *Art and Power: Europe under the Dictators, 1930–1945.* Exh. cat. London: The Hayward Gallery; Berlin: Deutsches Historisches Museum; Barcelona: Centro de Cultura Contemporània, 1995–96.

Cowling, Elizabeth, and John Golding. *Picasso: Sculptor/Painter.* Exh. cat. London: The Tate Gallery, 1994.

Daix, Pierre. *La Vie de peintre de Pablo Picasso.* Paris: Editions du Seuil, 1977.

———. *Picasso créateur: La Vie intime et l'oeuvre.* Paris: Editions du Seuil, 1987.

Delmas, Gladys. "French Art during the Occupation." *Magazine of Art* 38, no. 3 (March 1945): 83–88.

Desnos, Robert. *Picasso: Seize peintures 1939–1943.* Paris: Editions du Chêne, 1943.

———. *Picasso: Peintures, 1939–1946.* Paris: Editions du Chêne, 1946.

Dubois, André-Louis. *A travers trois républiques: Sous le signe de l'amitié.* Paris: Plon, 1972.

Duncan, David Douglas. *Picasso's Picassos.* New York: Harper, 1961.

Elsen, Albert. "Picasso's Man with a Sheep: Beyond Good and Evil." *Art International* 21, no. 2 (March–April 1977): 8–15, 29–31.

Eluard, Paul. *A Pablo Picasso.* Geneva and Paris: Editions des Trois Collines, 1945.

Ferrier, Jean-Louis. *De Picasso à Guernica: Généalogie d'un tableau.* Paris: L'Infini, Editions Denoël, 1985.

Freeman, Judi. *Picasso and the Weeping Women: The Years of Marie-Thérèse Walter & Dora Maar.* Exh. cat. Los Angeles: Los Angeles County Museum of Art; New York: Rizzoli, 1994.

Galassi, Susan Grace. *Picasso's Variations on the Masters: Confronting the Past.* New York: Harry N. Abrams, 1996.

Gasman, Lydia. "Mystery, Magic, and Love in Picasso, 1925–1938: Picasso and the Surrealist Poets." Ph.D. diss., Columbia University, 1981.

Gedo, Mary Mathews. *Picasso: Art as Autobiography.* Chicago and London: The University of Chicago Press, 1980.

Geiser, Bernhard. *Pablo Picasso: Lithographs, 1945–1948.* Trans. Walter Pack. New York: Curt Valentin, 1948.

Gilot, Françoise, and Carlton Lake. *Life with Picasso.* New York, Toronto, and London: McGraw-Hill, 1964.

Goeppert, Sebastian, and Herma Goeppert-Frank. *Pablo Picasso: Catalogue raisonné des livres illustrés.* Geneva: Patrick Cramer, 1983.

Goggin, Mary-Margaret. "Picasso and His Art during the German Occupation: 1940–1944." Ph.D. diss., Stanford University, 1985.

Gohr, Siegfried, ed. *Picasso im Zweiten Weltkrieg: 1939 bis 1945.* Exh. cat. Cologne: Museum Ludwig, 1988.

Groth, John. "Letter from Paris." *Art Digest* 19 (1 December 1944): 9.

———. "Picasso at Work, August 1944." *The Museum of Modern Art Bulletin* 12, no. 3 (January 1945): 10–11.

Heller, Gerhard. *Un Allemand à Paris: 1940–1944.* Paris: Editions du Seuil, 1981.

Hunter, Sam. "Picasso at War: Royan, 1940, Sketchbook No. 110, 1940." In *Je Suis le Cahier: The Sketchbooks of Picasso.* Exh. cat. Boston and New York: Atlantic Monthly Press, 1986.

Janis, Harriet, and Sidney Janis. *Picasso: The Recent Years, 1939–1946.* Garden City, N.Y.: Doubleday, 1946.

Jardot, Maurice. *Picasso: Peintures, 1900–1955.* Paris: Calman-Levy, 1955.

Jünger, Ernst. *Journal de guerre et d'occupation, 1939–1948.* Paris: René Julliard, 1965.

Kahnweiler, Daniel-Henry. *Les Sculptures de Picasso.* Paris: Editions du Chêne, 1949.

———. *My Galleries and Painters.* Trans. Helen Weaver. London: Thames and Hudson, 1971. Originally published as *Mes galeries et mes peintres: Entretiens avec Francis Crémieux* (Paris: Editions Gallimard, 1961).

Laporte, Geneviève. *Sunshine at Midnight: Memories of Picasso and Cocteau* Trans. Douglas Cooper. London: Weidenfeld and Nicolson, 1975. Originally published as *Un amour secret de Picasso: Si tard le soir, le soleil brille* (Paris: Librairie Plon, 1973).

Larrea, Juan. *Guernica: Pablo Picasso.* New York: Curt Valentin, 1947.

Lassaigne, Jacques. *Picasso.* Paris: Somogny, 1949.

Léal, Brigitte. *Musée Picasso: Carnets. Catalogue des dessins.* 2 vols. Paris: Editions de la Réunion des Musées Nationaux, 1996.

———, "'Le Taureau est un taureau, le cheval est un cheval': Picasso, peintre d'histoire, de *Guernica* au *Charnier.*" In *Face à l'histoire, 1933–1966,* 142–49. Exh. cat. Paris: Centre Georges Pompidou, 1996.

Lee, Francis. "A Soldier Visits Picasso." *View* 6, nos. 2–3 (March–April 1946): 16.

Leiris, Michel. *Journal 1922–1989.* Paris: Editions Gallimard, 1992.

Lhote, André. "Opinions libres . . . sur la peinture française." *Comoedia,* 13 June 1942, 1, 6.

Limbour, Georges. "Picasso au Salon d'Automne." *Spectateur des Arts* 1 (December 1944): 4–8.

Lord, James, *Picasso and Dora: A Personal Memoir.* New York: Farrar Straus Giroux, 1993.

Malo, Pierre. "Picasseries et Picasso." *Comoedia,* 30 August 1941, 6.

Malraux, André. *Picasso's Mask.* New York: Holt, Rinehart and Winston, 1976. Originally published as *La Tête d'obsidienne* (Paris: Editions Gallimard, 1973).

McCully, Marilyn, ed. *A Picasso Anthology: Documents, Criticism, Reminiscences.* London: The Arts Council of Great Britain with Thames and Hudson, 1981.

Miller, Lee. "In Paris . . . Picasso Still at Work." *Vogue* (15 October 1944): 98–99, 149–50, 155.

Oppler, Ellen C. *Picasso's Guernica.* New York and London: W. W. Norton, 1988.

Paris, Centre d'Art et de Culture Georges Pompidou. *Paris–Paris, 1937–1957: Créations en France.* Exh. cat. Paris: Centre Georges Pompidou, 1981.

Paris, Musée Picasso. *Catalogue sommaire des collections,* 2 vols. Paris: Editions de la Réunion des Musées Nationaux, 1985–87.

Parrot, Louis. "Hommage à Pablo Picasso, qui vécut toujours de la vie de la France." *Les Lettres françaises* 4, no. 20 (9 September, 1944): 8.

———. "Picasso au Salon." *Les Lettres françaises* 4, no. 24 (7 October 1944): 7.

Penrose, Roland. *Picasso: His Life and Work.* London: Victor Gollancz, 1958. Rev. eds.: New York: Harper and Row, 1973; Berkeley: University of California Press, 1981.

Penrose, Roland, and John Golding, eds. *Picasso in Retrospect.* New York: Harper and Row, 1973.

Picasso, Pablo. "Why I Became a Communist." *New Masses* 53, no. 4 (24 October 1944): 11.

———. "Pourquoi j'ai adhéré au parti Communiste: Une Interview de Picasso à la revue américaine New Masses." *L'Humanité 41, no. 64* (29–30 October 1944): 1–2.

Powell, Kirsten H. "'La Drôle de Guerre': Picasso's *Femme nue se coiffant* and the 'Phony War' in France." *Burlington Magazine* 138, no. 1117 (April 1996): 235–45.

Pudney, John. "Picasso: A Glimpse in Sunlight." *The New Statesman and Nation* 28, no. 708 (16 September 1944): 182–83.

Rolland, Andrée. *Picasso et Royan aux jours de la guerre et de l'occupation.* Royan: Botton Père et Fils, 1967.

Rosenblum, Robert. "The Spanishness of Picasso's Still Lifes." In Jonathon Brown, ed. *Picasso and the Spanish Tradition,* 61–93. New Haven and London: Yale University Press, 1996.

Rubin, William. *Picasso in the Collection of the Museum of Modern Art.* New York: The Museum of Modern Art, 1972.

———. *Pablo Picasso: A Retrospective.* Exh. cat. New York: The Museum of Modern Art, 1980.

———, ed. *Picasso and Portraiture: Representation and Transformation.* Exh. cat. New York: The Museum of Modern Art, 1996.

Russell, John. *Picasso: Painting 1936–1946.* London, 1946.

Sabartés, Jaime. *Picasso: An Intimate Portrait.* Trans. Angel Flores. New York: Prentice Hall, 1948. Originally published as *Picasso: Portraits et souvenirs* (Paris: Louis Carré and Maximilien Vox, 1946).

———. *Documents iconographiques.* Geneva: Pierre Cailler, 1954.

Sadoul, Georges. "Une demi-heure dans l'atelier de Picasso." *Regards,* 29 July 1937, 8.

Seckel, Hélène, and André Cariou. *Max Jacob et Picasso.* Exh. cat. Paris: Réunion des Musées Nationaux, 1994.

Seckler, Jerome. "Picasso Explains." *New Masses* 54, no. 11 (13 March 1945): 4–7.

Spies, Werner, and Christine Piot. *Picasso: Das plastische Werk.* Stuttgart: Gerd Hatje Verlag, 1983.

———. *Die Zeit nach Guernica 1937–1973.* Exh. cat. Berlin: Nationalgalerie Staatliche Museen, 1992.

Steinberg, Leo. "'The Algerian Women' and Picasso at Large." In *Other Criteria: Confrontations with Twentieth Century Art.* London and New York: Oxford University Press, 1972.

Stich, Sidra. "Picasso's Art and Politics in 1936." *Arts Magazine* 58 (October 1983): 113–118.

Szittya, Emile. *Notes sur Picasso.* Paris: Courier des Arts et des Lettres, 1947.

Téry, Simone. "Picasso n'est pas officier dans l'armée française." *Les Lettres françaises* 5, no. 48 (24 March 1945): 6.

Toesca, Maurice. *Cinq ans de patience (1939–1945).* Paris: Editions Emile-Paul, 1975.

Tuchman, Phyllis. "Guernica and *Guernica.*" *Artforum* 21, no. 8 (April 1983): 44–51.

———. "Picasso's Sentinel," *Art in America* 86, no. 2 (February 1998): 86–95.

Ullmann, Ludwig. *Picasso und der Krieg.* Bielefeld: Karl Kerber Verlag, 1993.

Utley, Gertje. "Picasso and the French Post-war 'Renaissance': A Questioning of National Identity." In Jonathon Brown, ed. *Picasso and the Spanish Tradition,* 95–117. New Haven and London: Yale University Press, 1996.

———. "Picasso and the 'Parti de la Renaissance Française': The Artist as a Communist, 1944–1953." Ph.D. diss., Institute of Fine Arts, New York University, 1997.

Vlaminck, Maurice de. "Opinions libres . . . sur la peinture." *Comoedia* 2, no. 50 (6 June 1942): 1, 6.

Warnod, André. "Pour la première fois Picasso va exposer dans un Salon." *Le Figaro,* 2 October 1944.

———. "En peinture tout n'est que signe, nous dit Picasso." *Beaux-Arts* 22 (29 June 1945): 1–2.

Weisner, Ulrich, ed. *Picasso Todesthemen.* Exh. cat. Bielefeld: Kunsthalle Bielefeld, 1984.

Whitney, Peter D. "Picasso is Safe." *San Francisco Chronicle,* 3 September 1944.

Wilson, Sarah. "Art and the Politics of the Left in France, ca. 1935–1955." Ph.D. diss. Courtauld Institute, London, 1993.

Zervos, Christian, ed. *Cahiers d'Art 15–19* (1940–1944).

———. "L'Homme à l'agneau de Picasso." *Cahiers d'Art* 20–21 (1945): 84–112.

———. "Pablo Picasso." In *Exhibition of Paintings by Picasso and Matisse.* Exh. cat. London: British Council and the Victoria and Albert Museum, 1945. Republished as "Picasso: Figures d'entre deux charniers" (*America* 2 [1945]: 54).

———. *Pablo Picasso.* 33 vols. Paris: Editions Cahiers d'Art, 1932–78.

Lenders to the Exhibition

Anonymous collectors
Art Depot, Sweden
The Art Institute of Chicago
Sammlung Berggruen
Mrs. Lindy Bergman
The Cleveland Museum of Art
Fine Arts Museums of San Francisco
Galerie Cazeau-Béraudière, Paris
Galerie Louise Leiris, Paris
Galerie Rosengart, Lucerne
Tony and Gail Ganz
Gecht Family Collection, Chicago
The Solomon R. Guggenheim Museum, New York
Henie-Onstad Art Centre, Hövikodden, Norway
The Alex Hillman Family Foundation Collection
The Israel Museum, Jerusalem
Collection E. W. K., Bern
Kunstsammlung Nordrhein-Westfalen, Düsseldorf
Los Angeles County Museum of Art
Menard Art Museum, Aichi, Japan
The Menil Collection, Houston
The Metropolitan Museum of Art, New York
Mr. and Mrs. Marcos Micha
Milwaukee Art Museum
Musée des Beaux-Arts, Lyon
Musée Picasso, Paris
Museo Nacional Centro de Arte Reina Sofia, Madrid
The Museum of Modern Art, New York
Nagasaki Prefectural Art Museum
Národní Galerie, Prague
National Gallery of Canada, Ottawa
National Gallery of Victoria, Melbourne
The National Museum of Modern Art, Kyoto
Philadelphia Museum of Art
The Phillips Collection, Washington, D.C.
Marina Picasso Collection
Pinacoteca di Brera, Milan
Noel and Florence Rothman, Chicago
Staatsgalerie Stuttgart
Michael Werner Gallery, New York and Cologne
The University of Iowa Museum of Art
Yale University Art Gallery, New Haven

Index of Illustrations

Note: Page references in **boldface** indicate the illustrations.

* Not included in exhibition

Photography Credits

Photographs of works of art reproduced in this volume have been provided by the lenders unless otherwise noted:

Frontispiece
© Peter Rose Pulham

Picasso, War, and Art
STEVEN A. NASH
Fig. 5 Prudence Cuming Associates Limited, London
Fig. 13 © Worcester Art Museum
Fig. 14 © Lee Miller Archives
Fig. 17 © Christie's Images, New York
Fig. 18 © Harvard University Art Museums
Fig. 20 © Mme Louis Izis

Picasso's Disasters of War: The Art of Blasphemy
ROBERT ROSENBLUM
Fig. 6 © Photo Arxiu Fotogràfic de Museus, Ajuntament de Barcelona
Fig. 7 Photograph © The Museum of Modern Art, New York
Fig. 8 Photograph © 1998 The Art Institute of Chicago. All rights reserved.
Fig. 16 Bernard Terlay

Death Falling from the Sky: Picasso's Wartime Texts
LYDIA CSATÒ GASMAN
Fig. 7 © 1992 Thames and Hudson Ltd, London, reproduced by permission of the publishers
Figs. 12–13 Courtesy Robert Colle

From Guernica *to* The Charnel House: *The Political Radicalization of the Artist*
GERTJE R. UTLEY
Fig. 3 © Dora Maar
Fig. 4 Galerie Fischer (Photo Shut), provided by Los Angeles County Museum of Art
Fig. 7 Archipel
Figs. 9–12 © Cahiers d'Art, Paris

Where Do They Come From – Those Superb Paintings and Horrid Women of "Picasso's War"?
BRIGITTE BAER
Fig. 17 Courtesy the Vilato-Ruiz Archive

Circumventing Picasso: Jean Paulhan and His Artists
MICHÈLE C. CONE
Fig. 10 © Courtesy Christie's Images, New York
Fig. 13 Sarah Harper Gifford

Reports from the Home Fronts: Some Skirmishes over Picasso's Reputation
MICHAEL FITZGERALD
Fig. 1 © Magnum Photos, New York
Fig. 6 Courtesy the National Archives, Washington, D.C.
Fig. 7 © Robert Doisneau, Angence Rapho, Paris

Catalogue of Works
Cat. nos. 4–6, 83 Archival photograph of Museo Nacional Centro de Arte Reina Sofia, Madrid
Cat. no. 7 © 1998 Museum Associates, Los Angeles County Museum of Art. All rights reserved.
Cat. nos. 13, 17, 19, 22, 30, 32, 34, 50 © RMN–J. G. Berizzi
Cat. nos. 25–26, 57–58 ProLitteris + SPADEM
Cat. no. 28 David Heald © The Solomon R. Guggenheim Foundation, New York (FN78.2514 T62)
Cat. no. 31 Photograph © 1998 The Museum of Modern Art, New York
Cat. nos. 35, 74 © RMN–Gérard Blot
Cat. no. 36 Javier Hinojosa

Cat. nos. 37, 52 Galerie Jan Krugier
Cat. no. 39 Courtesy Galerie Cazeau-Béraudière, Paris
Cat. no. 42 Steven Soloman
Cat. no. 43 Oto Palán
Cat. no. 46 © Walter Klein, Düsseldorf
Cat. no. 47 © Images Modernes–Eric Baudouin
Cat. no. 49 Robert E. Mates © The Solomon R. Guggenheim Foundation, New York (FN 55.1433)
Cat. no. 54 © RMN–Béatrice Hatala
Cat. no. 63 Ecco Wang, 1998
Cat. nos. 64–65 © RMN
Cat. nos. 69, 79 Hickey Robertson, Houston
Cat. no. 73 Ellen Page Wilson
Cat. no. 75 Zindman/Fremont
Cat. no. 76 The Art Institute of Chicago, Imaging and Technical Services Department
Cat. no. 77 Efraim Lev-er
Cat. no. 82 Photograph © The Museum of Modern Art, New York

Chronology
Pages 209, 223 © Gilberte Brassaï, Paris
Page 216 Centre de documentation juive contemporaine, Paris
Pages 218, 225 (above) Roger-Viollet, Paris. © Lapi-Viollet
Page 221 © Magnum Photos, New York
Page 227 (above) © Lee Miller Archives